The New Basics

The New Basics

A-to-Z Baby & Child Care for the Modern Parent

Michel Cohen, M.D.

WILLIAM MORROW
An Imprint of HarperCollinsPublishers

This book is designed to give information on various medical conditions, treatments, and procedures for your personal knowledge and to help you be a more informed consumer of medical and health services. It is not intended to be complete or exhaustive, nor is it a substitute for the advice of your physician. You should seek medical care promptly for any specific medical condition or problem your child may have. Under no circumstances should medication of any kind be administered to your child without first checking with your physician.

All efforts have been made to ensure the accuracy of the information contained in this book as of the date published. The author and the publisher expressly disclaim responsibility for any adverse effects arising from the use or application of the information contained herein.

A hardcover edition of this book was published in 2004 by HarperCollins Publishers.

HarperCollins books may be purchased for educational, business, or sales promotional use. For information, please e-mail the Special Markets Department at SPsales@harper-collins.com.

First paperback edition published 2005.

Designed by Alain Cohen

The Library of Congress has cataloged the hardcover edition as follows:
Cohen, Michel.
The new basics: A-to-Z baby & child care for the modern parent
Michel Cohen.—1st ed.
p. cm.
ISBN 0-06-053547-4 (alk. paper)
1. Child rearing. 2. Parenting. I. Title.
HQ769.C6317 2004
649'.1—dc22 2003056704

ISBN 0-06-053548-2 (pbk.)

21 22 SCP 20 19

To my parents,

who gave me life and taught me how to enjoy it

To Ben and Lela,

my inspirations

To my love, Jeannie,

without whom this book would not be

And to the joys of my life,

Abeline, Nora, and Fanny

Contents

d

e

f

g

h

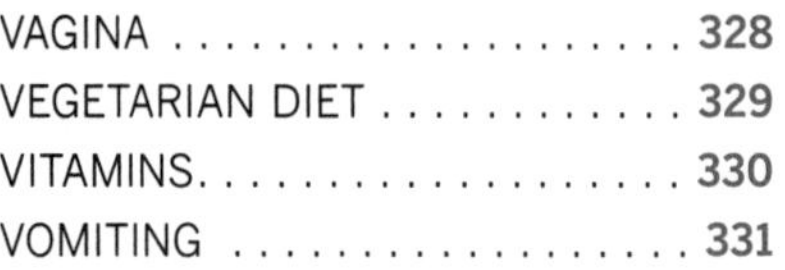

Acknowledgments

Thank you, little creatures who brighten my days with your smiles.

To your parents: Together, we have achieved our own little revolution in the world of medicine. This is your book as well.

To Judith Regan, the mastermind, for this wonderful opportunity.

To Aliza Fogelson, smart as a whip, gentle as a lamb. Your professionalism and thoroughness were a tremendous help.

To Laurie Liss, my very special agent, for your hard work.

And to you, Barak Zimmerman, for helping me find the words. You lost a few nights of sleep, but you sure saved the day.

Why another book?

Imagine a book that provides simple and reliable information on caring for your child, one that treats you like an adult and gives you what you need to know, no more and no less. Imagine a book that promotes a softer approach to pediatric care and takes a stand against overuse of medication; a book, in short, that doesn't drive you crazy at a time when, as a new parent, you're scrambling to process all the available information and make good choices.

Ten years ago, I established my pediatric practice in Manhattan's Tribeca district. My goal was to offer kids the best medical care while avoiding unnecessary intervention. Working with the thousands of parents who have entrusted me with their children, I developed the philosophy that informs this book: Less medicine is often the best medicine.

We are entering a new era in health care. On the one hand, technology has made possible amazing advances in treatment. On the other hand, there's a return to the basic principle of the Hippocratic oath: "First, do no harm." Slowly but surely, patients and doctors are realizing that we need not medicate *all* ills. Not every fever should be reduced if it helps fight a virus. Not every cough should be suppressed if it clears the airway. Not every bacterial infection should be attacked with powerful antibiotics if the body stands a good chance of fighting off the infection and thus strengthening its own immunity. This new thinking makes even more sense in regard to children, to whom nature is very gentle. Most childhood illnesses are simple and self-resolving. One should be vigilant to monitor symptoms but also to respect the body's natural defenses and to avoid unnecessary or even detrimental interventions.

The *New Basics* is the fruit of my ten years in practice, of raising my three kids, and of my experiences outside the realm of medicine. Within these pages, in a convenient A-to-Z format, you'll find the important medical and developmental issues you'll face in caring for your young child. To humanize this ocean of information, I have invented two imaginary patients: a baby named Lucy and a toddler named Jimmy. When facing challenging situations regarding your child, you'll know clearly when to worry, when not to worry, what to do, and what not to do. You'll receive guidance on when to actively intervene but also when a laissez-faire approach is your best option. You'll learn how to ignore the frivolous myths that can impair your judgment. In the end, I hope that reading this book wil help you relax as a parent.

Adenoids

See also | **Tonsils**

Adenoids are glands located behind the nose. (Don't bother looking; you can't see them without fancy equipment.) Along with the tonsils (which you *can* see in the back of the throat), the adenoids trap the germs we inhale. Occasionally, these glands cause more harm than good. They become enlarged, obstruct the airway, and provide a playground for viruses and bacteria.

Enlarged adenoids primarily affect young children, with the following possible consequences:

- Difficulty breathing through the nose, a nasal voice, or snoring, none of which is a major problem.
- Persistent colds: Some kids always seem to have a runny nose.
- Repetitive ear infections, because germs ascend from the adenoids up through the eustachian tubes to infect the middle ear [**See:** Ear Infections].
- Repetitive ear infections, which can in turn lead to a fluid buildup in the middle ear and cause temporary hearing loss.
- Sleep apnea, a condition in which a child stops breathing for more than five seconds (an eternity for the parent) several times during the night. These pauses may strain the heart by making it pump harder to meet the body's oxygen demand [**See:** Snoring and Sleep Apnea].

Years ago, almost all kids had their adenoids removed at the first little sneeze. These days, the thinking is more conservative. Since enlarged adenoids will most likely shrink with age, repetitive colds and snoring alone do not warrant removal. On the other hand, if your kid develops significant sleep apnea or a substantial hearing loss from frequent ear infections, surgery is probably indicated, but rarely before four years of age.

Removal of the adenoids is a simple outpatient procedure with swift recovery and extremely infrequent complications. When the tonsils are also removed, kids suffer slightly more postoperative risk and discomfort [**See:** Tonsils].

Adenoid removal is spectacularly successful in reducing sleep apnea. Recurrence of ear infections also decreases drastically after surgery, especially when ear tubes are indicated and inserted concomitantly. However, recurrent ear infections may not fully disappear.

REAL QUESTIONS FROM REAL PARENTS

Is there any alternative to surgery?

Some doctors prescribe antibiotics in an attempt to avoid surgery. This is a noble idea in theory, but it achieves very little. Nasal steroid sprays are another favorite treatment. Both of these approaches can buy you a little time, but they won't eliminate the need for the operation.

Can adenoids regrow?

Once removed, adenoids can regrow in a matter of months or years after the operation. By the time they do, however, the child is larger, with larger nasal passages and greater resistance to infection.

Adoption

Every pediatric practice cares for a large number of adopted kids from different countries. I love to see families bring home children from remote parts of the world, because not only does each adoption represent incredible opportunities for parent and child alike, but it's also fascinating to watch these kids adapt to their new lives. Here is what you can anticipate in terms of caring for your adopted child before, during, and after adoption.

Before

Care starts before the kid is actually in the family. Prospective parents bring me photos, medical records, and even videos of their future children. Some ask my advice concerning the health assessments they've received from adoption intermediaries. I advise them not to rely on these, because they are often inaccurate or deceptive. These kids can present a wide and sometimes undocumented variety of health concerns or diagnoses that are erroneous. However, kids adopted in the United States generally have complete health records, since they're usually adopted at birth from American hospitals.

For most parents, physical ailments would rarely deter them from adoption once they've been paired up with a child; they're ready to deal with these issues at home, no matter what. One exception of course is HIV status, because of the poor prognosis for afflicted children. In most countries, reliable HIV testing is performed at birth and made available to prospective parents. Other potential illnesses in developed countries, especially among older children, include rickets, vitamin deficiency, tuberculosis, and malnutrition. Effects of alcohol and drug use during pregnancy are less common in foreign-born children than in American kids. Family history is usually unavailable or unreliable for kids from overseas and to a lesser degree for United States kids. As with biological children, we deal with issues as they arise, no matter what family history comes into play.

During

In terms of medication or nutrition, there's not much you should bring with you to the happy occasion of meeting your child. No matter where in the world the adoption process takes you, while you're there you should feed her the same formula that she's used to [See: Formula]. If she's older, join her in eating the local food she knows until you come home, and then feed her whatever is appropriate at her age [See: Feeding].

In crowded orphanages or foster homes, kids are exposed to more than their share of colds, flus, and stomach bugs. Let the local doctor treat these conditions; even if the care is not optimal, it's your only option. I usually advise parents to call or e-mail me upon first contact with the child, and I'm sure your doctor will do the same. In a short conversation, I can get a fair idea of the child's health status and make any special recommendations if needed.

With older kids, especially, don't worry about bonding problems during the transfer of bonding from the foster home to yours. That little creature will feel your loving devotion and hang on to you right away. Within a day or so this perfect stranger will become your perfect child.

There is nothing in particular you should do on the way home; the air trip may not be easy, especially with an infant, but avoid sedative medication on the flight [See: Air Travel].

Right After

If Lucy is happy and healthy, don't rush her straight off the plane to the doctor. You can wait a couple of weeks for the first visit, when she will have a comprehensive health assessment.

Your doctor will examine her thoroughly, evaluate her development, draw some blood, and probably update her immunizations. Customary tests include the newborn screening that tests for AIDS and for a rare but preventable metabolic disease, a skin test for tuberculosis, a stool sample test for parasites, and blood tests for anemia, hepatitis B, and any other diseases specific to Lucy's country of origin [See: Immunizations; Screening Tests].

Immunization reports are usually adequate, so unless the chart looks unreliable, we complete the immunization schedule from where it left off.

After

Once any specific health issues are settled, care for this child just as you'd care for any child.

From a developmental standpoint, even when kids exhibit minor initial delays stemming from overcrowded orphanages, it's amazing to see how quickly they catch up and thrive in a loving environment, especially when they're adopted at a relatively young age. Language acquisition, for example, is miraculous. I've seen a two-year-old go from speaking the dialect of the Guangdong province in China to a decent command of English in just a few months.

Kids who are adopted are often put under a microscope and subjected to unnecessary—even erroneous—developmental interventions. I suggest you take a laissez-faire approach and use a light hand when it comes to such interventions: Allow the kid to recover on her own from the minor delays caused by neglect.

On the other hand, among the challenges adoptive parents face is to resist overcompensating with affection or attention and to be firm in enforcing the same boundaries that all children need. Refer to the "Discipline and Boundaries" entry for handling situations as they arise.

The Question

The issue of when to tell children that they are adopted is clear. As early as three or four years of age, when Lucy is able to comprehend the concept, tell her in simple and explicit terms that she was adopted. You don't need to wait for her to ask. At first, the concept will be abstract and she won't fully understand, but as she grows up and her comprehension deepens, she'll probably ask more questions that you should also answer clearly. In the United States, open adoptions allow parents of American-born kids to maintain contact with their biological parents. I've seen some unusual yet harmonious situations in which the biological parents and the child's family stayed in contact and formed a rare bond.

Air Travel

Ear Pressure

"The captain has just turned on the breast-feeding sign."

There are many myths about flying with a baby. For example, some parents believe that the change in cabin pressure will cause Lucy terrible ear pain and make her ears "pop" unless you diligently keep a nipple in her mouth during take-off and landing. Put simply, this is not true. For starters, cabin pressure is no longer the issue it was some twenty years ago; these days, computers control cabin conditions, and problems are rare. For minor changes, Lucy will just swallow her saliva and relieve the pressure without your assistance. If a little pressure builds up anyway, crying will open her eustachian tubes and relieve it. Therefore, if she's sleeping during altitude changes, you don't need to wake her up for "sucking," as some books suggest. Think of how you deal with your own pressure buildup: You yawn and yawn, almost to the point of dislocating your jaw, to equalize the pressure, with only moderate success. So if indeed a little pressure builds up in her ears, a few gulps on a nipple probably won't do the job. On the other hand, if she's awake and up for it, nursing at takeoff and landing could be a good way to distract both of you and "depressurize" her.

Flying and Crying

When you show up at the counter with a baby, the other passengers all start wondering if they'll have to sit next to you. As you know, babies can exhibit all kinds of bad behaviors that are only magnified by the cramped space of a commercial jetliner. If Lucy cries during the flight, just as she would at home, you're going to get some serious looks from the people sitting around you. Unfortunately, apart from gently rocking and feeding her if she's hungry, there isn't much you can or should do. Be aware that whether you're in-flight or at home, overfeeding and overrocking can worsen the crying. When nothing you do makes a difference, you have no options left; just let Lucy exhaust herself to sleep. As for the other passengers . . . aren't the headsets free these days?

When Can Babies Fly?

As soon as you can tolerate sitting for the duration of the flight. Sure, crowded places like airplane cabins carry an increased risk of colds and flu, but so does a kiss from grandma or an older sibling, and they'll come much closer to Lucy than your fellow air passengers will. Contrary to popular belief, Lucy can travel without all her immunizations and can even be exposed to the outside world. For the most part, the illnesses against which we commonly immunize have already been eradicated, thanks to the effectiveness of these vaccines.

Flying with Ear Infections

If Jimmy has recently been diagnosed with an ear infection, don't automatically cancel your flight plans. Most ear infections are mild and short-lived. Just bring along some pain medication in case he experiences discomfort. Even the worst-case scenario, in which the eardrum bursts, is often misunderstood. It's only a remote possibility, and it can happen on the ground as well as in the air. And no matter where it happens, it's not cataclysmic; in the vast majority of cases, it heals perfectly [**See:** Ear Infections].

Flying and Sleeping Aids

Nothing short of a heavy-duty sleeping pill will knock Jimmy out for five or six hours straight. Decongestants such as Benadryl may induce drowsiness, but their soporific action is temporary. To top it off, these medications can have an unexpected reverse effect, in which case you'll have to put up with a child who's bouncing around as if he's personally responsible for creating turbulence. Bring lots of toys instead; distraction is far better than drugs.

Flying and Car Seats

They give you the advantage of not having to hold Lucy for the whole flight, but they're cumbersome and require an extra seat, which could be pricey. In terms of safety during turbulence, holding Lucy in your arms is probably just as safe as a car seat (as long as your own seat belt is securely fastened, snug and low).

Anesthesia

The thought of putting your child to sleep for surgery or an MRI may make you think twice about the procedure. Rest assured, anesthesia and sedation are safe, even in young children. As with any drug, anesthetics and sedatives can have side effects, including severe allergic reactions. But this is very rare, and if a complication does arise, there are many interventions to counteract it. Once an operation or MRI is deemed necessary, don't let the risks of anesthesia dissuade you from going forward.

Antibiotics

Everyone agrees that antibiotics are overused, but everyone overuses them. The reasons for overreliance on antibiotics are psychological: Doctors need to earn patients' trust by prescribing something as well as to consider the distant specter of liability. And then of course there is the laziness factor. While it's easy to whip out the prescription pad, it's harder to spend fifteen minutes communicating actual medical knowledge.

I encourage parents to fully understand their child's condition and the range of treatments available before defaulting to an antibiotic, which has no positive effect when it's not warranted. I find that most people will forego unnecessary treatment once they understand the reasoning behind waiting. Questions like "If we don't treat this condition with antibiotics, is there a decent chance it will get better on its own?" should become part of your repertoire. Assuming your doctor is open to such back-and-forth, this attitude will help reduce undesirable side effects, such as yeast infections or allergic reactions, and give your child a chance to build up a natural resistance to infections. By the way, if your doctor is not open to such a discussion, I suggest that you find one who is.

The overprescription of antibiotics is an economic issue, certainly—drug companies get fat when their products are prescribed—but it is also a serious medical one. Those germs that survive a first round of antibiotics become resistant and more difficult to eliminate, posing a greater threat to the community.

What are the most common situations where antibiotics are improperly prescribed? First of all, there's the common cold. Antibiotics have no effect on colds, even if there's an everlasting nasal discharge and even when this discharge is green (which does not automatically indicate sinusitis). The same thing goes for the flu, unless there are complications. And antibiotics should no longer be used routinely for ear infections or lingering coughs.

Think of it this way: When you actually need antibiotics, you want them to work, so don't waste their potency by needlessly overusing them.

Apgar Scores

Apgar scores (named for Dr. Virginia Apgar, who invented them) are a set of numbers that are assigned upon examination of a newborn at the first and fifth minutes of life. Based on brief tests for heart rate, breathing, muscle tone, reflex response, and skin color, these numbers are not meant to indicate how healthy a newborn is. On the contrary, they help doctors decide what type of intervention is needed in case of a complication at delivery. By the time you're cozy in your room with Lucy, these scores are meaningless, because she's already been deemed healthy.

Appendicitis

See also | **Belly Pain**

Appendicitis, the inflammation of the small appendix of the intestine, causes a painful infection in the belly. It is rare in children under five but not unheard of. Typically, Jimmy will experience pain in the right lower part of his belly, just above the groin. It starts slowly but soon becomes excruciating, while fever and vomiting may develop. Appendicitis often shows up in an atypical fashion: The child could be feverless, and the pain could subside after increasing (not a good thing, because it could mean that the abscess has ruptured and the infection will spread). It may even happen in kids too young to point to their bellies. For these reasons, belly pain in kids always provokes suspicions of appendicitis. Still, the most reliable sign is the intensity of the pain. If Jimmy suddenly complains of intense abdominal pain, don't second-guess yourself. If you have any doubt, call your doctor for advice. The only way to treat a confirmed case of appendicitis is surgery.

Apple Juice

Commercial apple juices are composed mainly of sugar and water. In general, I don't endorse sugary drinks for infants and toddlers; they encourage a sweet tooth and reduce the appetite for nutritious foods. Also, when imbibed in excess they can act as a laxative and cause ongoing diarrhea. Of course there is no need for strict prohibition; a little diluted apple juice isn't going to turn Lucy into a sugar junkie. But there is nothing wrong with giving kids plain water.

Asthma

See also | **Colds; Pets; Respiratory Allergy**

Asthma is an overreaction and constriction of the small "pipes" of the lungs. It appears from time to time in a predisposed child in response to irritants that trigger mucus production and tighten the passageways.

Asthma is inherited. Typically, one of the parents either outgrew asthma as a child or still has occasional attacks. Although infants and toddlers can have breathing problems that resemble asthma, true asthma usually does not reveal itself until the end of the second year. The majority of asthmatic children will experience mild or moderate attacks that last a couple of days, during which breathing is difficult and the kid has a deep, productive cough. Respiration is shallow and is accompanied by a characteristic fine wheezing. Before age five, the likeliest triggering agents are by far colds and flus. Beyond this age, respiratory allergens such as dust, pollens, and animal dander can be factors, as can food allergens and even exercise.

Only a small minority of asthmatics are in any serious danger. Most folks outgrow asthma: The attacks become less frequent and less intense until they disappear completely, although some kids remain asthmatic into adulthood.

How to Recognize a Mild Attack

In a mild asthma attack, Jimmy can still talk and sustain an activity such as playing. His chest moves in and out quickly, but the muscles of the chest and neck do not "pull" hard. The skin remains pink.

How to Recognize a Moderate Attack

Jimmy breathes quickly, and you can hear some wheezing. His activity is reduced, but he's still moving around. He isn't working hard to breathe, and his skin is still pink.

How to Recognize a Severe Attack

In a severe asthma attack, Jimmy's breathing is labored, or in other words he has to work hard to inhale and exhale. He looks distressed and pale (maybe even blue around the mouth, with semiclosed eyes), and his only preoccupation is breathing. In addition, his neck muscles and those between his ribs become clearly visible in between breaths. A severe attack will require treatment at the emergency room.

How to Treat an Asthma Attack

Asthma treatment relies on two different classes of medication: muscle relaxants and steroids. When an attack occurs, it lasts for a few days and then subsides spontaneously. During that time, medication should be minimized; the child's comfort is paramount, but asthma medications have significant side effects, even in small doses. If Jimmy has mild difficulty breathing but is otherwise normally active, no treatment is warranted, since there is nothing to improve. For a moderate attack, asthma medications are administered according to the level of discomfort. A severe attack is treated in a hospital.

Medications That May Be Used

Muscle Relaxants

Muscle relaxants such as Albuterol increase airflow by relaxing the muscles around the pipes. They don't cure or prevent asthma; they simply improve the breathing until the attack wanes. They are best administered with a nebulizer, a device that delivers the medication in a fine mist. (They also come in handy manual pumps, which are great for older kids who have good coordination.)

In terms of side effects, the lungs are the only thing these medications relax. Kids become quite jumpy on them, and their hearts beat rapidly for an hour or so after the treatment. Compared to impaired breathing, this is a minor problem, but it's a good reason not to overuse them if respiration is only minimally compromised. These muscle relaxants act almost instantaneously but have short-lived effects. The instructions say to take them every four hours, but at the peak of an asthma attack, you can administer them frequently, as often as every twenty minutes for a few hours, since young children have strong hearts. However, if you reach the point where you're administering this kind of drug three or four times in a row before seeing a positive effect, it probably indicates a need for tighter medical supervision, so call your doctor for advice.

Steroids

Oral steroids act more slowly than muscle relaxants, but they tackle the problem at its source by reducing the inflammation of the pulmonary pipes. In the right situation (e.g., when an asthma attack lingers or if breathing seems to be worsening despite the muscle relaxants), short courses of steroids have tremendous benefits with no side effects. They greatly reduce the severity of the attack and can prevent a hospital stay. But if used too often, they can have short- and long-term repercussions, such as a predisposition to infection and disturbance of bone growth. Daily inhaled steroids should be reserved for children who suffer recurrent asthma attacks in spite of all other preventive measures.

Medications to Avoid

Muscle relaxants and steroids are the only two types of medicine that are effective in treating asthma. Avoid cough suppressants since coughing helps clear mucus from the breathing pipes. If Jimmy's nocturnal hacking is preventing him from sleeping, however, you can bend this rule.

What May Help Prevent an Asthma Attack

- Limit exposure to smoke, dust, and other irritants. Remove from an asthmatic child's room anything that can harbor these: carpets, stuffed animals, plants, books, curtains, and down pillows and comforters. Wrap his mattress and pillows in plastic or zippered antiallergen cases to control the level of allergenic particles and dust mites.
- Vacuum the house thoroughly.
- Severe asthmatics commonly receive the flu vaccination in an effort to minimize their chances of contracting a triggering virus, but the vaccine's effectiveness is very limited. Common colds, the main cause of asthma in children, can't really be prevented.
- In cases of allergic asthma, avoiding allergens is important. But don't rush to give away the family pet just because Lucy has had a mild reaction to cat hair [See: Pets].

What May Not Help Prevent an Asthma Attack

- Starting Jimmy on a nebulizer at the first sign of a cold is relatively inefficient in preventing an attack, and exposes him to side effects.
- For children who have frequent bouts, there is a fairly new medication called Singulair, which is supposed to prevent the irritation of the airway. Although it has few side effects, the benefits are inconsistent. Also, when a child on Singulair doesn't have an attack, you won't really know if it's the medication at work or if the child is simply outgrowing the condition.
- Herbal and homeopathic treatments have no proven benefits, nor do dietary changes. Parents often try these options, and I can tell you firsthand that, unfortunately, I have seen no clear benefit from any alternative therapies or specific diets.

REAL QUESTIONS FROM REAL PARENTS

Can I prevent my child from becoming asthmatic?
If your child is predisposed, there is little you can do to prevent asthma. Breast feeding may provide a small protective factor, but it is unclear to what extent.

If one of us has asthma, what are the chances our child will get it?
Hard to say. There will be a definite predisposition, but it's not a sure shot. You'll just have to wait and see.

Does eczema predispose to asthma?
Those with asthma often have eczema, but most people with eczema don't have asthma, so in a word, no.

Could a persistent cough be asthma?
The jury is still out on this one. For me, asthma has to include a significant amount of wheezing. In any event, asthma medications have little effect on these lingering coughs and should be avoided because of their side effects. Also, if it really is asthma you're dealing with, the cough helps by bringing up the mucus.

Attachment Parenting

See also | **Colic**

I have always thought that parents are instinctively attached to their babies. Apparently not everyone shares that point of view. In one of his many baby books, Dr. William Sears introduces a concept he calls "attachment parenting," wherein he teaches new parents how to develop a connection with their new baby, just in case they don't know how to do so on their own.

Dr. Sears's grand theory can be boiled down to one sentence: When your baby cries, it's always for a reason, and you should attempt to stop the crying, no matter what it takes. To assist parents with this task, he furnishes an elaborate set of rocking and jumping methods as well as an intricate square-dance routine. Unfortunately, I have encountered many parents who followed this philosophy and literally drove themselves and their baby crazy with guilt and frustration when it didn't work. And it will never work as well as he suggests.

There's no question that a young baby's cries often indicate hunger or a need for closeness, and that need should be tended to. But you'll find that no matter how loving a parent you are, Lucy will cry sometimes simply because she needs a release. She can't talk. She can't exercise. She has no creative outlets. So how does she blow off steam? By crying and flailing about. Attempting to suppress that crying at all costs worsens the problem by denying her a natural soothing mechanism. Ultimately, the obsession with avoiding crying will make the whole family anxious and unhappy. I assure you, you are attached. Just trust your instincts.

Attention Deficit Disorder (ADD)

See also | **Discipline and Boundaries**

Attention deficit disorder (ADD) is the medical term used to describe children who experience trouble focusing and concentrating and who exhibit hyperactivity and impulsiveness. The condition and its causes are poorly understood. Researchers are increasingly attempting to find a link to a brain dysfunction, but so far they have no conclusive evidence.

I believe ADD is both overdiagnosed and overtreated. Many children who don't have ADD are impulsive and have a low tolerance for frustration. The pattern can take root at an early age, when a toddler fails to acquire proper frustration-management skills and a sense of boundaries. Parents play a major role in the early acquisition of these skills, and inconsistent responses to a toddler's frustration can foster this behavior. These kids become so preoccupied with control issues that they lose their ability to focus on other matters, such as a school curriculum, an art project, or a play activity. This can lead to low self-esteem and unhappiness, which in turn reinforce the impulsiveness. Too frequently, these kids end up misdiagnosed and treated for ADD. This quick fix suggests that the problem stems from some faulty wiring in Jimmy's brain rather than from fundamental issues of parenting and discipline.

The treatment of true ADD relies primarily on brain stimulants (the most popular being Ritalin), which do not "cure" the condition; they simply help kids focus and calm down. We don't know exactly why these medications work and to what extent. It's hard to study them, because the initial diagnosis of ADD is so subjective and the tangible improvements hard to measure. Other classes of drugs are being investigated, such as antidepressants, but it's too early to judge their efficacy.

In my experience, in cases of true ADD, the medications are pretty good at producing significant behavioral modification soon after the start of treatment. Concentration improves more dramatically than impulsiveness and hyperactivity do, though they are related phenomena: Once a child can concentrate better, his improved self-esteem usually leads to less impulsiveness.

Children generally tolerate ADD drugs well. The few short-term side effects—decreased appetite, tics, and insomnia—can be managed by decreasing the dosage. Long-term side effects appear to be low as well, at least for Ritalin, which has been around for many years.

Most kids with true ADD grow up to become balanced adults. With proper support, they learn to manage their concentration spans and to choose activities that are appropriate to their skills and abilities.

One final word on the issue: It is estimated that up to 5 percent of American children show signs of ADD, a sharp increase in comparison with ten years ago. Drug companies don't seem to mind this increase, and while they will no doubt insist that they are simply doing what drug companies should do—help remedy a newly identified problem—it is clear that ADD treatment has become a huge industry. In the medical magazines I receive, the bulk of the advertisements are for ADD medication and are aimed at influencing doctors to be heavy-handed with the prescription pad. I believe children who truly have ADD should get all the help they need, but as parents, we must guard vigilantly against the interests of drug companies in directing how our children's behavior is understood and treated.

REAL QUESTIONS FROM REAL PARENTS

If my toddler is hyperactive, what are the chances that he will develop ADD?

While hyperactivity could be an early sign, most bouncing toddlers turn out not to have ADD.

What are the early signs of ADD?

Early signs can appear in preschool, when a teacher expresses concern that Jimmy is not sustaining interest in a specific activity or is particularly disruptive during structured activities. However, these signs are unreliable and do not solidify until a child is in primary school, around six or seven years of age, when measurable performance is affected. Also, toddlers are inherently different in terms of how they focus. The one who does not sit willingly in a circle or clap his hands on the beat in music class will not necessarily develop ADD later on. He may just have a different imaginary world or may not yet be interested in socialization.

Can I prevent ADD?

You can provide a consistent approach at the toddler stage for boundaries and frustration; this may help to avoid ADD-like behavior, but you can't prevent true ADD.

How can I know for sure if my child has ADD?

We have no definitive tests yet for a formal diagnosis of ADD. A psychological evaluation relies on subjective observations from parents, teachers, and the psychologist or psychiatrist conducting the evaluation. To tell the truth, the diagnosis for ADD is less scientific than you would think. These assessments are far from accurate, since diagnosis is often based on suspicion, and medication is tentatively prescribed. If that medication then results in a conspicuous shift in personality, it is determined ex post facto that the child most likely had ADD.

Is there any alternative to drugs?

I've seen people try all kinds of alternative approaches, many of which center on a child's diet. None makes a substantial difference in "real" ADD. Psychotherapy is unfortunately not that effective either. Again, the only alternative that I would recommend—whether or not "real" ADD is the culprit—is establishing consistent boundaries. These simple rules make a huge difference if Jimmy has boundary-frustration issues, and even if actual ADD turns out to be the problem, they are excellent management strategies that will help him cope with his moods [**See:** Discipline and Boundaries].

What if I am afraid to give my child drugs?

ADD medications have been the victim of bad press, and it's easy to see why. Too many teachers suggest them for kids who are simply hard to handle. Too many doctors are ready to dispense them liberally. And too many parents just go along with these recommendations following a "path of least resistance." If you and your doctor share a strong suspicion that Jimmy has actual ADD rather than simple impulsiveness, one option is to try medication, at least for a short while, and see if there's a difference. If not, then at least you know.

How long is the treatment?

That's the trick question. ADD drug treatments are not quick fixes, and they frequently last well into the teens. As with every chronic medication, doctors reassess from time to time by decreasing the dosage and monitoring the change in behavior.

Autism

See also | **Sensory Integration**

Autism is a rare, poorly understood condition in which children, usually boys, are disconnected from other beings to an extreme degree. It becomes evident if a child fails to acquire language by the second year of life. Although some perfectly normal children will talk late, autistic children characteristically have no receptivity to language and make only furtive eye contact. They always seem to be in their own world, won't cuddle, and may engage in repetitive, self-stimulating behavior, such as spinning around.

Autistic children can have exceptional abilities in specific areas such as music. Similarly, Asperger syndrome is a specific form of autism in which a child is highly intelligent but has great difficult relating to others. Finally, some children display autistic features to various degrees without being fully autistic, in what we call "pervasive disorders."

Neurologists believe autism to be a malfunction of a specific part of the brain in genetically predisposed individuals. Researchers are investigating possible links between autism and in-utero exposure to various hazardous substances, but so far no one has established definitive connections. In the last decade, autism has been on the rise, but this may be a function of improved diagnoses, not increasing numbers, since cases of nonspecific mental retardation have declined in the same period.

Sadly, there is nothing you can do to prevent autism, and it's unclear whether early diagnosis and treatment can change the outcome significantly. Treatment is palliative and relies on behavioral modification to help autistic children acquire some language.

A few years ago, a poorly conducted study raised the possibility of a link between autism and the vaccine for measles, mumps, and rubella (MMR). Since then, a number of other studies have demonstrated conclusively that MMR vaccines do not trigger autism, but those studies have received less attention in the press. In addition, thimerosal, a mercury-based preservative that was previously used in vaccines, has also been incriminated, though never very scientifically. As a result, many parents are still afraid to let doctors administer the MMR vaccines to their children, although the health benefits far outweigh these small and unconfirmed risks of autism.

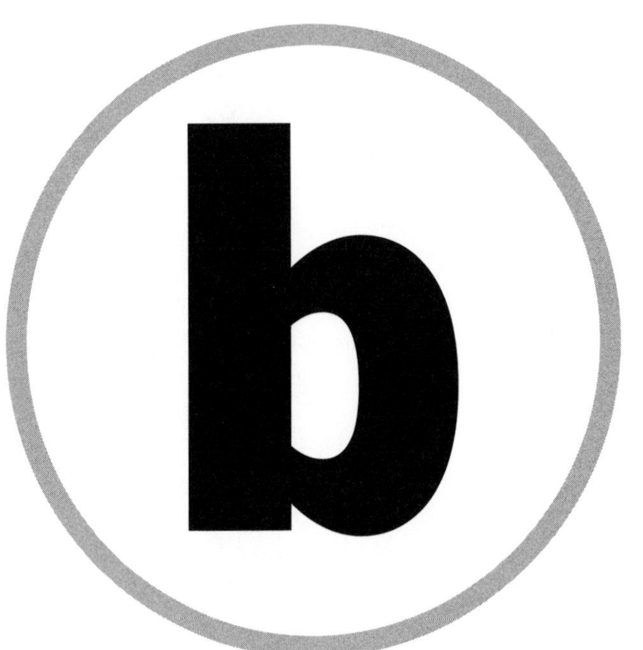
b

Baby Carriers and Slings

See also | **Strollers**

My neighbor is an ex-hippie who used to carry her baby in one of the earliest papoose-style carriers rather than using a traditional carriage. People heaped abuse on her and told her that she was hurting her baby both psychologically and physically.

Those nosey parkers were wrong. People still feel apprehensive when it comes to placing a newborn in such a primitive means of transportation, but rest assured Lucy will be comfortable and safe in a baby carrier or a sling. Remember, she was tucked into a ball for nine months and survived it just fine. Her back is just as flexible, so there's no reason to assume that after birth she'll suddenly want to lounge in a carriage like an adult in a bed. She'll be happy to be bundled up against you like in the good old days.

Baby-carrier labels advise caution for newborns lighter than eight pounds, not because of discomfort or possible back issues, but because a small baby can fall through the carrier's side opening. If you choose to use a papoose-style carrier before your baby reaches eight pounds, make sure you adjust the straps properly. No matter the baby's size, beware of her falling while you're putting her in and taking her out of a sling.

These baby carriers aren't just convenient; they're also lifesavers during Lucy's "cranky time," when nothing but a rocking motion can calm her. And after Lucy outgrows her carrier, you can move her into a backpack-style carrier if you're the hiking type.

Baby Food

See also | **Feeding**

Here's a good way to gauge the appeal of prepared baby foods: Take the jar and look carefully at the expiration date. The substance inside has been designed to last for two years past the date of purchase. By the time you've brought this squishy stuff home, it's been a while since this Earth's best selection was gathered from Mother Earth. How could it taste like anything other than paste? I have seen countless parents of ten-month-old babies who complain about their infant's lack of interest in new foods, when in fact what they're really witnessing is their baby's determination to spit up an unctuous puree that looks the same before and after it's been in the child's mouth.

There is nothing wrong with giving babies prepared foods for the sake of convenience, but don't believe these preparations are a healthier option. The healthiest baby foods are the ones you make by mashing up whatever you're having for your own meal. The result will certainly be fresher and tastier than anything manufactured by a giant baby-food corporation.

Don't be afraid to feed Lucy food that's spicy or strange. Try steak, fish, pasta, vegetables, salty foods, peppery foods, garlicky foods; all you need is a fork or a food processor and a little bit of imagination. You can also prepare a bunch of semisolid meals and freeze them in ice-cube trays for later. And don't worry that your system is less precise than the corporation's; their complex labeling system (stage one, stage two, etc.) might appear scientific, but it's really just a marketing gimmick.

Bad Breath

In infants, bad breath usually accompanies the advent of teeth. The gums become a little irritated and can smell foul when the new choppers pierce through. In older kids, bad breath could result from the appearance of back teeth as well as from mouth breathing at night, which dries the mouth and allows bacteria to flourish. Enlarged adenoids are the main cause of mouth breathing [**See: Adenoids**]. Finally, a persistent foul odor in Jimmy's mouth could indicate that he has inserted something in his nose, which should be removed by your doctor.

Bed Graduation

See also | **Sleep**

When should Jimmy make the transition from crib to bed? Persistent attempts to climb overboard are a sign he may be ready. Even if he doesn't attempt a breakout, most kids are happy to be freed from their crib prison around two years of age. When he's first getting used to his new bed, be prepared to find Jimmy on the other side of his room in the morning or in your bed in the middle of the night. If you don't mind either of these outcomes, pick an occasion, such as his second birthday, and go shopping for a new toddler bed. The bed could include an optional side rail that prevent falls, but remember, toppling out of a low bed a few times teaches children not to fall later on. You can also lay the groundwork for the crib-to-bed transition by buying a convertible crib that becomes a toddler bed thanks to an adjustable mattress and rail.

Kids usually greet "bed graduation" with joy. Don't press the issue if Jimmy doesn't. Keep both the crib and the bed in his room, and try to make the switch again a few weeks later. Just be patient . . . I have yet to hear of a five-year-old who still sleeps in a crib.

Bedtime

See also | **Sleep**

Parents often ask me how much sleep their child needs at night. There is just no magic number; it varies from kid to kid. The average for all kids, as early as the third to fourth month of age, is eight to ten straight uninterrupted hours, but this depends on how much they nap during the day. The ideal bedtime is when both parents have had an opportunity to giggle and read with the kids, then say good night and still have time for themselves and each other. For this reason, if one or both parents return home late from work it may be worth it to delay the kid's bedtime (within reason). That said, I find that school-age kids rarely wake up happy if they've gone to bed past ten the previous night.

The worst reason to let a kid stay up late is because he doesn't want to go to bed. Jimmy may fight sleep just to stay up and be part of the action, but you must be firm.

Bed-Wetting

As most children transition from diapers to potty training, they learn to hold their urine overnight. Some kids take longer. By the age of five, if they have bouts of nighttime incontinence, kids are considered "bed wetters." Bed-wetting is far more common in boys, and it runs in the family. In rare cases, the problem can persist into adolescence.

Besides the stress of excessive laundry, bed-wetting is a problem only to the extent that it may embarrass Jimmy, although his embarrassment could be a reflection of yours.

In the end, there's little you can do. Bed-wetting eventually resolves itself when Jimmy's bladder gets more mature. You can buy alarms that ring when the bed is wet, but they'll only wake *you* up; Jimmy will continue to sleep, drenched in blissful ignorance. Medications have proven ineffective so far. The latest fad is an expensive hormonal medication named DDAVP, which I have found to be just as useless as other bed-wetting medications, despite the company's claims. To control the problem, limit your child's prebedtime fluid intake. You might say, "Nothing to drink after 8:00 P.M." You can also teach him to change the bedclothes and run a load of laundry. The less of an issue the bed-wetting is for you, the less it will be for him.

If bed-wetting recurs after Jimmy has been dry for a significant time, it could be a reaction to a stressful event such as moving, starting a new school, or witnessing parents fight. When the stress subsides, the bed usually dries out again.

Belly Button

At Birth

At delivery, when Lucy's umbilical cord is cut and clamped, she is left with a funny piece of plastic on her abdomen. The clamp stays on for a few days, until the nurse ceremoniously removes it and reveals an inch of protruding skin that you'd rather not have to deal with. Don't let this stump intimidate you; it's just a piece of drying, dead skin. And when it's completely dry, it will break off at the base, leaving a white area in the middle, which will eventually become regular skin.

REAL QUESTIONS FROM REAL PARENTS

How should I care for the stump?
You can drip some alcohol on it for drying and cleaning, but you might as well leave it alone to heal naturally. Either way, the result will be the same.

When will it fall off?
Anywhere from a few days to a few weeks. Like any body part, some stumps are bigger than others. The thick ones take longer to dry and fall off.

When can I bathe the baby?
If you were to bathe Lucy for many hours a day, the umbilical stump would stay moist and have no chance to dry. But a little water here and there, and even a short bath daily, won't impede the drying.

What about the oozing?
At the base of the belly button, where the tissue is still alive, there is a slight oozing of clear secretions. This is normal.

What about the blood?
When the stump is about to fall off, or if it already has, there could be a little bit of bleeding that is of no concern.

How will I know if it gets infected?
Infection is quite rare, but if it were to occur, you would see an area of intense redness and swelling around the area. This is not to be confused with a mild irritation caused by the rubbing of the dry stump against the surrounding skin. If you suspect an infection of the navel area, call your doctor.

In Infants

Belly-Button Swelling

When the muscles around the base of the umbilical cord do not tighten enough after birth, the intestinal content bulges out and forms an "umbilical hernia." Though minimal at first, the bulging increases in the first few months as Lucy grows, and it can become quite large.

These hernias are totally painless. The belief that they are not springs from a simple misunderstanding. Whenever Lucy cries, the pressure on her belly increases and the hernia bulges. As a result, you might think that she is crying because of the bulging hernia, when in fact the reverse is true: The hernia bulges because she is crying.

Umbilical hernias, even large ones, will usually disappear of their own accord within the first year. In rare cases, they persist into late childhood and require surgical correction. Common folk remedies, such as taping a coin to the belly button, are worthless, may irritate the skin, . . . and don't even bring good luck.

Belly Pain

See also | **Appendicitis**

The most typical belly pain that children experience is a vague waxing and waning discomfort in the middle of the abdomen. In general, it's caused by stomach bugs, indigestion, or constipation. Serious belly pain, the most feared being appendicitis, is rare and intense. Certain signs will help you distinguish mild pain from other twinges.

WHEN **TO WORRY**

- **If the pain increases rapidly,** with no period of relief
- **If Jimmy is unable to sit,** stand, or walk
- **If he is unable to participate** in any other activity and focuses exclusively on the pain
- **If he can't sleep** because of the intensity of the pain

- **If the pain is in a specific spot** rather than a vague discomfort (the right-hand side of the groin would indicate appendicitis)
- **If there is high fever** and vomiting

If he suffered a recent blow to the belly, which could have caused an internal injury

If your child exhibits any of the above, a doctor should evaluate him immediately.

WHEN **NOT TO WORRY**

- **If the pain alternates** with periods of relief
- **If Jimmy can handle other activities,** such as watching TV
- **If he can sleep** through the pain
- **If the pain is vaguely localized,** or up near the navel
- **If he is able to jump** without extreme discomfort
- **If the pain improves** with a belly massage
- **If he has a good appetite**

For mild belly pain, you can give Jimmy a regular painkiller, such as acetaminophen, but don't give it too often; if you mask the symptoms, you may not get an accurate sense of the severity and duration of the pain. Other over-the-counter medications such as antacids have no real benefits in most cases of belly pain, since kids are rarely subject to hyperacidity.

"Belly Pains in the Head"

Belly pains in kids often originate in their heads, and for some reason are more common in school-age girls. You can recognize these mental belly pains if the child vaguely points to her navel but is otherwise in perfect health and shows no other signs of ill health (such as vomiting or diarrhea). Invariably, if you give the allegedly sore tummy a little rubbing and cuddling in response, the next time your girl is looking for a little attention she'll tell you her belly suddenly hurts again. As soon as you decrease the therapeutic pampering, these aches will magically disappear.

Bites

See also | **Pets**

If your child gets bitten, your main concern is infection from the biter's mouth. All mouths, whether human or animal, are heavily contaminated with germs. For a bite to bear the risk of infection, it must break the skin; if the teeth leave only an imprint, there's no risk at all. A penetrating bite, however, requires vigilance and should be evaluated by a doctor, who may prescribe preventive antibiotics. If the site becomes infected, you'll see significant redness, pain, and swelling, which will definitely require an oral antibiotic. To reduce the chance of infection and avoid trapping germs under the skin, doctors rarely suture open bite wounds, unless they're on the face (for cosmetic reasons).

If it's a penetrating animal wound, you also have to consider the possibility of rabies, a rare but potentially fatal disease. Since rabid animals become inexplicably aggressive, consult your physician immediately if your child is bitten without provocation by a dog or wild animal such as a bat. The only treatment for rabies is early vaccination, which should be administered as soon as possible after the bite.

Biting

See also | **Discipline; Teething**

Babies practice oral exploration from a fairly young age, first by gumming their hands and other objects and then, as early as six months of age, by biting. Biting involves all encountered objects, including you. The first bites are (probably) not premeditated, but Lucy soon discovers that biting can be a lot of fun. When she sinks her brand-new little fangs into your arm, the noise you make is far more entertaining than any sounds her toys can produce. As she develops the habit, she will, unfortunately for you, learn to distinguish the "squeakier" places, such as your nipple.

To stop her biting, just don't respond. As difficult as this sounds, it is effective. When Lucy bites you, just move your arm out of the way without screaming.

She'll quickly find another way to make noise, or she'll go back to her squeaky toys.

In Toddlers

Of course I'm upset! Here's how I found out. When I picked Jimmy up at nursery school today, Mrs. Campbell–you know, the school director–gave me the strangest look and said we needed to talk. Once we were in her office, that's when she told me Jimmy had bitten some other kid–our Jimmy! She even showed me a Polaroid of his tooth-marks on this poor little girl's arm. Mrs. Campbell was suspicious. She asked if everything's going well here at home, or if we've had any major changes in the family. She even offered to send Jimmy to the school psychologist! What should we do?

For toddlers, biting is guaranteed to get a reaction from parents, teachers, and other adults. It is true that the first bites stem from frustration, but Jimmy soon grows all too aware of the commotion that bites generate. To eradicate this anti-social behavior, you must limit the attention Jimmy receives for biting, because he understands it as positive reinforcement.

How to Stop a Toddler from Biting

- Try to head off the triggering circumstance. If you sense that a particular situation is about to take a turn for the worse, scoop Jimmy up before he gets his teeth ready for action. The fewer chances he has to bite, the less he'll bite.
- If he manages to bite at home, tell him this is not appropriate, put him in his room for a couple of minutes, and then let him out without any more discussion.
- Do the same thing at the park if he bites or tries to: Strap him in the stroller for a little while to cool off as you roll him along in silence.
- As embarrassed as you may feel in front of the other parents, don't lecture him. Jimmy enjoys the attention, even though he has no idea what you're talking about.
- Don't insist on an apology. Jimmy isn't sorry, but he also didn't mean any harm. He just was a little frustrated and didn't know how to handle it.
- Don't expect him to use words instead of biting (assuming he already has the ability to speak). He'll resort to words as he gets older. On top of that, the words that come out of Jimmy's mouth instead of biting may not make you too happy.

Biting and hitting are totally normal behaviors for a toddler. If you give these events minimal attention and enforce boundaries properly, you won't see more than a few exploratory bites. And before the end of his second year, Jimmy will have abandoned his canine inclinations and moved on to more "acceptable" ways of coping with frustration.

Blood

See also | **Ear Infections; Stomach Bugs**

In general, we would rather our kids' blood stay inside them, where it's supposed to be. In the unfortunate case that it doesn't, here's how to assess the severity of the problem and how to handle it.

In the Diaper

Blood can appear in the diapers of newborns for many of these benign reasons:

- Because eating is a new process, the intestine can become slightly irritated, resulting in a few temporary streaks of blood. Persistent blood in the stools of formula-fed babies can be a sign of intolerance.
- Some parents (but not you, right?) follow recommendations to stimulate a baby's rectum with a thermometer to help relieve the baby of stools. Besides interfering with the natural defecation process, this can obviously irritate the area and cause bleeding. I suggest you stay away from this barbaric practice.
- For Lucy, blood in the diapers may be the result of a natural but surprising hormonal process. She could have assumed some of your maternal hormonal profile and then shed those hormones, resulting in a quasi-menstrual process that can produce a tiny amount of blood in the first couple of weeks.
- Finally, not everything in a diaper that looks like blood is blood. The normal precipitation of the urine into crystals can appear as red-tinged stains, especially in newborns. This is not a reliable sign of dehydration, no matter what you may read in some books.
- Blood in Lucy's stools can also result, to a lesser degree, from causes that usually affect toddlers. Described below, these include stomach bugs and a blockage of the intestine called *intussusception*.

In Vomit

You may see blood in vomit or spit-up when a baby has been ingesting milk through a cracked nipple, even if the fissure is not obvious. There is no reason to be alarmed or to discontinue nursing. When the fissure heals, the blood will disappear.

In Stools

- For Jimmy, blood in the stool is usually the result of a fissure caused by constipation. If the stools are hard and his pain is intense, you can give him a glycerin suppository, repeating it daily until the fissure heals. It's more important, however, that you resolve the constipation by limiting the starch in his diet [See: Constipation].
- If blood in the stool is accompanied by diarrhea, this may point to a stomach bug [See: Stomach Bug].
- In rare cases, blood in the stool can be caused by a mechanical blockage called intussusception, which also causes intense belly pain and vomiting. It requires immediate medical attention.

In Vomit

The effort of vomiting can provoke a small amount of bleeding from a little tear in the upper digestive system. It usually doesn't recur; there's no cause for concern. For a large amount of blood, seek medical attention.

In Ears

If blood leaks from the ears, mixed with pus, it usually indicates a perforated eardrum caused by an ear infection, which you either already know about or will discover thanks to this unfortunate bleeding [See: Ear Infections].

In Noses

This is your average benign nosebleed, usually caused either by nose picking or by warm weather and dry air [See: Nosebleeds].

Blood Type

I often hear parents complain that they weren't told their baby's blood type at birth. I reassure them that there's no good reason to know and that most hospitals don't even run the test routinely any longer. Thirty years ago, blood type was a major issue. If, God forbid, you were in an accident and needed a transfusion, the hospital or paramedics had to rely on a card in your wallet that indicated your blood group; if they had to determine your blood type in real time, you might have been past needing the blood by the time they were done. Thanks to new technology, blood typing is now instantaneous, and as for that card, you can leave home without it.

Blue Extremities

Young babies' hands and feet sometimes turn blue, thanks to the tiny size of their blood vessels. When these vessels constrict they may limit blood flow, but the resulting bluish tinge doesn't necessarily mean your baby is cold. After the first couple of months these blue episodes will become less common.

Bones

In Infants

Clicks and Pops

Sometimes, when you pick Lucy up, you hear a popping sound coming from her shoulder or elbow. Don't worry; she isn't broken. It's just the sound of the cartilage and bone giving a bit, which produces a click.

Bone Injury

Since they have few opportunities to hurt themselves, infants rarely suffer broken bones. Nonetheless, breaks can happen, typically either from trauma or twisting. A broken bone usually produces a persistent crying and/or a noticeable deformation in the limb. In either case, make sure Lucy receives medical attention immediately.

In Children

Bones can break in many ways: direct trauma, a fall, or a trapped limb. After a limb injury, if there is no swelling and the pain subsides enough to let activity resume, it's probably not a broken bone. Any deformity or swelling, or a persistent limp, requires medical attention, especially if there is an associated open wound.

If Jimmy has sustained a fracture, your doctor will apply a cast to the affected limb for three to six weeks, depending on the nature and severity of the injury. When the cast is applied, the pain subsides markedly. Before that happens, you can give Jimmy acetaminophen or ibuprofen to alleviate the discomfort until the pain has diminished. Broken fingers and toes are often splinted together to restrict movement, while broken noses and collarbones are seldom immobilized, because of their inherently limited range of motion.

Bottle Feeding

See also | **Feeding; Schedule**

Look how happy Lucy is! Held in place at a steady thirty-degree angle, she sucks happily from her space-age "Riteflo" antireflux feeding device. This modern system is designed to provide a continuous flow and to detect any air bubble before it can reach the nipple. The nipple, by the way, is an exact molded replica of yours, with the same recoil coefficient as genuine skin. Each time the level of the fluid reaches a burping gradation, the Riteflo beeps to remind you to perform the ritual procedure. But that's not all! The system is loaded with Riteflo brand formula's latest blend, fortified for brain development and reinforced with mommy's personal amino-acid profile . . . enhanced, of course, to be better than mommy! You can already tell Lucy is getting smart by the sparkle in her eye.

Even without fancy equipment or formula, bottle feeding is simple and straightforward. Here's a how-to guide.

How?

Lucy may be a genius, but it doesn't take a genius to suck on a bottle. As soon as she's awake and shows an interest in sucking, put the nipple in her mouth. She will automatically move her jaw and suck out some of the milk. It's as simple as that.

How Much?

At first, Lucy will drink very little, maybe a couple of ounces per feeding. When she's hungry, the signs aren't subtle: She'll root or cry. When sated, she'll push the nipple away, slow her sucking, or fall asleep.

As she gets older, she'll steadily increase the amount she ingests, from about twenty-four ounces at one month of age up to about thirty-two ounces at six months. These are rough numbers; the best way to know if Lucy is still hungry is to offer her a little more than usual on occasion and let her decide if she wants it.

Around eight months, when she's eating a significant amount of solid food, Lucy will reduce her milk intake herself by simply not finishing her bottle the way she used to. Or she'll just take fewer bottles. However, there are considerable variations at this stage. Some babies drink barely ten ounces of formula and already eat a tremendous amount of solid food, whereas others are still swilling their five bottles daily and hardly touching the stuff that requires chewing. Both are fine.

How Often?

Bottle feeding, like nursing, should occur on demand. Initially, Lucy will wake up at different intervals, seemingly hungry, and you should encourage her to regulate her own feeding. If you try to impose a more rigid schedule, you'll find it rough going. She will end up imposing hers on you anyway, which will be on average every three hours until she is eating a significant amount of solid food at roughly six months [**See:** Schedule].

Around three to four months, the only noticeable change is that Lucy takes much less time to eat. She can gulp down her bottles in record time while looking around for distractions.

REAL QUESTIONS FROM REAL PARENTS

How much is too much?

Be aware that overfeeding is relatively easy with a bottle, because the supply is unlimited and Lucy may take it just for soothing purposes. In any event, if you do happen to overfeed her, you're likely to get the extra milk back in the form of spit-up.

How long can I leave a bottle out if it has been used?

Until the next feeding, which means as long as six hours.

Should I sterilize the bottle?

Washing of the nursing equipment is more than enough. Babies are able to fight germs and aren't meant to ingest only sterile nutrients.

What kind of nipple is best?

Lucy can suck on any kind. Don't pay attention to the brand or the shape; it's all marketing. The hole of the nipple should be big enough that she can feed with ease but small enough that it doesn't flood her mouth with milk. Don't bother with the antigas bottles that provide a specific inclination or an extra plastic bag to squeeze the air out; they're just more marketing rip-offs.

What about burping?

Babies swallow more air while bottle feeding, which causes more spit-up. This is easily remedied: Just keep Lucy upright for a while after feeding and massage her back. This will move the air up and the food down, even if she doesn't muster a full burp.

If my baby wakes up ten minutes after feeding, does it mean she's still hungry?

Not necessarily. She might simply crave comfort. The best way to know is to give her a little more food. If she takes it willingly, then she's hungry; otherwise, she's not. As with most feeding matters, common sense is the final authority.

When can I put cereals in her bottle?

Never. There's no obvious benefit. It won't help her sleep at night, and the additional calories are unnecessary. Worse, it can bind the stools.

Bottle Refusal

If you plan to feed Lucy one or more supplemental bottles daily while nursing, it may be a good idea to introduce the practice as soon as she's comfortable with breast feeding, which usually takes a week to ten days. With this early double exposure, she can remember how to suck on both devices and go from one to the other easily, as long as she gets to practice on both routinely.

If you aren't using a bottle on a regular basis, however, there is no point in introducing it until you need to, whether you're going back to work or decreasing nursing. After she's fully accustomed to your nipple, if she senses you pushing a bottle on her, she'll refuse it. Don't be surprised. Your breast is her preferred source of nutrition, and she won't take a substitute, especially from you. But don't be discouraged either. When you have to introduce that bottle, you can implement my simple and efficient strategy:

1 | Fill a bottle with either formula or pumped breast milk.
2 | Leave Lucy with someone else: your husband, your baby-sitter, anyone but you.
3 | Get out. Don't linger in the doorway. Don't look back. Don't call home. When you come back, you'll find that Lucy has magically taken the bottle. one hundred percent guaranteed.

Bottle Weaning

Who cares if Jimmy still has his bottle at fifteen months? Actually, he does. In their second year, toddlers still find significant comfort in sucking from a nipple. As long as he downs his "ba-ba" and doesn't treat its nipple as a pacifier, he's fine. A bottle before bedtime is fine too, provided he doesn't keep it in his mouth while sleeping (the milk sugars can cause cavities; [**See:** Tooth Rot]). During meals, offer him a regular cup of water to wash down the food.

As he gets older, he'll steadily decrease his bottle count per day until he's down to one or none. If, however, he drinks more than three or four daily, uses them as pacifiers, or is drinking so much from the bottles that his appetite for solid food is affected, then it's time do away with them.

How to Get Rid of the Bottle

Just throw it in the garbage. Sound tough? It's actually really simple, but you have to stand firm. Done right, it's the cleanest solution. The first afternoon without his ba-ba, Jimmy will be rather insistent. Don't take the bait. If you talk too much about the missing bottle, you might as well give it back to him. After a bottle-free day or two, I assure you he'll completely forget about it.

Having said all that, I have to confess that one of my kids had a bottle a day till the age of four, until we resorted to the above strategy. Since then, I've seen this approach to weaning help hundreds of my bottle-addicted little patients, and it works better than any other method.

Sipping Cups

People seem to like these, though I'm not sure why. They leak, which means more cleaning up. Also, if you move from bottle dependency to sipping-cup dependency, you're just adding another habit that will eventually require breaking. As far as I'm concerned, it's best to go straight from a bottle to a regular cup at around the first birthday.

Breast Feeding

It's a . . . it's a . . . GIRL!" Lucy gulps her first breath. By her third one, she already has your nipple in her mouth. You know that nursing right after birth will increase your chances of breast feeding without a hitch. The first day, under the nurse's strict supervision, you wake her up to feed every three hours on the nose, ten minutes on each breast, and you pump your breasts in between to increase your colostrum production. But it's not going as you expected. Lucy couldn't care less about the three-hour schedule. She wakes up when she wants to, sucks a little, and then falls asleep. At times she squirms or cries inconsolably and is unable to latch on to your breast. Finally, you tempt her with the forbidden fruit: a bottle of formula, which she gulps down ravenously, to your dismay. The nurse suggests you try the transverse position, and your husband suggests the football hold. But nothing makes a difference. A lactation specialist is summoned. She diagnoses Lucy as a lazy feeder and illustrates with her own tongue how Lucy's is pointing the wrong way. She recommends sucking exercises and feeding Lucy colostrum from a cup to avoid formula dependency or nipple confusion. In the end, you're both confused, and the whole experience of breast feeding begins to look like a disastrous choice.

A long, long time ago, nobody talked about breast feeding. People just did it instinctively. And guess what? Miraculously, it worked. In today's world, however, where every aspect of parenting is placed under a microscope, breast feeding has become more of a science. With its renewed popularity has come abundant data and misinformation as well as cautionary tales about everything that could possibly go wrong. Instead of reassuring you, all of this information can create unrealistic expectations and unnecessary apprehensions. But breast feeding won't work well if you're too skittish, and the less it works, the more anxious you'll be.

In this chapter I outline what you can expect at every stage of your nursing career. I also attempt to debunk all the nursing myths that could undermine your confidence and your pleasure. Breast feeding is simple and straightforward. Just go with the flow and follow your instincts. After the first couple of days, once you and your baby have gotten used to each other, it'll feel like you've been doing it all your life.

The First Few Days

Immediately after birth, Lucy is quite awake. She scans her new surroundings, bewildered, overstimulated, and seeking comfort. If you offer her your nipple, she'll take to it primarily for comfort and will be pleasantly surprised by a little bonus called colostrum, a white substance that tastes surprisingly good. Lucy logs the experience into her fledgling memory and falls asleep. The next time she wakes up she remembers vaguely what to do.

When this initial surge of adrenaline tapers off, Lucy dozes, making only occasional peeps. In her half-awake state, she continues to seek out the breast again, more for comfort than for food. The fact is, a newborn just doesn't need to eat much initially. In the first few days she'll wake up erratically, with no consistent pattern: sometimes asleep for hours, sometimes awake for hours, sometimes waking and sleeping every ten minutes. Whatever her rhythm, just keep her next to you and follow her lead. Doze when she does. Wake up when she does, and feed her when she seems interested.

WHAT **TO DO**

- **Whenever Lucy is up and wants comfort,** put her at the breast in the position that seems the most comfortable to you. Her sucking will gradually become stronger and her pattern a little more regular, and your production will follow suit.

WHAT **NOT TO DO**

- **Don't feed at set intervals.** Waking her up interferes with her natural cycle and will generate frustration for both of you. I can't count how many mothers I've seen who became discouraged and stopped nursing because they were told to feed according to a rigid pattern and then found their newborn wasn't interested.

- **Don't feed for a mandatory length of time.** Lucy could stay a full hour or let go after a few minutes; let her determine which.
- **Don't insist on feeding Lucy from both breasts** if she falls asleep after one. As a matter of fact, she's unlikely to be awake enough for both at first.
- **Don't pump milk to stimulate your breasts.** It's tiring enough to have one baby, let alone a second electronic one. Lucy is a much more efficient pump.
- **Don't be obsessed with positioning;** you will naturally find the one that is most comfortable.
- **Avoid supplementing with a bottle.** Although one bottle here and there is not a big deal, the artificial nipple is so much easier that Lucy won't make the effort at your breast if she gets the choice too often.

REAL QUESTIONS FROM REAL PARENTS

How do I know if I'm doing it right?

If Lucy takes to the breast a few times a day, latches on, and sucks a little here and there, then you're doing it right. Swallowing motions are nice to look at, but sometimes not that obvious. The amount of waste she generates is irrelevant at this stage. The stools are still the product of what was in her stomach before eating, and urine is very scant, because Lucy has little fluid to spare.

What if I don't feel anything happening when the baby is at my breast?

Colostrum does not flow as freely as the milk that you will soon be able to feel, along with the "letdown" sensation in your breasts that everyone talks about. Just be patient.

Why don't I get much when I pump?

You can't gauge your milk production by what you can pump. Lucy is much more efficient than the pump.

How do I know Lucy isn't starving?

To tell you the truth, Lucy probably is hungry, but for the moment she has other problems to deal with, such as recovering from the physical and emotional trauma of birth. But nature is clever: This nutritious substance called colostrum is the perfect nutrient for someone who's hungry and groggy at the same time and whose stomach can only handle so much.

To reassure you, when babies are on formula and the food supply is unlimited, anything more than a couple of ounces comes right back up.

Why does it hurt?
Simply because it does. It's not your technique. It's not Lucy's technique. That's just the way it is. Anyone who tells you anything else is misleading you. This is sensitive tissue she's sucking on, and it will take about a week to get tougher. Find the position that seems the most comfortable and try to breathe through the pain. Apply a little pressure to the back of Lucy's head so that her mouth covers more of the areola and less of the tip. Also, in between feedings, leave your breast out as much as possible; air is good for healing, and the nipple won't become further irritated by the friction of your shirt or bra. Some mothers have more sensitive nipples than others, and their comfort comes more slowly.

I don't recommend breast shields; they are cumbersome, increase your awareness of the pain, and only delay the moment when your breasts get tougher. By the way, preparing your breasts during pregnancy with daily rubbing, as some of the books suggest, is pointlessly masochistic and won't prevent the pain.

What if Lucy cries like she's hungry but pushes the breast away?
Stop feeding and try again a few minutes later. Your flow may be too strong at first, or she may be too excited. After a few attempts, if she's still pushing the breast away, the message is clear. She's not hungry right now. You'll have to get used to the fact that Lucy can cry for reasons other than the desire to nurse. If you take it too personally, you'll become anxious and develop a latching problem, and then Lucy could reject the nipple out of frustration, even when she is hungry. I truly believe a newborn can sense tension.

When can I use a pacifier?
Whenever you wish. This does not interfere with nursing; nothing comes out of it, and Lucy knows that.

Am I going to be able to breast-feed with inverted nipples?
If you place your pinky in Lucy's mouth, you can feel right away how strong the suction is. She can revert nipples of any shape. Similarly, the size of your breast itself has nothing to do with your ability to breast-feed; the milk comes from mammary glands, not from the fat around the glands.

How about if I had breast surgery?
Except for some specific breast reductions performed years ago, plastic surgery should not affect the gland. Give it your best try.

Can I nurse even though I had a C-section?

Most mothers who have had a C-section are able to nurse perfectly well, although the pain can make it a little more uncomfortable. General and epidural anesthesia as well as postdelivery painkillers (even morphine derivatives) are not a problem while nursing.

Can I nurse if I have a fever?

A postdelivery fever or the flu should not prevent you from nursing, even if you're on an antibiotic. Most of them are safe while nursing.

Breast Feeding After the Milk Has Arrived

You've managed to get through the first couple of days without too much panic. Around the third day, your breasts suddenly get larger between feedings, and you produce real milk, which is clearer than colostrum. Since you're following Lucy's natural rhythm, your production meets her needs, and you won't get engorged. She's feeding more efficiently and for longer times, and she gulps with obvious swallowing motions. You also see an incremental excremental increase (more stools and urine).

WHAT **TO DO**

- **Continue feeding on demand.** Feed her until she falls asleep after one or two breasts, depending on her appetite. At night, try to get the hang of nursing while lying on your side; it's the only way you'll get any rest.

WHAT **NOT TO DO**

- **Don't wake Lucy up to feed at set intervals;** give her a chance to set her own schedule. Gradually, it will normalize, and she'll feed every two to three hours. Occasionally, she'll sleep for longer periods (ideally, at night), but as long as she wakes up hungry and alert, she's healthy. If she's still sluggish and has no appetite after a long sleep, however, this lethargy could be an early sign of illness, and you should seek medical advice.
- **Don't insist on feeding for a fixed amount of time** or keep her awake by rubbing your pinky on her cheeks or other tricks. When Lucy dozes off in the middle of feeding, that means it's not the middle. It's the end.
- **Don't pump milk to spur your production;** it will only confuse the spontaneous flow.

▶ **Don't chart the number of stools,** the number of wet diapers, the amount of time spent on the breast, and so forth. While these efforts may feel scientific, their main effect is to raise anxiety levels.

REAL QUESTIONS FROM REAL PARENTS

How can I be sure that I'm producing enough milk?

Trust nature, and trust yourself too. If mothers didn't produce enough milk, humankind would not have survived this long.

How will I know if my baby isn't getting enough food?

If she's hungry, Lucy will scream all day, or at least act fretful, even after feeding. In extreme cases, she'll sleep all the time and barely wake up. You should also be sensitive to your own body signs. If your breasts won't fill up and don't leak, you may not be producing enough milk. See your doctor, and he'll probably recommend supplementation with formula, at least temporarily.

What should I be looking for in the way of stools and urine?

Frequent stools of a mustard-yellow color and a seedy texture are a good sign. Most infants will produce a stool each time they eat, but some won't. It doesn't necessarily mean they didn't get enough food; it's simply that most of the food was used and little went to waste. Frequent urine (eight to ten times daily) is average, but the urine can get mixed up with the stools and thus is hard to count.

Should I worry if my baby is losing too much weight?

Most babies lose weight just after birth and regain it by around the tenth day. But if your baby's weight doesn't come back by day ten, it doesn't necessarily mean you aren't breast feeding efficiently [**See:** Weight Concerns].

What about hind milk and fore milk?

Don't be so technical! Lucy is getting both.

What if one side is more comfortable than the other?

This is typical. The trick is to alternate religiously, even if one breast is a little less comfortable for you. The efficiency and comfort will even out over time.

My baby seems to feed at night and sleep during the day. How can I reverse the schedule?

It will reverse itself naturally. Don't bother trying to keep Lucy awake during the day so she'll sleep at night. It won't work, and you'll only get more frustrated.

Breast Feeding the First Month

By now you've gotten the hang of it. You can nurse while you're walking or on the phone. The pain has decreased, and everything is going well.

WHAT TO DO

- Continue doing what you're doing.

REAL QUESTIONS FROM REAL PARENTS

When should I think of putting the baby on a schedule?

Don't bother. One advantage of nursing is that it doesn't require much thought. If you pay no attention to timing, Lucy will settle into a routine of two- to three-hour intervals, not because you've imposed it on her but because it's natural. You needn't obsess about regularity, but you should already be thinking about establishing a low-intervention regimen at night, wherein you'll feed only when your little diner is really insistent. This will be your first step toward raising a night sleeper, and it will help you avoid the later struggle of "sleep training."

When will the nursing taper off?

After a few months, Lucy will hold off a little longer between feedings, and the feedings themselves will take less time. But there probably won't be a major change in habits until she's ingesting significant amounts of solid food, around eight months.

Can I pump now?

You can pump, but be clear on your motivation. Some mothers stockpile an entire freezerful of breast milk "just in case." Instead, pump only what you're going to need. If you want to skip a few hours a day, that means one or two feedings' worth of breast milk. Also, consider the possibility of supplementing with occasional formula, which is not poison and won't interfere with nursing once Lucy has adjusted to breast feeding. If you choose to skip nursing several times a day, pumping milk makes sense. But if you plan to do so only occasionally, a few ounces of formula here and there won't make a big difference [See: Pumping].

Should I introduce a bottle to prepare the baby for a future time when she won't be able to nurse around the clock?

There is no advantage to keeping Lucy interested in the bottle if you don't need or plan to use one [See: Bottle Refusal].

When can I use a mix of breast milk and formula?

As soon as you have successfully mastered the technique of breast feeding. But if you rely too heavily on formula, you may decrease your production and dry up.

What if it still hurts?

That means you are in the rare category of mothers who experience pain beyond a few weeks. If you have no fever and no swelling, you don't have a breast infection. For the most part, persistent breast pain is a matter of individual predisposition. In other words, your nipples are simply oversensitive. Eventually, the pain will get better, but it may take a couple of months [**See:** Breast-Feeding Problems].

Up to Six Months

By now you probably qualify as a pro. And so does Lucy; she gulps down her meal in minutes while distracted by all the excitement around her. This may raise doubts in your mind as to whether you're producing enough milk, exacerbated by the fact that your breasts no longer feel as full as they used to Don't worry; your supply will keep up with her demand. If you return to work, full- or part-time, one option is to pump milk while you're at work [**See:** Pumping].

Six Months to One Year

Once Lucy is eating solid foods, her nursing tapers off, both in frequency and amount per feeding. She's still the best judge of her own intake, but don't let her feed so excessively that milk interferes with her appetite for solids.

REAL QUESTIONS FROM REAL PARENTS

How long should I nurse?

Although nursing has nutritional and emotional benefits, they're less obvious after six to eight months. On the other hand, if it's still convenient, there's no reason to stop. It's the healthiest, most portable way to feed and soothe Lucy. You could also do both breast and bottle feeding, in which case you'd have to resort to formula supplementation until roughly ten months, when it's okay to switch from formula to nonbreast milk, such as cow's milk.

When I decide to wean, how should I do it?

Quickly. Don't linger on the transition; it only makes it worse [**See:** Breast Feeding and Weaning].

After One Year

Breast milk still represents a balanced nutrient, and the coziness associated with nursing is very welcome, but by now both are optional. If you and Jimmy still enjoy it, there's no reason to stop. However, breast feeding more than three or four times a day at this age may have some of the following negative repercussions:

- It can interfere with the appetite for solid meals. I have seen toddlers literally live on breast milk, which is not desirable nutritionally.
- Toddlerhood is when Jimmy experiences frustrations and learns how to resolve them. If, each time a frustration arises, you systematically attempt to avert a tantrum with a nibble at your nipple, he won't have the chance to acquire necessary coping mechanisms, and he could end up whining all day as a result.
- Frequent night nursing, which is a common crutch for dealing with problem sleepers, will delay Jimmy's development of the ability to soothe himself back to sleep at night. It can also lead to early tooth decay, as the sugars settle in the mouth [See: Tooth Rot].

As long as you watch out for these pitfalls, there is no reason to stop nursing at one year if it is pleasant for you and Lucy.

REAL QUESTIONS FROM REAL PARENTS

How do I wean at this age if I decide to?

I can assure you that by now Jimmy will not lose interest on his own—not at twelve months, not at fifteen, not at eighteen—so it's going to require some strategy on your part. In addition to being able to ask explicitly and insistently for the breast, Jimmy is now strong enough to jump up and rip open your shirt. This makes weaning all the more difficult, so do it quickly and efficiently, because kids don't understand the concept of moderation. Decrease nursing to twice a day, then once a day, then nothing, all within a week. If you give in once, he'll remember what made you change your mind and redouble his efforts.

What about at night?

Same thing. Once you've decided to stop nursing at night, you might have to get Jimmy out of your bed and even put up with a little struggling [See: Sleep].

Breast Feeding and Diet

"Stop eating refined sugar and flour."
"Eat only unrefined starches."
"Eat before you get hungry."
"Eat several eggs daily."
"Chew slowly and thoroughly."
"Stay away from aluminum."
"Don't eat unnatural fats."
"Drink good water."
"Watch for new behaviors after each feeding."

These are examples of the typical nonsense nursing mothers will find on certain Web sites, where various self-appointed experts make it sound like you'll poison the baby if you eat anything more adventurous than wheat germ. The idea that certain spices or types of food will bother Lucy is a total myth. Breast milk is manufactured from the blood in your milk ducts. If you eat curry, for example, your blood won't taste like Indian food, and therefore your milk won't either. The myth goes as far as suggesting that gassy foods like beans will cause Lucy gas or discomfort. The most misogynistic of these "experts" get downright dirty and include chocolate on their list of forbidden foods, knowing full well that chocolate is a much better best friend to a girl than diamonds, especially when she's nursing.

I've seen many mothers confine themselves to a stringent diet, with one result: unhappiness. First theirs, then the baby's. And I've seen thousands of other mothers who ate whatever they felt like, just as they did before they were pregnant, without any problem. For the benefit of everyone around you, don't deprive yourself. Enjoy varied meals, and maintain a good diet. Don't think in terms of specific nutrients like protein, iron, calcium, or fluoride. They're all included in well-rounded meals. And I would remind you to drink lots of water, but you probably won't need the reminder. Like most nursing mothers, you're probably thirsty all the time.

Some say nursing helps you lose weight; some say the contrary. I say there's just no rule whatsoever. Some mothers take a year to shed the pounds, while others are back to their normal weight in weeks. It's all a matter of individual predisposition. This is no time to try a slimming diet or train for the marathon, since you need all the extra calories you can get to feed yourself and Lucy. Running and other sports are okay, if you can deal with your extra weight up top.

Coffee, Tea, and Alcohol

In reasonable amounts (a glass or a cup a day), all of these are harmless if not encouraged. With this kind of moderation, the amounts that will find their way into the milk are small enough to have no effect on Lucy. Beer (Guinness in particular) is sometimes said to stimulate milk production. To my knowledge, there's no scientific research to support that, but the relaxing effect of half a pint could in itself explain the increased production.

Breast Feeding and Medication

As a general rule, a drug that is nontoxic for you is nontoxic for Lucy too. Many medications carry a warning label, not because they are known to be detrimental but because drug companies simply haven't bothered testing the drugs' safety in conjunction with nursing.

Nursing and Anesthesia

The local anesthesia you get at the dentist presents no danger. Anything more complicated would be administered by an anesthesiologist, who would take your condition into account.

Over-the-Counter Medications

Almost all over-the-counter medications such as painkillers and cold remedies are safe while breast feeding, when used in recommended doses.

Antibiotics

Most antibiotics are safe while breast feeding, especially those that are prescribed for breast infections.

Antidepressants

Antidepressants have not been formally endorsed as safe for breast-feeding mothers, but I have seen many women who took small doses of Prozac or other antidepressants for postpartum depression while nursing, and their babies suffered no consequences. The problem is not simple. Often, the thought of discontinuing nursing is just too much, and it induces a sense of failure and worsens the depression. On the other hand, mothers who already have a tendency to depression will turn even bluer with the postpartum let-down and really need some help to get over the hump. When in doubt, discuss the matter with your doctor [**See:** Postpartum Letdown].

Breast Feeding and Weaning

See also | **Milk, Cow's**

"Child-led weaning" happens mostly in fairy tales. Babies rarely lose interest in nursing on their own. When you have decided to wean Lucy, nurse her morning and night for a few days, then cut the schedule to once a day, and within a week stop altogether. Stick to this regimen. If you give in to Lucy's first cranky spell and nurse her one extra time during the weaning week, she'll discover how much fussing it takes to get what she wants and will become more insistent the next day. Once you start weaning, your milk production will rapidly wane. If your breasts become painful, just express the excess and take occasional pain medication. If you wean before ten months, you'll have to use bottles of formula as a supplement. After that, you can go directly to an adult milk: cow, soy, rice, or goat, depending on your preference [**See:** Milk, Cow's].

Breast-Feeding Consultants

Breast-feeding's resurgent popularity has given rise to the new profession of lactation specialist. The ideal person for this job would be your mother or an older sister. The specialist's primary task is to hold your hand and give you the emotional support and guidance you need when things get rocky. Most breast-feeding problems, especially that of latching on, are caused by apprehension about doing it improperly. A reassuring presence can help you gain confidence.

Beyond the expert hand-holding, however, I take a dim view of their professional equipment and theories. In particular, if Lucy develops latching difficulty, a specialist might advise you to give poor Lucy sucking lessons with your finger in order to reeducate her "disabled" tongue. They might show you some awkward nursing positions that will likely make you even more anxious or hook you up to a "supplemental nursing system," a tube that's taped to your breast and connected to a pouch filled with milk. It's completely unnatural for Lucy to suck from a tube, and not only will this bionic contraption teach her nothing about nursing, it also will discourage you further.

Last but not least, they might recommend clipping Lucy's frenulum, the thin membrane under her tongue. This idea is based on an incorrect, mostly discredited belief that a short frenulum can cause nursing problems by creating a restrictive "tongue tie," which is in fact just a normal variant in tongue shape. This costly surgical procedure won't improve nursing either [**See:** Tongue].

Clearly, there is a market for the lactation specialist's services. I'd still recommend a female family member or friend first, but if they aren't available, you can hire a lactation specialist to come help out at your house, as long as she leaves her equipment at hers.

Breast-Feeding Problems

As described in the BREAST FEEDING entry, nursing usually works out fine; you overcome minor early hurdles, and the process ends up being a pleasure for mother and child alike. In case some complications arise, here's a quick guide to typical breast-feeding problems.

Engorgement

This may occur around the fourth day, when your breasts look like balloons and feel like rocks because production outpaces demand. It's a self-perpetuating problem, because when the areola is distended, it's harder for Lucy to latch on, so she feeds less, which causes more engorgement.

This condition could be caused by waking her up to feed at set intervals, which interferes with her natural schedule. It may also stem from stress or fatigue, both of which disrupt the letting down of the milk you're producing.

If you experience engorgement, massage your breasts in a warm shower, or apply warm compresses before nursing. Manually express milk, just enough so that your breasts are back to normal softness. (Don't pump, as that will only increase production.) And try to relax. I know this is easier said than done, but being too tense will decrease the milk flow and you'll stay engorged. When it occurs, engorgement typically lasts no more than a couple of days.

Difficulty Latching On

When Lucy has difficulty latching on to your breast, it causes frustration for you both, and the more tense you become, the less she'll latch on. Early bottle introduction is often to blame, since Lucy doesn't see why she should switch back to the relatively difficult human nipple once she's had a compliant rubber one.

No matter how the difficulty started, getting back to nursing if Lucy is hooked on the bottle or just having trouble getting ahold of the breast is easy. Let Lucy work a little harder for her meal. Each time she acts hungry, offer at least fifteen to twenty minutes at the breast, even if it's a struggle. If she's absolutely hysterical, calm her down for a moment and then try again. At first, you should only expect a few sucking movements. Be patient and determined. Once she gets it, it'll be easier the second time, and those first few sucks will translate into many more. After she's spent fifteen to twenty minutes at one or both breasts, offer her a bottle of pumped breast milk or, if pumping is too awkward, a bottle of formula. Let her drink whatever she wants to after that, from nothing to many ounces. There is no point in starving her.

You supplement here for two reasons. First, you quench her thirst. Second, you gain reassurance that Lucy is not hungry, which ultimately gives you more confidence to nurse. As her reliance on the breast grows, and both of you become confident, decrease the number of supplemental bottles each day. Within a week, you should be able to breast feed almost exclusively.

Overnursing

In this situation, which may develop after a week or two, Lucy feeds constantly in a series of tiny sessions. She snacks for a few moments, then sleeps a little, nurses upon waking, then sleeps again. While a few of these cycles can occur normally, if she nurses all day long you will rapidly become exhausted. You can break the cycle by making Lucy wait at least two hours between feedings (finish to start), even if that means a two-hour stroller ride. You may have to put up with some crankiness, but it's worth it. The next time around, she will be hungrier, feed longer, and then sleep longer, which will make both of you happier.

Fissures and Cracks

If Lucy has been too greedy, you could experience cracks and fissures in your nipple. If the pain is bearable, continue nursing. The cracks will heal soon, and if you stop nursing, breast engorgement will delay healing. These fissures can bleed a little, creating what seems like a horrifying problem—a baby who spits up bloody milk—which is in fact no problem at all, at least for her.

There's no miracle cure for these fissures. Air exposure, coupled with the application of a greasy ointment such as lanolin, will soothe your skin after nursing, and the fissure will heal spontaneously within a week.

Breast Infection

A fissure, even a small one you don't see or feel, could be a port of entry for an infection, which shows up as shooting pains, swelling, redness, and occasional fever. Your doctor will treat this infection with antibiotics that are safe while breast feeding; you should continue to nurse, unless the pain is overwhelming.

Intense Pain

In the first few days, pain in the nipple is expected. It usually lasts a week, but in some mothers it is particularly intense and lasts longer. No matter what you may have read elsewhere, this is not because of your technique or Lucy's inability to suck properly; you may simply have very sensitive nipples. It could also be that you two have become such good nursing partners that you're doing it continuously. If the pain is too excruciating to nurse effectively, give yourself partial or complete breaks, and in the meantime, pump your milk to keep producing. During that break, feed Lucy a bottle of breast milk or formula, whichever is more convenient. As soon as nursing becomes bearable, reintroduce even if it's a bit of a struggle (see above).

Sometimes, the pain persists beyond a few weeks, or reoccurs after a few months. Here are a few possible causes:

- A blocked milk duct may be causing a sharp localized pain without any obvious inflammation. This will resolve on its own after a couple of days.
- A breast infection (see above).
- A fungal irritation. If a fungus is the problem, your nipple will be red and extremely irritated, but there will be no swelling, and the irritation will not extend beyond the areola. You also may find evidence of a fungal infection called thrush in your baby's mouth in the form of white deposits on the inner cheeks and sides of the tongue (see above).

Apply an antifungal cream such as Lotrimin on your nipples after each feeding, and if Lucy is affected, have your doctor prescribe an antifungal suspension such as Nystatin for her. Ingesting the remnant of the cream on your breast won't harm her. If the fungal infection on your breasts is stubborn and resists external treatment, your doctor will prescribe an oral antifungal that you can take while nursing without fear of harming Lucy.

Fungal irritation of the breast is frequently overdiagnosed as an easy answer to a frustrating problem. If the pain remains after an unnecessary antifungal treatment, you could become even more frustrated. Keep in mind that if there is no redness to the nipple, you're unlikely to have a fungal irritation.

When the pain persists, it's usually a matter of individual predisposition; in other words, you're more sensitive to pain, and you feel it more acutely. I've seen many mothers who suffered for months, and for what it's worth, they all told me it got better when they decided to stop thinking about it.

Breast Milk vs. Formula

I'm going to repeat what everybody knows about breast feeding: Breast feeding is good, both psychologically and emotionally. It strengthens the baby's immune defenses, allows you to get more rest at night, and is far more practical and economical than its store-bought alternative. These benefits are greatest in the beginning, so even if you only nurse for two or three months, it's well worth it.

The question many parents ask is: "How superior is breast feeding to bottle feeding from a health standpoint?" The answer is hard to quantify. Mixed properly, formula contains the same amounts of water, protein, sugar, and fat as breast milk, but it lacks the immunoglobulins and enzymes that breast milk provides. On the other hand, formula is reinforced with vitamins and iron in quantities greater than those breast milk supplies, even if these extra quantities aren't crucial. But if you're eating and nursing properly, you're providing just the right amounts of these same nutrients anyway [**See:** Bottle Feeding].

Though breast feeding is very good at transferring immunity, it obviously doesn't prevent all illnesses. Some medical evidence, for example, points to a decrease in respiratory infections in breast-fed babies, but in my practice, where the vast majority of babies are breast fed, we see our share of the usual coughs and colds every winter. A few years ago, another study stirred up media attention by reporting that nursing decreases the frequency of ear infections. As a result, I occasionally get calls from parents (usually late at night) seeking an explanation for their child's sudden onset of ear pain. "How could his ears be infected? He was nursed for a full year!"

Another common misconception, that breast feeding guarantees acceptance to an Ivy League school, springs from an inconclusive but highly publicized study that argued that IQ is slightly higher in breast-fed children. I cannot provide much anecdotal evidence on that one, as very few of my patients have applied to college yet. In any event, almost all the kids I see are geniuses; their mothers can vouch for that.

In summary, if you think nursing isn't for you, I recommend that you give it a chance. You may like it more than you think. If you've already given it a good try and disliked it (or if you don't even want to try), your baby still stands a very good chance of being healthy.

Breast Swelling

Newborn babies of both genders can have swollen breasts that even produce small amounts of milk. This infant lactation is caused by the maternal hormones acquired through the placenta, which stimulate the baby's mammary glands. The lactation will markedly decrease or disappear a few weeks after birth. Later on, girls may have mild swelling of the breast buds years before puberty. As long as these breast buds are small and unaccompanied by other signs of sexual development, such as pubic hair, they are not worrisome.

Breath Holding

At times Jimmy may get so upset and cry so hard that he stops breathing for half a minute. When this happens, he'll look pale or even blue around the mouth and occasionally go limp . . . before he takes a deep breath and starts crying again. The first time you witness such an episode you may feel like crying too. Rest assured, when his oxygen gets low enough, he'll breathe again.

As dramatic as these spells look, they are not harmful, either in the short or long term. They can happen normally as early as eight months of age, are most common in toddlers, and are not seen after age five. You can actually reinforce these episodes by overreacting; Jimmy will pick up on the commotion or your attempts to distract him and later reproduce the fit to reproduce the attention he received. In other words, if you try too hard to avert these breathless fits, you'll see more of them.

Children who have a low red-blood-cell count are supposedly more prone to these spells, so if the fits recur despite the fact that you're not reinforcing them with attention, your doctor may want to check Jimmy's blood for anemia.

Breathing

See also | **Adenoids; Asthma; Bronchiolitis; Croup; Nasal Aspirator; Pneumonia**

In Infants

Noisy Breathing

Virtually all parents ask me why their new baby makes so much noise while breathing. The answer is simple: The noise is in the nose. Everyone, including newborns, produces nasal secretions. You and I unconsciously clear them by coughing or swallowing. But Lucy doesn't bother to clear her passages unless the accumulation is causing her serious breathing trouble. Also, her nasal passages are so narrow that a tiny bit of obstruction produces a tremendous amount of noise. The result is rumbling, grunting, and other monstrous sounds that seem wholly out of keeping with her delicate and cute appearance. This rumble is amplified by the silence of the night.

Nasal secretions do not indicate a cold, allergy, or discomfort. They are normal products of an infant's respiratory system, and there's no need to try to fix them by changing the sleeping position, using nose drops, or, worst of all, wielding a nasal aspirator [**See:** Nasal Aspirator]. Nor will a humidifier reduce the noise. When she feels like it, Lucy clears her passages by swallowing, sneezing, and coughing without any assistance. Expect this noisy congestion to last several months, until her nasal passages grow.

Rapid and Slow Breathing

An infant's respiratory system is immature (like the rest of the infant). Lucy didn't have to breathe in your belly, so when she emerges, she doesn't have a perfect grasp of this new exercise. She exhibits all manner of respiratory idiosyncrasies, sometimes breathing rapidly for no reason, at other times pausing for what seems like an eternity. This is normal. Don't be concerned.

Stridor (Squeaky Breathing)

In the first few months, if you hear Lucy make a squeaking noise that sounds like a dog toy, it's usually caused by the soft tissues of her airway. In some infants these tissues are unusually soft, and they vibrate during forceful breathing such as crying. This condition, which goes by the fancy name of laryngomalacia, almost never causes breathing difficulties and usually disappears on its own by six months of age.

Wheezing

Wheezing, especially combined with cold symptoms and rapid breathing, usually indicates bronchiolitis, a viral illness that mimics the symptoms that asthma produces in older children [See: Bronchiolitis].

In Children

Nasal Congestion

A cold or allergy can produce congestion and noisy breathing. You'll hear nasal congestion in the chest, not because that's where it is but because the sound is transmitted and resounds in the lungs. Continuous nasal congestion in children could be a sign of adenoid enlargement [See: Adenoids].

Wheezing

Asthma impedes breathing by tightening the small pipes of the lungs in reaction to an irritant. The characteristic sound is a wheeze when Jimmy exhales. The difficulty breathing corresponds to the severity of the attack [See: Asthma].

Stridor (Squeaky Breathing)

Croup, a viral illness, creates cold symptoms that produce a specific barky cough and breathing difficulty that includes stridor, a squeaky sound upon inhalation [See: Croup].

Rapid Breathing

A child with high fever may breathe rapidly because of a reflex mechanism that attempts to lower his body temperature. Antifever medication slows the breathing. It may be challenging to distinguish the cause of the fast respiration, however, because pneumonia also causes a high fever and fast breathing. The differences are that in pneumonia, the breathing is more labored, the child looks much sicker, and lowering the temperature doesn't fully bring the breathing rate down to normal [See: Pneumonia].

Bronchiolitis

See also | **Bronchitis**

Bronchiolitis is a viral illness that occurs in infants and occasionally toddlers. Any respiratory virus can cause it, the most common being RSV (respiratory syncitial virus). Seen most frequently in winter, bronchiolitis is transmitted by parents and older siblings, in whom it only looks like a flu. Bronchiolitis starts out by looking like a bad cold with noticeable secretions, and in its more pronounced forms it produces breathing difficulty that resembles the symptoms asthma produces in older kids.

Mild bronchiolitis causes profuse nasal secretions and a cough, while respiration remains normal. In moderate forms, the breathing is faster than usual but not labored, skin color remains normal, and Lucy is still able to eat, although her appetite is reduced. In more severe forms, the neck and belly muscles pull in, respiration is labored, the skin is pale, and appetite decreases further.

Most cases of bronchiolitis are mild or moderate, take five days to run their course, and show a fresh outbreak of symptoms around the third day. Within a week, appetite and breathing improve rapidly, but be prepared to see nasal secretions persist for weeks and weeks.

Severe cases requiring hospitalization are rare in healthy babies; they are more likely in those born prematurely and in those who have underlying cardiac or pulmonary ailments. At the hospital, the treatment goal is to support Lucy's breathing while the virus runs its course.

Unfortunately, there's not much you can do at home to reduce the discomfort of bronchiolitis. Antibiotics are inefficient. Asthma medicines such as nebulized Albuterol are rarely helpful. The same goes for oral steroids. Cough medicines and decongestants are never recommended at this age, and saline drops in the nostrils don't help. Even humidified air doesn't make much difference. Your best bet is to keep feeding Lucy smaller amounts more frequently, keep her propped up to facilitate respiration, and watch for symptoms of deterioration, such as an inability to feed, or labored breathing. If her condition gets worse, call your doctor, who may consider hospitalization.

In terms of prevention, a new vaccinelike medication is available. Because it's expensive and has to be administered by muscle injection every winter, it's only indicated for babies who are at high risk of severe illness.

Bronchitis

Why do so many people seem to have bronchitis? Let me unveil a secret of the trade: Whenever a bad cough lingers endlessly after a cold, a doctor may be tempted to appease an exasperated patient by treating it with antibiotics under the label of "bronchitis." This accomplishes nothing, but it gives the patient patience to wait for a spontaneous resolution, and of course it also contributes to antibiotic overuse.

Unless they're smoking three packs of cigarettes a day, kids don't suffer from bronchitis. Or you could look at it another way: Every time a child coughs, it's a symptom of bronchitis, because the word simply means "irritation of the airway."

One final note: Don't confuse bronchitis with bronchiolitis, which is a viral inflammation typical of young children [**See:** Bronchiolitis].

Bubble Baths

Now it's time for a lesson in "bubble math." Bubble bath equals soap. Soap plus skin equals dryness. Dryness equals itching. Itching equals irritation. No bubble bath equals no irritation.

It doesn't matter whether the bubble bath comes from the health food store or the supermarket; it will dry out Lucy's skin no matter what. Worse yet, bubble baths also dry out little girls' vaginas. The dryness leads to itching, which creates a characteristic vaginal irritation and discharge. Stop the bubble baths, and the problem disappears.

Bug Bites

In Infants

A bug bite is less problematic than the reactive inflammation it triggers in the body and the potential that the inflammation might become infected. Scratching worsens inflammation, which continues the cycle.

Bug bites rarely produce much inflammation at this age, presumably due to the fact that babies don't really scratch. As a result, any significant swelling or increased redness you do see is a good indicator of a potential infection. This would require medical attention and probably antibiotics.

In Children

Young children are more prone to inflammation, which shows up as rapid swelling, redness, and itching. This is particularly true when the bites occur on the face and around the eyes; these regions have lots of blood vessels, and the swelling can be pronounced. Spider bites in particular produce conspicuous swelling. Inflammation responds to oral antihistamines such as Benadryl, which control the itching but cause drowsiness as a side effect.

If scratched, inflammation can turn into infection, which presents as increased redness, pain, and sometimes even yellow pus. Infected bites are treated with topical antibiotic creams and, on occasion, oral antibiotics prescribed by your doctor. If your child has been stung, remove the stinger if it comes out easily. Otherwise, leave it in, and the body will take care of it in time. If it's a tick, remove it as well as you can by scraping it with a credit card. Just accept that a little piece will probably remain under the skin, and don't dig for it, because you risk introducing infection.

In terms of symptom relief, short-acting antihistamines such as Benadryl are the most efficient way to treat the itching of a bug bite. Topical lotions and creams are relatively inefficient, but plain old ice can provide temporary relief.

An allergy to bug bites such as bee stings is rare in older children and even rarer in infants, but it can be serious. You'll recognize it by an intense immediate swelling which can be accompanied by difficulty breathing. Jimmy's allergic reaction to his first bite or sting is usually not as intense as the later ones will be, so take that first bite as a good warning to avoid stinging insects as best you can (see "Prevention," below), and to carry an epinephrine-filled syringe (sold prepackaged at the pharmacy) while outdoors.

Prevention

Chemical insect repellents all contain the same active principle, DEET, at different strengths. They stink, and they may be toxic if overused, but they do work. Children's formulas are slightly less concentrated, so they're safer but less effective. Avoid applying these products, no matter how low their strength, on children younger than a year; the chemicals can penetrate Lucy's thin new skin, thus magnifying the side effects. As for natural insect repellents, they have very nice names that evoke the forest and purity and so on, but they don't work at all. A mosquito net can be helpful at night, unless one mosquito finds its way inside the net and spends the entire night with your child.

One final tip: You can minimize the risk of infection by keeping Jimmy's nails short, thereby limiting his ability to scratch the inflamed area and introduce infection.

Burns

Most children get burned by accidentally touching something hot, like an iron or a radiator, or by accidental scalding. A burn will initially present as an area of redness. If it doesn't blister within the next day it's a first-degree burn. Pain medication is the only thing you need to administer—no ointment, no ice, nothing else.

If it does blister, it's a second-degree burn, and while it's probably still not a big problem (unless it's on the fingers, face, or genitals), your doctor should look at anything more than simple redness. Second-degree burns expose the skin to infection as a result of blisters, so antibiotic cream should also be applied. If the burn is more severe and the deep tissues are affected, it's an emergency.

Burping

Contrary to popular belief, a baby's burp, though reassuring, is not all that important. Burping happens when the stomach releases air that was swallowed while feeding or crying. Newborns don't often burp, since they eat slowly and sleep most of the day, allowing little chance for air to enter the stomach. Bottle-fed babies tend to ingest more air, because artificial nipples aren't as easy to seal a little mouth around. Therefore, as a good rule of thumb, if there's no air, there's no burp. So don't go pounding on Lucy's back for hours in search of audible results. And if she drifts off after a meal, you might as well let her sleep; even if you don't tap, the air will still make its way up, if less dramatically.

The recommended procedure for burping is simple and gentle. After feeding, just hold Lucy upright against your chest and rub her back or tap it softly. You don't need to wake up at night to burp her if she feeds while you're sleeping, since feeding at night is slow, and little air is ingested.

The de-emphasizing of the burp is a fairly recent development. In earlier years, pediatricians believed—and parents feared—that babies might choke if they missed out on this climactic event. They even thought such negligence could lead to SIDS. Much of the anxiety had to do with feeding habits. Earlier generations of parents were typically instructed to feed set amounts (of formula, if possible) at rigid intervals, but the prescribed amounts exceeded most babies' ideal intake. Major vomiting sometimes ensued, putting babies at risk for milk inhalation and causing parents to fear that their babies might choke. This fear only served to reinforce the burping myth.

Nowadays, we recognize that babies should be fed on demand. Since Lucy regulates how much she eats, you needn't be vigilant about burping and vomiting. And if she does spit up a little milk while sleeping, it won't lead to choking.

It's also worth putting to rest the myth that failure to burp a baby encourages colicky behavior [**See:** Colic]. This stems from a faulty, if understandable observation: Parents notice that a burp can stop a crying episode, but they don't notice that the silence is just a lull in the storm and that the crying usually resumes with added gusto. In fact, constant back patting or bouncing can become annoying and agitate Lucy.

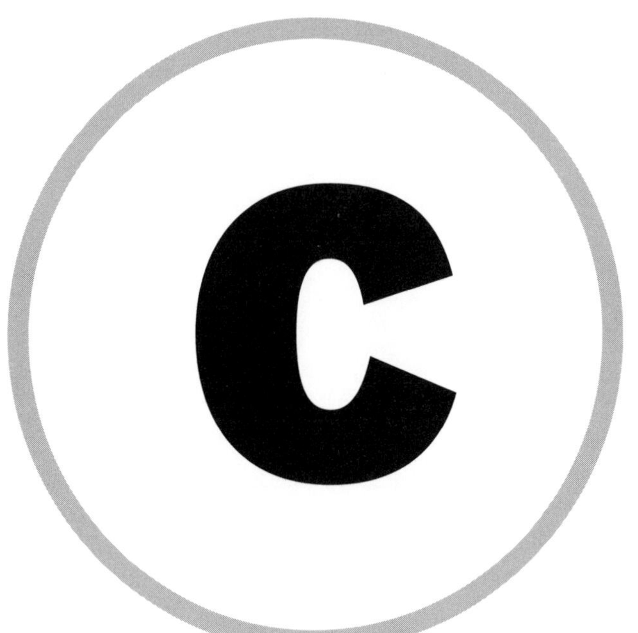
C

Calcium

At this moment, as I type this sentence, calcium is the most fashionable mineral. Stay current with the trend, because before you know it, selenium or zinc could steal the spotlight.

Calcium is, of course, an essential element for young children and infants as they build strong bones, but it is readily available in a wide variety of sources: dairy products, fish, broccoli, and many other common foods. And some of the ones that don't have natural calcium, like orange juice and breakfast cereals, are reinforced with this element. Even if Jimmy doesn't drink his milk, eating a normal, balanced diet will provide plenty of calcium . . . and zinc and selenium too!

Car Seats

Owning a car seat is one thing: using it properly is another. Many injuries occur when the seat is improperly fastened. It may sound obvious, but to limit the risk to your child, read your car seat's instructions carefully.

Babies who weigh less than twenty pounds (under one year, on average) should ride in the back of the car, facing backward in an infant seat. Kids who weigh more than twenty pounds should be moved to a front-facing seat. Use some common sense in deciding when to switch. Some very slim kids won't weigh twenty pounds before eighteen months or so, but if they become strong enough to support themselves, you can let them face forward at one year of age in a properly fitted car seat. Similarly, a heavy eight-month-old who happens to pass the twenty-pound mark should not be switched to a front-facing seat too early. At forty pounds, you can switch Jimmy to a booster seat with a seat-belt reducer. Finally, kids can ride in the front seat when their feet touch the floor (usually by age twelve) and the seat belt fits comfortably. At any point before this, the front-seat air bag is a serious hazard, even with a rear-facing car seat.

Car Sickness

If one of your family members is stricken with car sickness, your best bet probably remains the plastic bag. The medications prescribed for motion sickness have few benefits and aren't even approved for children under two. When Jimmy vomits, avoid making a big deal out of cleanup; get it over with quickly and get back on the road again. Kids don't like vomiting, but they like the attendant drama even less.

Cavities

See also | **Dentist; Fluoride; Toothbrushing**

If you don't want your kids to have any cavities, it's relatively easy to do your part: Just limit candy, frosted cereals, cookies, raisins, and anything else that's sticky and sugary. With toddlers, avoid feeding throughout the night; both bottle feeding and breast feeding from dusk till dawn increase the risk. Feeding before bed, however, doesn't significantly increase the risk of cavities.

Your second line of defense, of course, is oral hygiene: regular brushing and flossing, especially when the kids get older and more coordinated. Dentists believe fluoride supplementation in small amounts has some preventive effects. But that's about all you can do to help your kids keep their teeth healthy. You can't eliminate genetic predisposition, which is unfortunately one of the main factors that determine enamel fragility. Regular visits to the dentist starting in the second year of age will detect early predisposition and help treat cavities before they get worse.

Cereals

See also | **Feeding**

Years ago, eating solids early in life was considered essential. And among the principal beneficiaries of this philosophy were manufacturers of the baby cereal. Bland and slightly sweet, cereal is easily ingested by a young baby who does not need to eat solid foods yet. Nowadays, babies start on solids around six months of age, when they're ready to chew and are more coordinated, and by that point they have little interest in largely tasteless cereals. As the following facts illustrate, kids don't need to eat cereals, which lead to a host of problems in the present and future.

Cereal Facts

- Babies don't need to start with bland and tasteless solid foods. On the contrary, Lucy will love interesting tastes early on. Don't be thrown off by the funny faces she makes when she savors new foods.
- Fear of allergies need not motivate you to give Lucy formal, isolated introductions to each of the different types of cereal, e.g., barley, oats, rice, etc. Cereal allergies or intolerance are extremely rare [**See:** Wheat]. As her diet expands, include cereals in the food you prepare normally, and you'll introduce her to them as part of an organic process.
- Cereals are high in starch, which is a slow sugar. I've observed that an early emphasis on starch contributes to both a predilection for white foods (rice, potatoes, etc.) and the acquisition of a sweet tooth later on.
- Cereals contain iron, but the amount they provide is negligible unless Lucy eats a whole box daily. Anyway, she doesn't need extra iron; there's enough in formula and breast milk.
- Solid foods generally lead to harder stools, but when they become really hard at this age, cereals are usually the culprit. Instead of fixing the problem with a gentle laxative such as prune juice, avoid it in the first place by laying off the cereals.
- Other sources of starch, such as bananas and sweet potatoes, serve the same dietary purpose and taste much better than cereal.

Chicken Pox

See also | **Immunization**

In the last five years, chicken pox has been almost obliterated, thanks to the introduction of a new vaccine. Not so long ago, I saw dozens of cases each spring. Now, it's down to a handful a year.

Chicken pox, even in its mildest forms, is unpleasant. The symptoms start with a few pimples or "poxes" distributed over the whole body. As these poxes dry and crust over, more appear, and then they proliferate for the next five days. They are itchy and painful, especially on the eyeball or inside the mouth or vagina. Other symptoms include those typical of viruses: mild fever and decreased appetite.

In some rare cases, chicken pox can be quite severe, with hundreds of poxes and a high fever. The illness has some rare but serious complications, the most frequent being skin infection due to scratching. In uncomplicated cases of chicken pox, the treatment consists of limiting the itching with antihistamines such as Benadryl and preventing infection with an antibiotic cream. Oatmeal baths have a soothing action, but calamine lotion is totally ineffective.

Doctors vaccinate against chicken pox after the first year. The vaccine was in use for many decades before it became routine, and while it has proven safe and fairly efficient, it has some limitations. In very rare cases, immunized kids can still contract a mild case of chicken pox. Also, the vaccine's efficacy decreases with time, unlike the lifelong protection the disease itself provides its victims. Since the vaccine has very few side effects and offers relatively good protection, however, I recommend routine immunization for chicken pox.

REAL QUESTIONS FROM REAL PARENTS

When is chicken pox contagious?

From about twenty-four hours before the rash occurs until the end of the disease, when all the lesions are crusted. The whole process takes five to seven days.

Who is contagious?

Only a person who has the illness currently. People who have already had chicken pox or the vaccine are immunized and therefore not contagious, even if they come into contact with somebody who has an active case of chicken pox.

How long is the incubation period?
Up to three weeks after contact, although most cases appear within two weeks.

What if a very young baby catches chicken pox?
Usually, the mother has already had the disease and transferred maternal antibodies to her infant. The result is either total protection or a very mild case whenever a young baby is exposed in the first six months. After that time, the baby is at risk, but the younger the baby is, the milder the chicken pox. The exception is that very young infants (under a month) can have a rough course.

What if a pregnant woman gets chicken pox?
There is a small potential risk of malformation for the fetus. This is another reason doctors encourage vaccination. As you know, if she's had chicken pox before, there is no risk of contracting it.

Wouldn't it be better for my child to get chicken pox early in life?
These days, it's hard to find a young child with chicken pox. Therefore, if you don't immunize Jimmy against chicken pox, there's a greater chance he'll contract it at a later age, when its effects will be more severe.

Chin

When our first child, Abeline, was born, her chin was tiny. I was still in the midst of my medical training, and I clearly remember searching through the textbooks for more information on the development of babies' chins, hoping for some clue that would help me figure out if she had some type of syndrome. It turns out the problem wasn't with her chin; it was in my head. Babies just have very small chins. If you have a similar concern, rest assured; my Abeline just turned twelve, and her chin is beautiful.

Choking

See also | **Feeding**

In Infants

Do you know why people don't choke when they eat? Because when they were babies, they inhaled pureed carrots down the trachea (the windpipe) rather than the esophagus (the food pipe), and the discomfort stayed with them as a lesson well learned. Lucy has to make a few mistakes to learn to eat solid foods without incident. The first foods introduced are soft enough that a vigorous cough reflex can easily expel them; later, when the offending item is a larger, harder piece of food that can plug the airway, Lucy will know what to do. By ten months, most babies can handle chunkier foods.

If Lucy starts choking on solid food, give her a chance to cough it up. Use your finger to remove from her mouth only the food you can see, without digging. If choking persists, turn her upside down and tap on her back to help her cough up the lump of food.

"CPR for Baby" classes feature various lifesaving techniques and are widely available. Why not take one?

In Children

The most hazardous foods tend to be smooth and round, which makes them easy to inhale when a child changes his breathing suddenly, like when he's laughing. Have your doctor show you the Heimlich maneuver, a simple technique that could mean the world to you if you ever face this situation.

Circumcision

From a medical standpoint there are no good scientific reasons for circumcision. As much as it may prevent certain sexually transmitted diseases and penile cancer, these conditions are too rare to justify routine surgery. Religious, cultural, or personal reasons, on the other hand, may compel you to do so. But if you're going to trim your son's foreskin, just be clear about your reasons.

You may want Jimmy circumcised so he'll look like everyone else in the locker room. But these days, a third to a half of all kids are uncircumcised. You may not want him to look different from his father. This, too, seems specious; it wouldn't take long to explain to him why you decided to spare him foreskin-removal surgery. If he decided at some point that he really wanted to look like his daddy, he could always elect to have the procedure done at that point.

In the end, much of the fuss over circumcision seems like mountains out of molehills; both options have been practiced for tens of thousands of years. Whatever decision you make will be the right one.

Pain of Circumcision

If you decide to circumcise Jimmy, there's still the pain question. Are you subjecting him to a formative physical and psychological trauma that will scar him in later years? Hard to say. Since it happens so close to the shock of delivery, the procedure is probably just another hardship. Painkillers are not particularly effective. A penile anesthetic block requires about three shots in the penis before it takes effect, and in the end that's just as painful and traumatic as the circumcision itself. Anesthetic creams have a limited effect. Finally, Jewish people use a drop of sweet wine on the baby's tongue during traditional circumcisions, but last I looked, there's no Manischewitz at my local hospital's pharmacy. Having witnessed lots of these procedures, I think that what boys most hate is being held tight for a long period of time. But since they aren't in a position to articulate their complaints, it's hard to know for sure.

Circumcision Aftercare

After a circumcision, the baby's penis will be wrapped and left to heal. This wrapping presses on the wound to stop bleeding in the first couple of hours following the procedure. It should be removed within the first day, or it will stick to the penis. After it's off, apply a greasy antibiotic ointment liberally on the penis for a couple of days. This has the virtue of limiting the wound's contact with stools and urine as well as preventing infection. Healing is usually unproblematic, apart from a little redness and a small yellow crust that lasts about a week. This crust does not represent infection, which is actually quite rare. If infected, the penis becomes much more red, swollen, and painful.

"Incomplete" Circumcision

It may surprise you to learn that circumcision is not an all-or-nothing affair. The amount of skin that gets cut varies. Sometimes the foreskin still covers the head of the penis and it looks like nothing was done. Other times, there's more skin left on one side than the other. This occurs because it's not easy for the person performing the procedure to control the exact amount of skin snipped, and he or she is wary of cutting it too close. Not to worry. Many years later, after the penis has grown and the extra skin has evened out, it will look just like you think a circumcised penis should.

Clumsiness

See also | **Muscle Tone**

This is one of the areas in which I often see unjustified concern and intervention. It starts with the preschool alerting parents to the fact that their child is lagging behind in physical activities. Jimmy doesn't jump as well as the other kids. He still climbs the stairs one by one. He doesn't run with as much ease as he supposedly should.

Muscular strength and coordination differ widely among kids. Clumsy children are usually able to jump, climb, and run, but a little less skillfully. Chubbier toddlers have to deal with extra mass, which impairs their range of motion somewhat. No need to worry; this awkwardness does not correlate with their future abilities in any reliable way.

If Jimmy is clumsy but your doctor has not found any major motor deficit, you needn't intervene with occupational therapy. Just send your solid little citizen off to a good soccer league, and you're sure to see improvement when he's ready.

Colds

See also | **Bronchiolitis; Ear Infections; Eye Infections; Fever**

Get used to the idea that your little darling is going to have plenty of colds during the first few years. A cold is an infection of the nasal passages that is caused by any number of different types of viruses. These viruses induce inflammation of the mucous membranes, which then produce secretions and nasal redness. Other symptoms can include low-grade fever, decreased appetite, loose stools, and pinkeye.

Nasal congestion is very noticeable in infants. Lucy is lying down most of the time, so mucus accumulates in the back of her nose. When she's awake, she doesn't bother clearing her nose, as an older person would, by coughing, sneezing, or swallowing. Finally, the tininess of her nasal passages ensures that even a little blockage is clearly audible. All of this adds up to make Lucy's cold look and sound pretty dramatic. But what seems dramatic to you isn't necessarily traumatic for her. She can function just fine in the midst of a bad cold. She'll probably have slight discomfort but will otherwise eat and rest normally.

In infants, a cold can be the start of bronchiolitis, a respiratory illness that mimics asthma's effects, and shows up as a difficulty in breathing far worse than the nasal discomfort a normal cold causes [**See:** Bronchiolitis]. This requires medical attention.

In kids older than one year, after the danger of bronchiolitis has passed, colds produce more of an irritating cough, along with nasal congestion.

Colds have few complications, the most common one being ear infection, which would bring on increased fever, ear pain, or general discomfort in younger kids.

Cold Treatments Debunked

Colds are self-limiting; that is, the discomfort they cause only lasts for a couple of days even if the nose stays runny much longer. The best treatment option for a cold is just three words: *Ride it out*. This is important, because it will help you resist using "treatments" that not only don't help but can make matters even worse. Here is a roundup of some common cold remedies and my assessments of their effectiveness:

- Nose drops push the mucus down the throat but only temporarily; there's much more where that came from. These drops are also unpleasant for a baby's nose. An aspirator is even worse [**See:** Nasal Aspirator].
- Propping up Lucy may harness the awesome power of gravity to drain mucus from her head. This effect is limited, however, by the fact that a propped-up baby will wiggle and slide down to the bottom of the crib sooner or later.
- Humidifiers and vaporizers make you feel proactive. Hissing and misting, they purport to loosen up the mucus, but as you know, the thickness of the

mucus isn't really the problem . . . it's the quantity. And no amount of humidity can affect that [See: Humidifiers].

- Decongestants, which are all similar in nature, are generally useless. In the best scenario, they dry out the secretions for an hour or two, but as soon as the effects wear off, the mucus returns with a vengeance. These medicines also have side effects: You may not mind a little drowsiness at night, but reverse effects are very common, and they could keep Lucy awake and restless all night. My advice? Stay away, no matter how enticing the copy on the packaging makes these drugs sound.
- Acetaminophen and ibuprofen can help lower the fever, but since the fever is already low grade, there isn't much to bring down. You could, however, use these to decrease your child's overall discomfort.
- Alternative treatments: I haven't seen anything in the health food store that makes a difference in regard to the prevention or treatment of cold symptoms. That includes echinacea, one of the all-time homeopathic favorites, as well as vitamin C.

Lingering Colds

Don't expect to see Lucy's nose drying out after a few days. You should get used to the idea that the mucus-secreting stage of a cold will last for a long, long time. Even after the virus itself disappears (and along with it, the attendant fever and discomfort), the irritation it caused will persist. And because there's still mucus, there will still be coughing for two, three, sometimes even four weeks. This is not worrisome and does not indicate that the cold has turned into something worse.

Recurrent Colds

Sometimes, Lucy moves straight from one cold into another, and you may wonder if she has a weak immune system. But multiple colds are caused more by repetitive exposures than by increased susceptibility. This is especially true when children start day care, before they build up their immunities. It's also typical of the second child, who's exposed to every bug the first one brings home from school. The advantage is that the younger creature builds up her immunity much earlier than the first one.

Colds and . . .

Allergies

Colds are not allergies, even if they look alike. For starters, seasonal allergies take a few seasons to develop, so you rarely see them in kids under five. Second, they occur in late spring and early summer, which is the end of the common-cold season. Nonseasonal allergies, such as those to foods and mold, are even rarer.

Mucus Color

Typically, colds produce secretions that start clear and, over time, turn yellow or green. No matter what you've heard, the color of the mucus has nothing to do with the severity of the illness. Although thick, green mucus is associated with rare cases of sinusitis in children, many colds lead to green mucus production without sinus involvement. The green mucus myth contributes largely to antibiotic resistance, because antibiotics are all too often prescribed solely on the basis of mucus color.

Teething

Teething does not cause cold symptoms, but cold symptoms worsen teething by adding to the general discomfort.

Diet

The myth persists that dairy foods somehow increase the production of mucus. This is not true. Mucus is produced by irritation related to your child's virus, not by diet. The only grain of truth in this superstition springs from the fact that milk can be a little difficult for a sick child to digest because of its high fat content [**See:** Milk Cow's]. Unfortunately, no specific foods—not even chicken soup—seem to help with cold prevention, let alone treatment. The same goes for vitamins C, D, E, and K, as well as zinc and selenium.

Contagion

After a couple of days of illness, a cold becomes much less contagious. Even though the nose is still running, the virus has moved on. In addition, colds are so widespread that avoiding them is impossible; don't bother trying. As soon as Jimmy regains energy, he can and should resume normal daily activities without fear of imperiling other kids.

Colic

See also | **Attachment Parenting; Developmental Milestones; Sleep**

Colic is a generic term used to describe the condition of a young baby who cries more than normal. As far as I'm concerned, colic does not really exist. First of all, it is unclear what the normal amount of crying should be. Second, some of this excessive crying is actually caused by the obsession to suppress crying. Let me explain.

The Bad News

Whoever told you newborns are happy creatures was lying to you. Look, Lucy is pissed off. Wouldn't you be? She was nice and cozy in your belly, minding her own business—not too cold, not too warm, no hunger, no light, no sound—just perfect. This may not be evident the first couple of weeks, when Lucy is in the suppressive stage, snoozing most of the time to avoid dealing with the outside world. Don't rejoice too soon.

The sleepy stage passes, yielding to the adaptive stage. This is when Lucy wakes to the world and realizes she doesn't necessarily like what she sees. Light, sound, touch, hunger—all of these stimuli are just too overwhelming. And that's not even counting the intervention of other beings: the bouncing and rocking, the staring, the touching, and the diaper changing. During the adaptive stage, she learns to cope with this flood of new information, but the overabundance of new sensations (even pleasant ones) can make her whiny. When she cries, your instincts tell you to satisfy her needs. Sometimes she has a need; sometimes she doesn't.

Think of a simple scenario: Lucy is hungry. You feed her, and things get better immediately. That's easy. Think of a slightly less simple case, in which you think that she's hungry but realize that she isn't after she rejects the nipple. You think she just wants to be held, so you rock her a bit, and she calms down. Again, problem solved.

Now imagine a trickier situation: She's crying her head off at three in the morning. You know she isn't hungry, because she takes the nipple for a second but then starts kicking you as her face turns red. She does the same when you rock her and sing to her. What's the problem? You've just discovered what all new parents have learned throughout the ages: Every now and then Lucy cries, not because of hunger and not because of a need for closeness but simply because she needs to cry. We associate her horrendous cries with pain or suffering and immediately feel compelled to stop them, but that's not always the best thing to do. For newborns, crying is as much a tension-relieving mechanism as a sign of discomfort.

WHAT TO DO

- **When you have reasonably exhausted all methods** of soothing, leave Lucy to cry in dim light and warmth in the bassinet [See: Sleep].
- **After ten minutes,** you can attempt to soothe her again.
- **If she is still frantic,** put her back in the bassinet. She'll eventually fall asleep or return to a calmer state. Be prepared for two or three bouts of crying.

WHAT NOT TO DO

- **Once it's clear that Lucy isn't hungry,** don't feed her. She may take the nipple, but then her belly will fill up more than she can handle and you'll eventually generate more discomfort and more crying.
- **Bouncing or rocking her relentlessly** may calm her down temporarily, but it will also compound the problem.
- **Leaving Lucy to cry herself to sleep may sound harsh,** but once you understand that you won't always be able to calm her, life will become easier for everyone. If you were to get caught up in this go-round of overfeeding and overstimulation, you could end up with what people call "colic"—a situation in which a baby never gets the opportunity to cry in order to lower her frustration, so she cries all the time.

REAL QUESTIONS FROM REAL PARENTS

How long can I let her cry?

You are the limiting factor, not her. The ideal scenario is when she falls asleep after crying, because the next time around she'll have learned that she can calm herself. Having survived three newborns myself, I know how excruciating this can be for you. With the first two at least, I was often up all night singing and walking around to no avail. I learned the hard way.

Why is my baby crying so hard?

There is only one way for Lucy to cry: She holds her breath, gets all red, and then lets out an ear-splitting shriek, all the while flailing about. It looks intense, especially if you're related to her, but that's just how your average newborn cries.

Could she have a belly pain?

When Lucy cries, you look at her, and the first thing you see is her big belly. Lucy cries by contracting her abdominal muscles, which makes her raise her legs toward her belly. The effect is to create the impression of a bellyache. In fact, this is the origin of the word *colic*.

What about gas?

The belly-pain myth gets worse. Everybody produces intestinal gas, including Lucy. During a crying fit, Lucy raises her legs up to her belly, and the resulting pressure provokes the release of this gas. After a flatulent outburst, she may stop crying momentarily as a result of the pleasant sensation or the surprise. You may think she is crying because of gas, but in fact, it is exactly the opposite: She passes gas because she's crying. Do not give in to temptation to help Lucy get rid of gas by massaging her belly, pumping her legs, or aggressively burping her. This will only bug her even more [**See:** Gas].

Why is she fussier in the evening?

You're trying to get some sleep at night, so you spend less time doing things with her. This, combined with the fact that the day's normal stimulation can accumulate to a state of overstimulation, generates what people call the cranky hour or witching hour, that time when Lucy both wants more attention and can't really handle it. It usually starts in the evening and can last into the wee hours of the night if you stimulate her further or keep overfeeding her [**See:** Witching Hour].

Is it true that you can't spoil a baby?

You can't exactly spoil your baby, but you can spoil your life or your marriage. I have seen so many parents go over the edge following the "you should always try to soothe your baby" motto. No matter how loving a father or mother you are, you won't be able to soothe your baby at all times.

What about medications or teas?

Since there's nothing wrong with Lucy, there's no need for colic medications. Symethicone, gripe water, homeopathic remedies, herbal teas, and other remedies are deceiving. The sweet taste may stop the crying for a short moment, and give you a false impression of efficacy. But the crying resumes quickly and both of you end up even more frustrated.

Could it be reflux?

I have seen countless babies treated unnecessarily with anti-heartburn medications. In case you haven't noticed, babies always regurgitate some milk. Real reflux is seen in those rare babies who can't hold on to their food after eating and just vomit. They do not usually cry more than the other babies unless they get hungry because they've vomited too much [See: Reflux].

Could it be something I'm eating?

I have encountered nursing mothers who literally eat white rice all day, fearing that any other nutrient will be too harsh on their baby's tummy. But it's an old wives' tale that your diet has anything to do with this crying process. Since your baby's undoubtedly going to cry, you may as well at least enjoy your meals [See: Breast Feeding and Diet].

Could it be the formula?

Same thing. The type of formula has nothing to do with the crying. You're going to drive yourself crazy by trying all the brands in the supermarket, and then you'll just end up more discouraged. Allergy or intolerance to formula are very rare, and they produce other symptoms, such as vomiting, blood in the stools, and poor weight gain [See: Formula].

Now the Good News

This crying business always gets better. Around two to three months and almost overnight, Lucy figures it all out. She has finally acclimated to her new environment. She smiles, laughs, and becomes the happy baby you thought she was going to be. The adaptive stage is over, and with it, her so-called colic. And those babies who have been a little more temperamental turn out to be even more delicious. They've done all the crying they needed, so now they don't get red in the face when they face life's unavoidable little hurdles.

Collarbones

In Newborns

Collarbone or clavicle fractures can happen at birth, especially to large babies, for whom the birth canal is a tight squeeze. Because this bone is soft, the break rarely presents any symptoms, not even pain. Lucy's collarbone will just have a bump, which becomes less noticeable within a few weeks.

In Children

When an older child breaks his collarbone, it's usually the result of rough play. Some telling signs include pain on moving the arm and deformity of the collarbone. If you think Jimmy has a broken collarbone, take him to the doctor. The injury is moderately painful, but it's easily managed with pain medications in the first couple of days. Simple breaks are treated with a bandage around the torso to keep the arm and collarbone down and reduce the pain. Your doctor may even choose to leave a broken collarbone alone, since these bandages have limited effectiveness.

Color Blindness

By three years old, on average, a child starts naming colors with some accuracy. At this age, however, if you show Jimmy green and he tells you it's red, he may be seeing the right color but mixing up the names.

With real color blindness, most people can't distinguish between red and green. This condition can be diagnosed with a color chart by an eye doctor, but it's hard to identify it before age four. In any case, there is no treatment, so early detection is not crucial and people adjust very well to this minor impairment.

Constipation

See also | **Cereals; Picky Eater; Stools; Stool Retention**

Before we talk about what constipation is, let's talk about what it is not. An infant who only passes stools infrequently is not necessarily constipated. The nutrients in breast milk (and to a lesser degree in formula) can be absorbed almost entirely, such that no waste is produced. Lucy's stool pattern can change abruptly, from several stools in one day to none for ten days, and vice versa.

If Lucy's stool pattern becomes infrequent, don't resort to prune juice, glucose water, or rectal stimulation to activate her bowels; she'll become more regular eventually. (On the upside, you're saving on diapers and wipes.) Even when Lucy gets cranky and raises her legs, it doesn't necessarily mean she's constipated. It's more likely just a normal episode of fussiness that you attribute to her lack of stools, for want of a better explanation. However, if the pattern persists for many months and her stools are abnormally large, you should mention it to your doctor, because this could indicate a rare condition in which the rectum is distended.

Now, let's talk about what constipation *is*. For that, we'll go to Webster's, which defines it as "abnormally delayed or infrequent passage of usually dry hardened feces." That about covers it, although it shows up somewhat differently at different ages.

Constipation Before Solid Food

In formula-fed babies, stools can be hard as a result of extra iron. Try a low-iron formula first, since the extra iron is optional. If that doesn't do the trick, you may have a constipated infant.

Before settling on this diagnosis, however, let's address another cause of hard stools in infants. Many parents are told to introduce cereals with a spoon or in a bottle around four months, but this additional nutrient often causes constipation. If this is true in your case, simply discontinue the cereals, and the stools will regain a softer consistency. Simply put, baby cereals are unnecessary [**See:** Cereals].

Now, if Lucy is not on an iron-rich formula and is not eating cereal, you can safely declare her constipated. While rare, this can happen even if she's breast feeding, although the likelihood is slimmer, since breast milk is more laxative than formula.

Constipated infants just have a predisposition to reabsorb more water, which leaves the stools drier and harder. Unfortunately, this can lead to pain and even a little bleeding from small tears on the rectum. You can ease the problem by giving Lucy a couple of ounces of prune juice daily in a bottle. If the stools are very hard, your doctor will prescribe a mild laxative until the constipation resolves, which usually happens naturally when she starts eating fruits and vegetables at six to eight months.

As I've noted many times, rectal stimulation is not advised.

Constipation After Solid Foods

Now the diagnosis becomes easy. In the vast majority of cases, kids become constipated at this age because they're eating too much bread, potatoes, and cereals. Reduce the starch, and you'll reduce the chance of constipation. Again, a couple of ounces of prune juice given in a bottle each day will help, as will a mild laxative, which your doctor may prescribe.

Constipation in Older Children

When Jimmy points to his stomach and starts bawling that he's in pain because he can't go number two, it's too late for a laxative. It's time for crisis intervention: an over-the-counter glycerin suppository that will produce relief within hours.

Okay, crisis averted. Now that he's back to playing, let me have a word with you. Try not to make suppository relief a habit. Prevention is far better than cure. If Jimmy has a tendency to become constipated, do whatever it takes to change his diet so it doesn't happen again. Too much starch is almost always what causes constipation. Starch means pasta, bread (white *and* brown), potatoes, crackers, cereals, rice, and beans. I can hear you saying "But that's everything he likes!" That's right; kids like starch because it tastes sweet, but the solution is simple: Lay off the starch, and you've solved the problem.

Giving him a laxative to ease the problem won't do any good in the long run, since the effects wear off over time. And there's another, far scarier dimension to constipation: It can lead to stool retention, a situation in which a child becomes fearful of defecating, regardless of the consistency of the stools. If you have a few minutes, go ahead and read the stool-retention topic, and you'll understand why you want to avoid starting that cycle at all costs.

REAL QUESTIONS FROM REAL PARENTS

What if my child doesn't overconsume starch?
Give even less starch until the stools become softer. There could be a gap between our definitions of how much is "too much."

What can I give my child instead of starch?
Fish, meat, vegetables, fruit, dried fruit, eggs, tofu, yogurt . . .

What if he won't eat anything?
The first day won't be fun, but the second day will be a little better. The third day will be better still and so on [**See:** Picky Eater].

What if I give him more fluid?
That won't fix the problem if you don't decrease the starch.

How about if I add vegetables and fruits to his diet?
That's good for general health, and they do have laxative properties; however, you must decrease the starch to alleviate his constipation.

What about milk? Will it contribute to constipation?
Rarely. But if you've decreased the starch and the constipation persists, ease off the milk for ten days and see if there's a change.

Cord Blood

On a visit to your obstetrician, you may see an inviting brochure that proposes the possibility of banking your baby's umbilical cord blood at a private laboratory in case your child develops cancer or blood disease later in life. While this space-age concept sounds appealing, there are many reasons to think twice before shelling out hundreds or thousands of dollars for this service. First, the likelihood of your child contracting one of these diseases is very low. Second, it has not been positively proven that cord blood is superior to donor blood for treatment of these illnesses. Third, most of these labs are unregulated, and you just don't know how (or even if) the blood is stored.

This kind of marketing to new parents can be effective, but until we learn more about the benefits of cord blood and this preservative technology, I suggest you ignore this dubious offer and its appeal to your protective feelings.

Cosleeping

See also | **Family Bed; Sleep**

"Should we let our new baby sleep in our bed during the first few months of her life? Is it safe? Once we start, how will we know when to stop?" As with so many aspects of parenting, there is no "right" answer to the questions surrounding cosleeping. Whether you do it or not depends on your desire to have Lucy close at night and the practical costs of such an arrangement, not to her but to you. From Lucy's point of view, there's no doubt she'll be happy to join the party if you invite her. If you don't, however, she won't take it too personally, and she'll simply get used to sleeping in her bassinet. Hence, the choice is yours.

Extensive research on cosleeping's long-term benefits has so far failed to yield conclusive results. Based on my personal observations as a doctor, it doesn't make a difference. In the long run, the little guys who shared their parents' beds for the first few years are just as intelligent and emotionally well developed as those who slept in bassinets. Another bit of common sense applies here: What you do when your kids are awake matters much more than what you do when they're asleep.

One of the big advantages of sharing your bed with Lucy is that you'll be able to get some rest while nursing. When she's hungry, all you'll have to do is roll over on your side and feed her while lying down. That way, you won't even have to get up to burp her, since she feeds more slowly when you're both half-awake. The alternative is exhausting: You wake up, retrieve her from the crib, feed her in a rocking chair, rub her back for a few minutes, and then put her back in the crib. Repeat that routine a few times a night, and just watch those circles darken under your eyes.

In terms of safety, sharing a bed is controversial. Some inconclusive research says you run a small risk of smothering Lucy by rolling over onto her. That said, mammals have slept with their progeny since the dawn of evolution. I find it hard to imagine that something as instinctive as sleeping together could frequently lead to tragedy. As a father, I remember being keenly aware of that little presence when our kids slept with us in the early months. My feeling is that cosleeping is perfectly safe, barring such extenuating circumstances as alcohol, drugs, extremely heavy sleep, or anything else that would impair your ability to sense a newborn.

If you can't decide on one arrangement over the other, consider using a cosleeper, which is a small mattress that fits alongside yours. That way, you can have your cake and eat it too: Lucy will stay close to you for easy access at feedings, and you can roll her back onto her own little bed when she's done.

REAL QUESTIONS FROM REAL PARENTS

If we decide to cosleep, will we ever be able to get the baby out of our bed?
It's true that Lucy will attempt to extend her welcome, and regaining your independence may be a bit of a struggle. But don't let this concern prevent you from enjoying the experience of cosleeping for however long you choose to do so [**See:** Sleep].

When should we stop?
As soon as you feel the need for independence. It really varies from one family to another. In my practice, I see several five- and six-year-olds who still sleep in their parents' beds. The kids are fine, although I'm not sure how happy the parents are [**See:** Family Bed].

Will our baby become a bad sleeper?
Having Lucy close to you could create a routine wherein you soothe her each time she wakes up, usually by breast feeding. To avoid causing sleeping problems, try not to respond to her every little peep early on. Feed her only when she's ravenous. She'll gradually learn to soothe herself back to sleep when she wakes up, even if she's sleeping right next to you.

Cough

See also | **Asthma; Bronchitis; Cough Syrups; Decongestants; Pneumonia**

Coughing is a reflexive response to stimulation of the airway by an irritant that results in the forceful expulsion of air. Mucus that drips down into the airway during a common cold is by far the most common irritant. Technically speaking, coughs are good at clearing unwanted particles from the airway.

Although coughing rarely indicates a severe illness, it is among the most worrisome of childhood symptoms; it's often very noisy, which reminds you constantly that Jimmy is sick, and it interferes with restful sleep, both his and yours.

In Newborns and Infants

Lucy clears her normal mucus production by sneezing. But if she has a cold and additional secretions build up, she may develop a cough. If the irritation persists, the coughing can last for many weeks, even after the virus itself is gone.

WHEN TO WORRY

- **If Lucy's breathing is labored**
- **If she is unable to eat**
- **If she looks very pale**
- **If she has a high fever for her age** [**See:** Fever]

In these cases, she may have an infection such as bronchiolitis, and she should see her doctor [**See:** Bronchitis].

WHEN NOT TO WORRY

- **If Lucy has profuse nasal secretions and coughs,** but her breathing, though normal or slightly faster, is not labored.
- **If she's able to eat,** even if the amount is smaller than usual, and she gurgles a lot.

For her comfort, prop Lucy up when possible to help drain some of the mucus out of her airway. I don't endorse other remedies: Humidifiers are useless, and cough syrups and decongestants are not recommended for infants, owing to their limited benefits and fairly prominent side effects [**See:** Cough Syrup; Decongestants; Humidifiers].

In Children

New Onset

Jimmy's cough is most likely the result of a cold or flu. It's important to understand that in these cases, the cough does not originate in the lungs. The virus induces a postnasal drip that provokes the cough. A cough in itself is not a reliable indicator of pneumonia, and as a matter of fact, kids who have true pneumonia often barely cough at all, because they're so weakened by the condition.

WHEN TO WORRY

- **If Jimmy has had a high fever for many days,** with significantly less activities. Although it may be a simple flu, pneumonia could sometimes present in a similar way.
- **If his breathing is labored,** it could indicate an asthma attack or pneumonia.

In either situation, your doctor should listen to Jimmy's chest.

WHEN NOT TO WORRY

- **If Jimmy has no fever** or if his fever lasts no more than a couple of days
- **If he remains active**
- **When the cough sounds horrendous.** You can't gauge the severity of Jimmy's illness by the intensity of his cough. Some simple viruses produce awful-sounding coughs and in fact are not so serious; croup, for example, sounds like a raw bark [See: Croup].

The cough is only a symptom; before you rush to suppress it, it's important to understand that it serves a useful function by helping to expel unwanted particles out of the airway. Also, kids are surprisingly capable of sleeping while hacking away (as you toss and turn, of course). If the cough is particularly disabling, you can suppress it with an over-the-counter cough syrup, or call your doctor for a prescription variety. In terms of treatment, most coughs have a viral origin, which means antibiotics are useless.

Cough, Persistent

Years ago, a "lasting cough" was indicative of tuberculosis until proven otherwise. TB has almost disappeared, but the fear of a lingering cough has not, and it motivates many unnecessary antibiotic prescriptions.

The mechanism of a persistent cough is twofold. Either Jimmy has a strain of a virus that induces a long-lasting cough (several weeks, in some cases), or he has suffered from a string of recurrent colds, each of them with a new onset. In either case, the cough, which becomes dry with time, gains momentum at night when the mucus drips down the airway. To make matters worse, the constant forceful expulsion of air (the cough) becomes an irritant itself, which triggers additional coughing. The cycle becomes self-perpetuating.

Three or four days into a viral illness, the cough is no longer contagious, but you may have a hard time convincing the parents of Jimmy's classmates of this fact.

WHEN **TO WORRY**

- **If Jimmy has a persistent fever**
- **If he has lost weight**
- **If he is significantly less active**
- **If his breathing is labored**

If Jimmy has any of these symptoms, a doctor should listen to his chest and decide whether a lung infection is at work.

WHEN **NOT TO WORRY**

- **If the cough persists for a long time** without any other symptoms (duration is not indicative of severity)
- **If Jimmy maintains normal activity,** even if he seems a little tired from his disturbed sleep

"Cough in the Head"

As with any symptom that produces parental attention and anxiety, coughs can become psychogenic. In other words, when Jimmy has been hacking away for a while, he notices that two heads turn in his direction every time he coughs. This attention can reinforce the cough and turn it into a tic. In order to prevent or break this cycle, try to avoid displaying too much concern for your child's barking, even if it's painful to ignore.

Treatment of a Lingering Cough

A persistent cough results from an irritation, not an infection; therefore antibiotics are not useful in such cases. If you insist strenuously enough, you're likely to get one, but I guarantee it won't make a difference, and it will expose Jimmy to possible side effects. Other medications prescribed needlessly in these cases include asthma medications (these coughs are rarely related to asthma) and steroids (which can weaken the immune system). Once you've established that the problem is simply a lingering cough with no underlying illness, administer cough suppressants only if the cough becomes unbearable to Jimmy, and wait patiently for the resolution.

REAL QUESTIONS FROM REAL PARENTS

How will I know if the cough turns into pneumonia or bronchitis?
A lingering cough without any other symptoms does not turn into something worse. It just lingers. The chief symptoms of pneumonia are not coughing but high fever and a very sickly, pale, weak child. In that case, the condition is worse to start with. As far as bronchitis, any time Jimmy coughs, he has bronchitis, which is a catchall term that simply describes an irritated airway [**See:** Bronchitis].

Why do I hear it in the chest?
The sound is amplified by the air in the lungs.

Could it be an allergy?
Lingering coughs are rarely allergies. Nasal allergies can produce persistent coughs, but they are also associated with sneezing, tearing eyes, and skin rashes. Also, most nasal allergies are usually pollen-related and occur in summer, while lingering coughs are most common in the winter.

When will it get better?
It could take a while. A winter cough could be caused by a succession of colds, and it could last all winter.

In summary, as frustrating as it can be to hear your child hacking for long periods, a cough rarely represents a serious illness, nor will it turn into one. Your best option is to wait patiently until the irritation of the airway settles, avoid unnecessary medications or overt attention, and hide your anxiety to prevent the cough from moving out of the chest and into the head.

Cough Syrup

See also | **Coughing; Decongestants**

Cough syrups simply suppress Jimmy's urge to do so. This is not necessarily a good thing, since coughing keeps unwanted substances like dust and germs out of the airway. In asthma, especially, the cough helps by bringing up excess mucus. As a rule of thumb, if Jimmy is coughing without complaint, don't interfere with his expectoration process.

If the cough is quite disabling, however, you may have to consider a cough suppressant. The over-the-counter varieties have a limited effect, which wears off after a couple of hours. If possible, choose a plain suppressant without an expectorant or a decongestant; these additives have potential side effects and few benefits.

Prescription cough syrups are more efficient, especially when they contain codeine. A remote cousin of morphine, codeine can be habit-forming in adults (especially those who take it more for the side effects than for a cough), but this addiction is not an issue in kids. Used in appropriate doses, codeine is perfectly safe.

My approach is to prescribe cough syrups sparingly, but when I do prescribe them, I use the ones that really work. The codeine-based syrups are the most effective, and they have relatively minimal side effects.

Coxsackie

Don't panic when Lucy's school posts a Coxsackie alert; the name is the scariest thing about this virus. Coxsackie (named after a town in New York State) is exceedingly common and responsible for many different illnesses. Most of them are mild, while others are severe but rare. Indeed, many nonspecific flus are caused by one of the Coxsackie species. Symptoms include moderate fever, scratchy throat, loss of appetite, and sometimes pinkeye. The treatment is the same as for all common viral illnesses: Ride it out.

Coxsackie is also responsible for two common mild conditions with equally scary names: herpangina and hand-foot-mouth disease.

Herpangina

Herpangina, a result of the Coxsackie virus that primarily affects young children, causes painful lesions in the mouth. In general, it starts with a moderate to high fever and decreased appetite, followed by the appearance of small sores in the mouth and the back of the throat.

Herpangina runs its course in a few miserable days. Treatment centers on managing the pain. You may have to resort to painkiller suppositories if Jimmy clamps his mouth shut because of the painful sores. Oral soothing lotions and mild topical anesthetics aren't very helpful. As far as eating goes, a few days of decreased appetite don't pose a big problem, as long as Jimmy manages to sip fluid so he doesn't become dehydrated.

Herpangina is sometimes confused with another equally painful febrile illness, herpes of the mouth. The confusion is not important, because both ailments call for the same treatment. The only noteworthy distinction is the fact that oral herpes can reappear in the form of a fever blister many years later [**See:** Herpes of the Mouth].

Coxsackie is quite contagious and usually appears as an epidemic in the summer and in the fall. Prevention is unrealistic, since, like almost every other viral illness, contagion is at its peak in the early phase of the illness, when symptoms are minimal.

Hand-Foot-Mouth Disease

Another short-lived and relatively mild Coxsackie virus, this disease primarily affects young children but can be caught at any age. Sufferers find their hands, feet, and mouth covered with raised lesions that can occasionally blister and become painful. The rash can also show up on the buttocks (where it won't blister). This condition usually disappears spontaneously within a week. As with herpangina, contagion is hard to control, and pain management is key. Note that it has nothing to do with foot-and-mouth disease, which afflicts livestock.

Cradle Cap

Cradle cap is the equivalent of dandruff for babies. It's a very common condition that appears around two months of age, peaks at around six months, and then slowly disappears. The most bothersome things about it are the smell of the olive oil that's sometimes used as a cover-up and the fact that it can wreck lots of cute baby pictures. In its mild form, it causes just a few flakes. Occasionally, it looks more like a thick white crust covering the whole scalp; that's the "cap."

Cradle cap is a hormonal process, not an illness. Though it improves on its own, it's remarkably persistent, and flakiness occasionally lasts until as late as the third birthday (by that age you really have to look for it). Breast-feeding mothers often wonder whether their diet or the hormones in the breast milk have triggered or exacerbated the condition. The answer is no. Cradle-cap babies produce excess sebum, which turns into flakes.

As for treatment, oil will make the scalp look better for a few hours because it moistens the flakes, but it won't affect the root cause at all. Furthermore, if your baby is blessed with a full head of hair, the Elvis option isn't practical. Rubbing the flakes with your hand or a soft brush will remove some of them, but more will show up the next day. In brief, since the discomfort is minimal and these treatments are fairly inefficient, the laissez-faire approach is a good alternative. When the time comes to impress Grandma, of course, go ahead and apply a little unscented baby oil, just for looks.

Crawling

There are many ways for an infant to crawl: classic (on all fours), commando (on the elbows), lopsided (on one side), or not at all. If Lucy happens not to crawl on schedule, some books will make you worry unnecessarily that she's missing a milestone, is mentally delayed, or suffers from some other terrible condition. The same books also suggest that you encourage her to crawl, although you'll certainly feel silly down on all fours giving her crawling lessons. The babies who choose to crawl usually begin on average around the eight-month mark. But crawling is far from mandatory; many kids just skip it altogether and go straight to walking. If all other aspects of development are on par, there's no need to worry if Lucy does not learn this optional mode of locomotion.

Creams and Lotions

See also | **Skin in Babies**

One of the big advantages of being a baby is having beautiful skin without using any creams, treatments, or lotions. Many products profess to keep your baby's skin soft with aloe or other magical ingredients, but none of these are necessary, unless your child has a skin condition such as eczema.

In the first few weeks after delivery, however, you will see intense flaking as Lucy's skin sloughs off the several layers of dead cells that were kept hydrated in utero. This is normal and will soon stop on its own, without any creams.

Crib Paraphernalia

Here is a short review of the accessories you might add to a crib, most of which are unnecessary:

Bumpers: By the time Lucy moves around enough to bump her head on the crib, she'll also be old enough to know that bumping her head hurts. After a few bumps, she won't do it anymore. Because early knowledge is valuable, if slightly painful, I don't recommend bumpers.

Proppers: These items have not been proven to add any protection against SIDS. The safest way for Lucy to sleep is on her back, which requires no propping. The only exception is babies who suffer flattening of the head from lying on one side too often; in that case, proppers can help keep them off the flat spot in the first couple of months, before they become too wiggly [See: Head Shape].

Blankets: They end up covering the head instead of the body, which isn't ideal. A sleeping bag that zips around the body is much more convenient at a young age.

Pillows: They can be potential hazards for the same reason as blankets.

Stuffed Animals: They're fine, as long as they're not too fluffy.

Mobiles and Hanging Toys: These are fun for Lucy and provide visual stimulation while she's lying on her back. But don't overdo it. The world is new to her, and she is curious enough that she won't need much help to stay interested in it.

Croup

See also | **Coughing**

Croup is a viral illness that causes irritation of the trachea (the main airway leading to the lungs). Its audible symptoms include a characteristic barking cough, various degrees of difficulty breathing, and a squeaky sound on inhalation called "stridor."

Croup occurs in kids from three months to almost six years, and it tends to strike in winter. It often starts like a flu, with a fever as high as 102° or 103°F but may appear suddenly, usually at night, without any prior signs of cold or flu. Croup can sound quite impressive, especially when Jimmy barks like a seal and breathes like a train whistle. Despite these dramatic aural features, croup is usually mild and resolves after a couple of days. Some cases can be more severe, however, with significant respiratory distress.

In mild cases of croup, you'll only hear the stridor when Jimmy breathes rapidly or coughs. In moderate croup, Jimmy has to work hard to breathe, and the stridor is audible even when he's at rest. With severe croup, his breathing is constantly labored.

WHEN TO WORRY

- **If Jimmy gulps for air,** despite relief treatment [See Below: "What to Do"].
- **If his breathing difficulty is constant**
- **If he seems to pull in air** with his neck or belly muscles
- **If his skin is pale** or his lips are blue
- **If you suspect he has inhaled an object into his lungs** (He may manifest the above crouplike symptoms in this case.)

Any of the above will require a trip to the hospital.

WHEN NOT TO WORRY

- **When Jimmy has a barking cough** or difficulty breathing but is able to sleep, drink, or cough
- **If his breathing improves markedly** with the moist-air treatment described below

WHAT TO DO

- **During croup, the trachea swells up and airflow is reduced.** The faster and more intensely Jimmy breathes, the more difficult breathing becomes. The goal is to help break the nerve-wracking cycle and induce deeper, slower respiration.
- **First, try not to panic;** this will only increase Jimmy's anxiety and rate of respiration. Then you can help him ease his breathing.
- **Have Jimmy breathe the steam of a running shower.** You may also want to open the windows or take him out for a short stroller ride. Both activities improve airflow by encouraging slower breathing.
- **Lower his fever** (if he has any) with acetaminophen or ibuprofen. A high temperature speeds up the respiratory rate, which makes breathing even more difficult [See: Fever].
- **If the episode occurs at night,** put him back to sleep when he's calmed down, and place a vaporizer or humidifier turned on at full strength by his bed.
- **If there is no relief and his breathing is still labored,** you may need to take him to the hospital.

While mild croup requires no further treatment and subsides within a couple of days, your doctor will treat moderate forms by prescribing a short course of oral steroid medication, which is safe and efficient. Severe cases of croup are treated in the hospital.

Some kids will experience periodic recurrences of croup, especially the type that manifests no flu symptoms. One minute Jimmy's fine; the next he has that distinctive cough and labored breathing again. This could happen a few times a year until the end of childhood (ten years old or so), and if it does, you'll become an expert at treating the condition.

Cup Feeding

See also | **Breast Feeding; Nipple Confusion**

The latest trend in feeding newborns is giving breast milk from a cup, as if babies were party guests with martinis. This brilliant idea was conceived to avoid nipple confusion while foisting nutrition on newborns, who are normally quite sleepy in the first few days. Have you ever seen a baby feed from a cup? It's cute, but it's not very efficient. If you insist strenuously enough, you may get Lucy to take a few sips, but this method of feeding goes against nature. The simple fact is, babies need to suck.

This hyperconcern over early nutrition is ludicrous. Most babies don't feed much during the first few days anyway, so there is no need to confuse them with either a cup or an artificial nipple. Babies have nursed for ages without cups, so why start now? My advice in terms of nursing is that you follow Lucy's lead; she'll tell you when she needs to eat and how.

Cuts

The first thing you do to a cut is stop the bleeding by pressing on the wound. When the bleeding has stopped, your next focus is to establish whether or not the cut requires stitches. If the sides of the wound are touching consistently, the skin will heal on its own, and all you need to do is apply antibiotic cream regularly to prevent infection. If, however, there is a significant distance between the two edges of the cut, or if the edges are close but spread apart easily when the affected body part moves, this may require surgical closure, both for cosmetic purposes and to limit infection. There is some urgency, because a cut can still be treated several hours later, but by the next day it may be too late to repair the skin without significant risk of infection. The newest technique for superficial wound closure is a sterile glue, which is very similar to Krazy Glue and allows painless closing of superficial wounds only.

In the Mouth

Cuts inside the mouth (buccal wounds) appear white and puffy instead of red, as external cuts do. Since they heal well and scarring is not an issue from an aesthetic standpoint, buccal wounds are rarely stitched unless they are large. Also, no kid will let you inside his mouth with a needle and thread, so stitches require sedation. Fortunately, cuts in the mouth rarely become infected, thanks to saliva's cleansing properties.

Scars

Once you've dealt with the cut, you worry about the scar. In general, a red puffy area will persist for many months, so you won't be able to gauge the healing skin's final appearance for a while. While you wait, there's not much you can or should do. Applying vitamin E to the scar, while popular, won't really improve the outcome. Keep the wounded area out of the sun as best you can, and use sunscreen on it; the new skin of the scar is unpigmented and will burn easily.

If it's any consolation, the scars we get in childhood are generally invisible by adulthood.

DAY CARE
DECONGESTANTS
DENTIST
DEVELOPMENTAL MILESTONES
DIAPERS
DIAPER RASH
DIARRHEA
DIMPLE IN THE BACK
DISCIPLINE AND BOUNDARIES
DOCTOR VISITS

Day Care

See also | **School Anxiety; Stimulation**

Many parents feel pressure to send their children to preschool because of its reputed cognitive benefits. You hear that day care makes for better-socialized kids, higher-testing kids, even smarter kids. But don't let that sway you too much. A loving home environment with a few activities and play dates will be just as good for Jimmy at a young age if not better. While there's nothing wrong with structured activity and challenges, it's just as important for him to learn to balance work and play and to develop a healthy appetite for learning.

I always favor smaller, more intimate environments. A two- or three-year-old is not meant to be around twenty other kids during the day. Kids adapt remarkably well to various situations, but large facilities can be factorylike and impersonal, and they can foster aggressive behaviors. Having five or six close friends to play with builds stronger peer relationships by reproducing a family setting. For that matter, day-care facilities in private homes can be an excellent option (assuming they're well run), because they provide a more intimate and lower-pressure environment.

But won't Jimmy catch every viral infection under the sun at day care? Maybe, and that could happen whether he's with five kids or twenty-five kids, but look at it this way: He'll either develop immunity now, or he'll develop it later. When I started my residency, I caught virus after virus for the first six months. Now I barely ever get sick, even though I kiss a good dozen coughing toddlers daily. Jimmy may as well get started early.

Decongestants

See also | **Colds**

In theory, decongestants are supposed to dry the secretions produced by the nose. Children's formulas come in different colors or flavors, often in combination with other medicines such as expectorants, cough suppressants, or painkillers. It sounds like a dream if you read the box, but the reality is far different. All decongestants basically have the same active ingredient, pseudoephedrine, whose questionable effectiveness is short-lived and limited at best. Although pseudoephedrine products are some of the most widely used drugs (and a huge source of profit for pharmaceutical companies), they are increasingly controversial. In infants, especially, their side effects can be pronounced. They usually affect energy levels, either making a baby sleepy or, conversely, exciting the central nervous system. In older children, side effects are less pronounced, but the drugs don't work any better to clear the secretions. Still, many doctors prescribe the drugs, knowing that even if the pills won't do much for the symptoms, they'll at least give parents the impression that something is being done to help their child's runny nose. In my experience, a rational explanation of the side effects of decongestants is enough to convince most parents to avoid them.

Dentist

See also | **Cavities; Fluoride; Teeth**

If you've stuck to a reasonable diet low on sugar derivatives and have resisted feeding your toddler throughout the night, your first visit to the dentist will be a happy one. In exchange for a pair of cool sunglasses, a few action figures, some flashy stickers, and a gooey creature he can throw against the wall, Jimmy will agree to open his mouth, and the three of you will count his teeth, one by one. These teeth will be inspected and cleaned, and for an additional premium you might also buy a fluoride treatment that is supposed to help protect against cavities. Then you'll leave with more treasures: a toothbrush, a sample of kid's toothpaste, and a pamphlet depicting the monster bacteria that will attack your kid's teeth if he ever dares suck on a fruit roll-up again. You should have this first visit toward the end of the second year or so; before that, you're still night feeding.

Developmental Milestones

Encouraging children to develop according to a schedule would be admirable if children were a figment of your imagination. They are real, however, and they are individuals who tend to develop at their own pace. The developmental process is extremely complex, of course, but suffice it to say that babies develop according to nature's clock. Children are not perfectly designed robots who change and reach milestones in lockstep with one another. A parent's reaction to her child's pace of maturation is, in the end, a matter of philosophy. Does it really matter if one child is a chatterbox at eighteen months while another can barely say "dada" or "mama"? By the time they're three, both of those kids will be able to converse. For that reason, guidelines are not tremendously useful.

That said, I understand how much importance my patients and many other parents place on the exciting milestones in their children's lives and when they occur. So here's a short outline of what you may see happening at specific times over the course of the first year. As each child is different, remember to wait patiently before drawing conclusions about yours.

Birth Through the First Couple of Weeks

It's hard to know what newborns are supposed to do, since they rarely want to do much. The first week or so is called the *suppressive stage*. Overwhelmed by all the new stimulation and overtired from the delivery, Lucy sleeps most of the time. When she wakes up, she either looks around for a while and goes back to sleep, or she cries for food or comfort. By this point, she can already respond to noise and scan her surroundings, taking special interest in the face of the person who feeds her. In terms of strength, she has more muscle tone than you may think. She can hold her head up, and she may even be able to pull her body partly upright, but she's no showoff; she's too busy sleeping all the time.

From a Couple of Weeks to Three Months

This is called the *adaptive stage*, and this is when perfect little babies tend to turn into whiny creatures as they encounter unfamiliar stimuli of all types and attempt to make sense of the world. As a result, Lucy will be more awake but not necessarily any happier. Noise, light, touch, hunger, her full belly (to name a few)—all the new sensations she's experiencing rattle her. As part of the process, however, she's learning that the noise will stop, the lights will dim, her full belly will empty, and her empty belly will soon be filled again. Her neck is even stronger, and she is capable of more facial expressions. She has better coordination, responds to visual and auditory stimuli, and loves looking at faces, which helps her learn to smile and laugh. This increased muscle control can also have negative implications: It means Lucy can cry louder and longer.

At this point, your shared goal is to get through this stage one day at a time and make it to the next phase. Read on.

Three to Six Months

The adaptive stage lasts for a couple of months, and then, as if overnight, Lucy becomes the kind of baby you see in advertisements: happy, cooing, laughing, playing. She has grown accustomed to the notion of being alive, especially since she's being served hand and foot by an all-powerful parental force. Since basic needs (food, cleanliness, and comfort) are taken care of, Lucy can start exploring the world and not only take in stimuli but also produce new ones. This is called the *exploratory stage*. Her first tool for exploration is her mouth, and the first thing she explores is her hands, since they're right there at the ends of her (still very short) arms. In terms of physical development, she's exhibiting increased neck and trunk strength and greater manual dexterity.

Six to Eight Months

Much of the development here focuses on the hands. At around six months of age, Lucy can grab objects and look at them before she shoves them into her mouth and eventually throws them on the floor. Because her drive to explore exceeds her understanding of the world, she may become overstimulated and frustrated, which can lead to early tantrums.

Physically, she can sit up if you help her balance, and she may or may not be able to roll over on her own. She's starting to coo (though some babies are quieter than others) and to sustain interest in objects. With your help, she is even able to stand up on her increasingly strong legs.

Eight to Ten Months

Around eight months, your time with a happy, stationary baby comes to an end, as Lucy's interest in exploring intensifies. She now explores her own voice by babbling and observing the effects her babbling has on you. She grabs everything in sight and performs a thorough visual analysis before putting everything she can into her mouth.

She can sit steadily, and when she gets bored, she attempts to crawl or drag herself across the floor in her own style. As much as she wants to go to new places, she does not necessarily want to meet new people; as a matter of fact, she'd rather not [See: Separation and Stranger Anxiety].

Ten to Twelve Months

Lucy is intent on standing up, and she's starting to think about walking, something she gets a taste of when she's cruising around the house, holding on to the furniture. You may recognize some words emerging from her babble, especially the ones that identify you. Her motor coordination is even more refined, and her thumbs have begun to come into play. She may also add waving to the repertoire.

Twelve Months

Lucy stands up steadily on both legs, cruises, and sometimes even walks under her own power. "Mama" and "dada" (or other two-syllable words) anchor her growing vocabulary, though these words do not necessarily refer to her beloved parents. She may be able to feed herself, or try to, and she probably demonstrates an appreciation for music, or at least clapping.

Diapers

See | **Diaper Rash**

In many ways, the best diaper would be no diaper at all. But since you have to use them, it's worthwhile to choose well. What's the difference, you may wonder, between cloth and disposable diapers? Absorbency. Cloth diapers tend to soak up more urine. Unless you change them often, the moisture can lead to diaper rash. As for the environmental issues, it's true that cloth diapers don't fill up huge amounts of space in landfills, but washers use lots of energy and water. In the end, it's probably a toss-up and a matter of personal preference. As this book goes to press, a third generation of diapers allegedly made out of recycled paper has just emerged. It remains to be seen how their brownish color will affect our gleaming white landfills.

Diaper Rash

See also | **Diapers**

A diaper is a receptacle that holds stools and urine, and therefore moisture. The combination creates wetness, which irritates the skin of the penis and vagina. Diaper rash typically shows up as an inflammation on the exposed area, and it can be quite pronounced. Later on, it can become scaly or peel. Sometimes a fungus exacerbates the irritation, in which case, the redness is surrounded with little vesicles (a type of blister) originating in the creases and extending to the prominent parts.

Diaper rash is not as painful as it looks. Most babies go about their business, even if their behind resembles a baboon's. The rash is notoriously stubborn, however, and can persist for weeks on end, so prevention is key.

How to Prevent a Rash

- Avoid soap; it's too drying for babies. I know you may feel you need to thoroughly clean any skin that's been in contact with stool, but lots of running water will do the same job [**See:** Washing].
- Use wipes as little as possible; they're abrasive and remove the skin's superficial protective coating.
- Leave the diaper off or loosely attached as often as you can. Airflow will help dry off the area and prevent moisture in the diaper.
- Avoid using creams and ointments such as Desitin. They're supposed to prevent diaper rashes, but by trapping moisture they may actually interfere with the way the skin breathes. Once a rash has set in, these diaper creams can delay the healing, which requires air. In short, use them as little as possible.

What to Do for Diaper Rash

- Since the rash is caused by the diaper and what's in it, if you remove the diaper or leave it on loose and open, you're tackling the problem at its source. Air is the cheapest and most effective treatment. Obviously, this is easier said than done when you have expensive furniture and rugs that you want to protect from baby urine and stool.
- A short course of steroid cream such as hydrocortisone works wonders on a stubborn diaper rash. See your doctor for these.
- Fungal diaper rashes generally respond to antifungal creams such as over-the-counter Lotrimin. Bear in mind that a fungus is a slow-growing organism—slow to multiply and slow to die—so be patient.

Diarrhea

Diarrhea is a condition in which more stool is produced than usual. Since newborns can have up to ten stools a day, often watery, it's difficult to define what diarrhea is at Lucy's age. Stomach viruses are the most common cause, but they're rare, because she has to pick them up from other kids, and so far her social schedule is pretty clear. Another rare cause would be an intolerance to her formula.

WHEN TO WORRY

- **If the amount of diarrhea is enormous** (more than ten times a day and extremely liquid)
- **If Lucy is also vomiting**
- **If she has blood in her diaper**
- **If she has a dry mouth,** lethargy, and poor appetite, which could indicate dehydration.

See a doctor if your baby has any of these symptoms.

WHEN NOT TO WORRY

- **If the diarrhea is explosive.** This is normal in infants.
- **If Lucy is drinking appropriately and not vomiting**

WHAT TO DO

- **There's nothing you can do to stop an infant's diarrhea;** it will resolve itself, but that takes a while. As a rule, diarrhea is tenacious. Continue feeding her as usual. If the diarrhea is part of a stomach virus, it will last an average of a week before it settles. If it lasts longer, it requires attention.

Diarrhea is easier to diagnose at this age, since normal stools are usually more formed. Anything over roughly four stools a day qualifies as "the runs."

WHEN TO WORRY

- **If diarrhea is accompanied by high fever** (103°F or higher)

- **If there is blood in the diarrhea**
- **If there is an unusually large amount** or it is produced constantly
- **If Jimmy has intense belly pain**
- **If he's vomiting repetitively,** which could increase the risk of dehydration
- **If Jimmy shows signs of dehydration,** such as lethargy, dry mouth, or low urine production

Take him to the doctor for evaluation if he presents any of these signs.

WHEN **NOT TO WORRY**

- **If Jimmy is eating and drinking well**
- **If his diarrhea persists many days to many weeks.** In older children, diarrhea is notorious for lasting days or even weeks after a stomach virus. The intestine has to heal for normal digestion to resume.

Years ago, doctors treated diarrhea with the so-called BRAT diet: bananas, rice, applesauce, and toast. These "binding" foods were supposed to make the stool harder, but in truth their effect is limited. No matter what your little patient eats, the diarrhea will follow its course until the intestine heals. Feed Jimmy normally and regularly when his appetite resumes. Allow him to replace his fluids with diluted juice or soda such as ginger ale. Anti-diarrhea medications such as Imodium are ineffective and can be dangerous for kids.

In summary, diarrhea is messy but usually not serious, and once it shows up it's here to stay for a bit, so be patient.

Dimple in the Back

In the womb, a baby is formed much like a sleeping bag that's zippered from the head to the bottom. Some babies display a tiny hole on the lower back, the result of that "zipper" failing to close all the way. This is called a *sacral dimple*, and it's located in or just above the cleft between the buttocks. It's not uncommon, and it is usually of no importance.

In extremely rare cases, however, these harmless dimples can be associated with spinal abnormalities, especially if there's a tuft of hair on the area or on the dimple itself, or if it's located high on the back. In other rare instances, the dimple can extend deeper into the body, forming a small opening that carries a risk of infection. Both of these would prompt your doctor to order tests to assess the dimple and the surrounding anatomy: either an ultrasound (simple but not very reliable) or an MRI (much more conclusive but requiring sedation).

Discipline and Boundaries

BANG! "Okay mister, that's it! I've told you not to bang on the TV! What if you break it? TVs cost a lot of money, you know, and Mommy had to work very hard to buy that TV. Oh, look at the kitten!" BANG! "Jimmy, I told you—that's it! You know better than that! Why don't you play with your train set? When we get to the park well get a cookie if you're a good boy and—" BANG!

When infants become toddlers, around the first year, they start exploring more complex matters. Some of those matters are topological or geographical: what spaces look like, how it feels to climb over something, or what it's like to squeeze behind it. Another object of exploration is you. Early on, you become the primary experiment in Jimmy's emotional laboratory. As his range of motion expands, he determines that it is being limited by larger people who don't wear diapers and tell him that some of his actions can be dangerous, inappropriate, or naughty. Consequently, Jimmy attempts to assert his individuality and independence by exploring your resilience.

I use the term laissez faire often in this book, but you won't see it in this section. Discipline is hard work, and it's one area of child care that will not take care of itself, much as you might like it to. You have to stand up to your kids early and consistently.

One of the phrases you'll hear over and over again from parents of young children is "the terrible twos." Throughout this book, I have said that many widely held beliefs about parenting are myths. "The terrible twos," I regret to inform you, is not one of those. Toddlers rebel against rules in unpredictable, hilarious, and supremely stubborn ways, and if you don't handle them properly, you may soon have a bona fide revolutionary on your hands.

Preventing the Terrible Twos

The best way to prevent the terrible twos is to counteract the terrible ones. If you watch closely, you can see the early signs of a rambunctious toddler around twelve to fifteen months. That's when you should begin setting up boundaries. In order to understand how, you must first realize that Jimmy won't listen to reason.

Rational explanations may be soothing to you as a parent. They may remind you of your own ability to maintain control during a difficult situation. To Jimmy, however, a rational explanation sounds like gibberish. Why would he not topple the trash can if he feels like it? Because you have the means to enforce the rule, that's why. This sounds like despotism, and it may very well be, but it's your only way to set house rules. Someone's going to be the despot, so it might as well be you. The earlier you start implementing boundaries, the smoother and more seamless this part of his development will be. To help you in this task, I've provided case studies that reflect the challenges you're going to encounter.

Case Study #1

Let's start with the simplest case: Jimmy is playing with something that's either dangerous, fragile, noisy, or all three.

1 | Jimmy is banging a glass on the table.
2 | You tell him not to.
3 | Jimmy stops.
4 | Two minutes later, Jimmy is banging the glass again, and now he's looking at you.

WHAT **TO DO**

- **Take the glass away from him.**
- **If he has a fit, let him.**
- **If he starts hitting you, treat it like an inappropriate behavior, as described below, in Case Study #4.**

WHAT **NOT TO DO**

- **Don't waste your time on "Don't do that" rhetoric;** it quickly becomes a motivation to touch things anyway.
- **Don't launch into lengthy explanations** about the inappropriateness of his actions.

As soon as he can move around, Jimmy wants to explore everything around him: every switch, every knob, and every latch. This is obviously an extremely important developmental stage; he is unlocking the secrets of the physical world. But it can also be dangerous or expensive, as those switches and knobs are connected to stoves, lights, stereos, computers, and other delicate pieces of equipment. Place expensive things out of his reach. Get locks for knobs and safety latches for toilet seats.

By limiting Jimmy's opportunities to get into trouble or destroy things, you limit your own reactions and his opportunities to display oppositional or contrary behavior. However, no matter how resourcefully you Jimmy-proof your house, there will still be occasions when you can't physically limit access to certain appliances or other forbidden items. For what to do in those situations, consult Case Study #4.

Case Study #2

This slightly more complicated situation illustrates when Jimmy does not want to do what you want him to do.

It's a crisp winter day, and you're getting ready to take Jimmy out.

1 | You want to put his coat on.
2 | Jimmy doesn't want his coat on.
3 | You tell Jimmy he needs a coat.
4 | Jimmy does not let you put on his coat.

WHAT **TO DO**

When it's time to leave, you:

1 | Pin him down.
2 | Put the coat on.
3 | Go out.

WHAT **NOT TO DO**

- **Don't spend half an hour discussing the need for a jacket.**
- **Don't bribe him.**
- **Don't talk while you're putting the coat on him.**
- **Don't scream.**
- **Don't get upset.**
- **Don't laugh.**

Keep it simple, keep it short, and keep it stern. If you introduce any kind of playfulness into the situation, even negative playfulness, Jimmy will begin to enjoy the battle of wills, and he has much more time to waste on these battles than you do. As he gets slightly older (over eighteen months), there is an interesting variation on this strategy. After a few attempts to put on his jacket, you can simply say, "Suit yourself. Let's go." This allows Jimmy to experience directly the consequences of his actions, and a few minutes later, after he's discovered how cold it is outside, he'll put his coat on himself (or ask you for help).

Case Study #3

Before we get to the real deal, let's consider one more classic scenario: Jimmy rejects his food.

1 | You and Jimmy are sitting at the table.
2 | You place his favorite meal on the tray.
3 | Jimmy throws the whole plate on the floor.

WHAT TO DO

1 | The meal is now over. Take him out of his chair.
2 | Put him down.
3 | The next meal service is snack time, in two hours.

WHAT NOT TO DO

- **Don't serve him more food now.**
- **Don't serve him more food ten minutes later.**
- **Don't insist he eat.**
- **Don't get upset.**

After three of these cycles, Jimmy will understand very quickly that when he throws his food overboard he gets hungry.

Case Study #4

I saved the best for the last. The most challenging situation is when Jimmy does something you don't want him to do and you can't remove the object of his interest the way you could in Case Study #1.

1 | Jimmy slaps your computer.
2 | You tell him to stop.
3 | Jimmy slaps the computer again.
4 | You tell Jimmy in a level tone: "Stop banging on the computer."
5 | Jimmy slaps the computer again.

WHAT **TO DO**

1 | **Since you can't move the computer,** you have to move Jimmy. Put him in a place where it will be impossible for him to return to the scene of the crime. His crib is an excellent option.

2 | **Leave him in there for a couple of minutes.** Whether he cries, sleeps, plays, or settles down for a nap isn't important. What is important is that he gets a chance to chill out without you around to distract him or give him attention.

3 | **When the time is over, go pick him up,** even if he's still crying.

4 | **Put him down,** send him off to play with no discussion of what happened, and move on. You've made your point.

5 | **If he starts slapping the computer again,** repeat the cycle without any warning; i.e., don't say "Do you want to go back to your crib?"

WHAT **NOT TO DO**

- **Don't get into lengthy explanations of how expensive the computer is.**
- **Don't attempt to distract him with another activity.** It will work at first, but as Jimmy figures out your technique, you'll end up spending hours developing new distractions before you butt heads again anyway.
- **Don't give him a hug after you pick him up.** The only thing he'll remember is that banging on the computer equals a hug.
- **Don't apologize, and don't make him apologize.** He's not sorry, and he doesn't know what apologizing means.
- **Don't scream, scold,** or do anything that will give him a reason to associate his bad behavior with either positive or negative attention.

REAL QUESTIONS FROM REAL PARENTS

Isn't Jimmy going to develop a negative association with his crib?

Don't worry about the crib becoming associated with punishment. First of all, this is not a punishment. You're actually helping him by putting him in a place where he feels safe and cozy, as opposed to, say, a dark closet. Second, if you put him in a place where he could escape and come back to bang on the computer, you'd end up in a power struggle, which would undermine your efforts and produce the wrong effect entirely.

Couldn't we use his high chair?

You could, but he wouldn't be removed from the situation, which is what he needs in order to chill out.

How about the corner?
It's humiliating, he won't stay there, and you'll end up chasing him around.

How about sitting on the sofa?
It's not humiliating, but otherwise the same things apply: He won't stay there, and you'll end up chasing him around.

Out in Public
All these methods apply when you're in the privacy of your home. If you're outside, do damage control. If Jimmy is being inappropriate, strap him into his stroller, get moving, and let him wail for a few minutes while you roll along in silence. This may stir some attention from passersby, but you'll stir up even more attention if you argue and reason with him for half an hour. Unless you refrain from comment, he'll quickly learn how to profit from the fact that you're hesitant to let him cry because you don't want strangers to think you're some kind of child abuser.

Parents often laugh and tell me they've used the techniques described above to train their puppies. Indeed, this is very similar. Your dog only listens to you because he knows you're bigger and stronger, and a source of food and shelter. By providing repetitive and predictable responses that don't turn into increased attention, you can suppress your dog's inappropriate behaviors and encourage his appropriate ones. Young kids are the same way; once boundaries have been integrated, life becomes easy or at least easier. You won't be locked in a permanent power struggle.

This is not to say that Jimmy won't try a few tricks. But after a while, he'll be able to foresee the entire disciplinary process, and that foresight will make shenanigans much less enticing to him. He simply won't bother slapping your new laptop again after you tell him not to. And just like your dog, he'll feel loved and cared for.

How to Treat the Terrible Twos

If you've established boundaries properly, these kinds of discipline issues should be largely settled by the time Jimmy is two. At that age, testing and oppositional behavior should have markedly diminished or disappeared. If not, there are a few possibilities: Either Jimmy is experiencing a late burst of contrariness, or you may have been inconsistent in enforcing boundaries. There's no cause for panic. Here's how you can regain control.

Case Study #5

1 | Jimmy hits Lucy.
2 | You tell him not to, or else he will be put in his room.
3 | Jimmy hits her again.

WHAT TO DO

1 | **Without any discussion,** put Jimmy in his room for a few minutes.
2 | **When the time is up,** open the door and let him out.

I recommend that you choose your battles. Only engage Jimmy on the most essential issues, and let the little things slide. If you discipline him twenty times a day, the process will lose its effect.

WHAT NOT TO DO

- **Don't get overly angry.**
- **Don't obscure the discipline with explanation.**
- **Don't lecture him on how cute Lucy is and why he should love her.**

This discipline plan could get complicated. Jimmy is now able to open a door and escape from a room. If he does attempt an escape, your only—admittedly unpleasant—alternative is to lock the door while he's in there. If he hits Lucy again, put him in the room again, and this time you can proceed according to plan. I guarantee you won't have to lock it the second time, because he'll know you mean business.

You may balk at the idea of turning Jimmy's room into a high-security detention center for a fairly common infraction, but you have to realize that if you tell Jimmy to stay in a room and he escapes instantly, you undermine your credibility, and your disciplinary actions become meaningless. And if you resort to other tactics—holding the door shut with your hand or carrying him back into the room every ten seconds—all you're doing is initiating a power struggle, and he likes that. He's getting your undivided attention, and even if it has some negative aspects, it's still attention.

In Tribeca where I live, many of us live in converted factory lofts with open rooms (i.e., no walls or doors). Because of the simple fact that some parents have been physically unable to remove their kids during power struggles, I have seen the boundary-setting phase drag on much longer than usual. If this describes your situation, find a safe and reassuring spot in your house where you can place Jimmy for a couple of minutes when you need to implement boundaries. It should be a place he can't escape from, such as an area confined with child gates.

After ten consistent days of this regimen I guarantee that your life and Jimmy's will be much more pleasant. Although he'll still have plenty of moments when he affirms his will and personality, the day won't be one long permanent struggle. If you're inconsistent, however, you've probably made things worse, and I'll see you in the next section. Read on.

How to Treat the Terrible Threes and Fours and . . .

You have no idea how many parents of four-year-olds come to me complaining that their child is difficult to handle, hits other kids at school, and has very little tolerance for rules or frustration. Invariably, a teacher or doctor has raised the specter of hyperactivity and mentioned the "R" word (Ritalin). And so, here we are, sitting in my office. During the consultation, the kid does his thing: He opens every drawer, flips every switch, and interrupts constantly, all the while eyeing us to monitor the effects of his disruptions. In the vast majority of children, this kind of behavior results from insufficient early setting of boundaries.

Jean Piaget, one of the great development psychologists, articulated a model of child development that includes the concept of "trust," which develops when a parent consistently responds to a situation with the same set of behaviors. As early as infancy, a predictable reaction is reassuring, and allows the child to build confidence and to know what to expect. For boundary setting, this is equally importent. If—for want of time or to avoid a conflict or out of simple fatigue—you vary your responses to Jimmy's behavior, you'll find the strategy is utterly impotent. Or, worse, you'll find that it's counterproductive. A misused "time-out" can devolve into an extreme form of pointless reasoning or confrontation that destroys the effects of discipline, sends contradictory messages, and destabilizes Jimmy emotionally.

An obstreperous four-year-old isn't a lost cause, though. Far from it. In many ways, these kids function on this level just as eighteen-month-olds do; therefore, the only way to get back on track is to do what you would with a toddler.

WHAT **TO DO**

1 | **When a problematic situation arises,** give a very short, firm warning.

2 | **If Jimmy doesn't listen,** put him in his room with no talking for four or five minutes. Let him throw things, cry, or fly into a rage. All of these responses help him to lower his tension level, and he can't really hurt himself in his room.

3 | **If he escapes more than once,** put him back in and lock the door.

4 | **When the time is up,** open the door and resume your normal activities.

WHAT **NOT TO DO**

- **Don't scream or get upset.** This emphasizes the issue, and you want to minimize it.
- **Don't reason too much with him.** This type of behavior is beyond reasoning, no matter how smart your kid is, and reasoning just equals attention.
- **Don't discuss the punishment.** Keep talking to a minimum, because here your actions really do speak louder than words.
- **Don't revoke privileges.** When a tense situation arises, the prospect of not watching TV later won't be enough to keep Jimmy from throwing a fit.
- **Don't reward him when he does behave.** Same as above: This won't be a deterrent when the crisis occurs. Who cares about those gold stars anyway?

Here again, consistency is the key. If you provide the same calm, controlled response to all phases of Jimmy's erratic behavior, you'll see a tremendous change in him within ten days. He'll be much happier and able to start focusing on issues other than boundaries.

Doctor Visits

See also | **Immunizations; Screening Tests**

The frequency of your visits to the doctor may depend on your insurance. I like to see babies at least twice in the first month, monthly until six months of age, and then every other month until the first birthday. After that, quarterly for the second year, semiannually for the third, and annually from then on. During these routine visits, we examine the baby, administer immunizations, perform blood tests and hearing tests, and answer questions.

These routine visits are less medical than developmental; feeding, sleeping, and socialization issues take up the lion's share of the time. And it's good that they do. If you take any drastically wrong steps in any of these areas, you may be seeing the effects years from now. Regular doctor visits will help you get your children back on track.

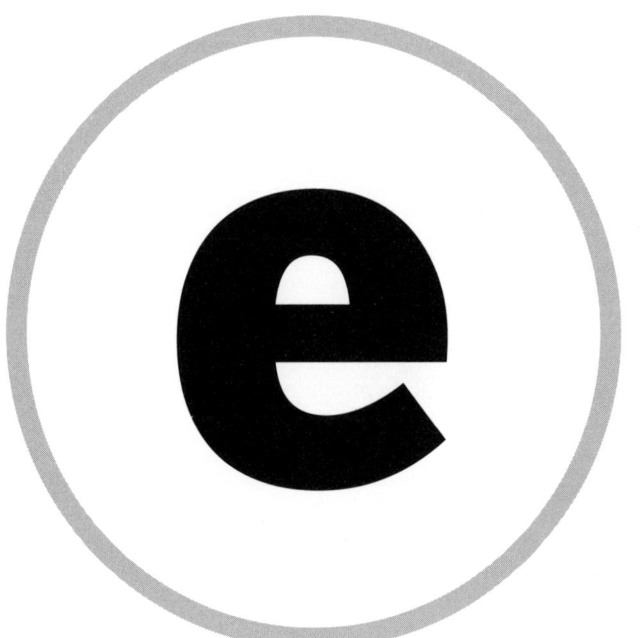

Ear Infections

See also | **Ear Fluid; Swimmer's Ear**

If you were to look into Jimmy's ear with an otoscope, you'd see the tympanic membrane, or eardrum, deep within the ear canal. The eardrum both seals the middle ear and transmits sound to the brain. Behind it, the middle-ear cavity connects to the throat via the eustachian tubes, which control the pressure in the middle ear. They also form a convenient passageway for germs to move from the throat and into the middle ear, where they may cause infections.

Every child suffers at least one ear infection, and some experience several. Rare before six months of age, ear infections primarily afflict toddlers, and the frequency tapers off as children get older. They frequently follow a cold or flu, because such ailments create a germ-friendly environment. Ear infections are not contagious, although the associated cold that can trigger them is.

The buildup of pressure in the middle ear is responsible for the discomfort. The degree of pain varies: Some ear infections may go unnoticed, while others can be excruciating. The pain peaks in the first twenty-four hours, and it rarely lasts for more than a couple of days, but a sensation of fullness or ringing in the ear may linger for up to a week after the infection has gone.

Fevers are also typical of ear infections, and infants especially may suffer temperatures as high as 104°F. Like any fever-producing illness, ear infections can cause febrile convulsions in predisposed children [**See:** Febrile Convulsions]. The child may experience vomiting, diarrhea, and poor appetite may occur in varying degrees of intensity.

Temporary hearing loss is the most common complication of an ear infection. Following an episode, you will probably hear Jimmy say "what?" even more than usual, until the fluid remaining in his middle ear drains and he recovers his full range of hearing.

In extremely rare cases, serious complications can arise when the infection spreads to the surrounding bone or the brain. This condition would be indicated by a persistent, very high fever and a very sick child.

Treatment

Once upon a time, doctors believed antibiotics were the only way to alleviate symptoms and prevent complications from ear infections. Since these infections are so common in children, the widespread use of antibiotics for this very purpose has largely contributed to antibiotic resistance. Recent research has demonstrated, however, that whether the cause is viral or bacterial, most infections will heal without any antibiotics and without any complications.

Increasingly, the standard of care for children over six months of age is to soothe the pain with acetaminophen or ibuprofen and observe for signs of a persisting infection. Pain medications are magical in their immediacy: Jimmy goes from crying to singing as soon as they take effect. You can use the highest recommended child's dosage, and repeat these medications as needed (every four hours for acetaminophen and every six hours for ibuprofen).

If the infection does not subside on its own within a couple of days, as indicated by persistent fever and pain, an oral antibiotic prescribed by your doctor is warranted. When the treatment is instituted at this stage, the ear infection clears up rapidly, although it's hard to know if you're seeing a delayed effect of the body's own immune system or the antibiotic at work. For infants younger than six months of age, we always use antibiotics when treating ear infections for fear of complications.

The laissez-faire approach—treating only those few ear infections that do not resolve instead of all of them—is far more logical. This approach spares your child the potential side effects of medications and helps keep his resistance to antibiotics low. Even when the infection doesn't clear up, waiting and watching for a couple of days has the benefit of allowing the body's natural defenses time to take effect. Unfortunately, despite the scientific evidence, doctors are still heavy-handed with the prescription pad when it comes to ear infections, probably because of a fear of liability, the ingrained habit of dispensing gallons of pink medication, and their own aversion to feeling useless.

Perforated Ear Infections

On occasion, the pressure in the middle ear will make the eardrum pop spontaneously, just like a pimple on the skin, and a bloody liquid will drip from the ear canal for a few days. This sounds and looks far worse than it is: The puncture relieves painful pressure almost immediately, and the draining promotes faster healing. You may be surprised to learn that before antibiotics existed, doctors regularly slit eardrums to treat ear infections. After a perforation, the eardrum usually heals in just a few weeks, and hearing is fully restored. Until the ear stops draining fluid, Jimmy should not bathe or go swimming, as water could seep into the middle ear and cause serious complications. Note: If the drainage persists more than three or four days, an antibiotic may be necessary.

Recurrent Ear Infections

One of the most frustrating things for parents (and children!) is a recurrent ear infection, which can start in infancy and continue through childhood. In such cases, anatomical disposition is generally to blame, rather than a weak immune system: The afflicted ear canal is configured in such a way that the germs ascend easily through the eustachian tubes to infect the middle ear. Enlarged adenoids are another predisposing factor [See: Adenoids]. These glands, which are located behind the nose and are supposed to clear the germs in the throat, sometimes become infected.

Recurrent ear infections primarily afflict younger kids, starting in infancy and tapering off as late as six years of age. My approach is to treat the most serious episodes—those involving prominent pain and fever—but to ride out the moderate episodes and let the child's natural defenses fight the germs. Contrary to what you may think, not treating a recurrent ear infection won't increase the chances of recurrence. Predisposed children will develop further infections or persistent ear fluid, whether or not each occurrence is treated. The unmedicated kids at least have the advantage of not developing antibiotic resistance. As a result of recurrent ear infections, fluid can accumulate in the middle ears, and impair hearing, which is critical for speech development. If Jimmy is predisposed to recurrent ear infections, no medicine, diet, or alternative treatment will decrease the occurrences of ear infection until he outgrows this stage. Abnormally repetitive ear infections incurring fluid buildup can be prevented with the surgical insertion of ear tubes [See: Ear Tubes].

Persistent Ear Fluid

After an ear infection, the fluid that's accumulated behind the eardrum usually empties slowly into the eustachian tubes. If, for any reason, these tubes become blocked, the fluid will remain in the middle ear and affect hearing, which can in turn impede language acquisition. This chain of unfortunate events may take place without your ever being aware of it, as ear infections and their aftereffects frequently go undetected.

If the doctor's examination shows that your child's ear is retaining fluid, the first step should be to have his hearing evaluated [See: Hearing Tests]. If it is only mildly impaired, there is no urgency, and the best approach is to wait and reevaluate the progress in a couple of months. The fluid will usually drain on its own. If it doesn't and hearing is markedly impaired, your doctor will probably suggest a simple surgical procedure that involves inserting ear tubes into the eardrum to drain the fluid and help avoid subsequent ear infections.

Long courses of antibiotics have little or no effect in drying out the fluid, although some doctors will sometimes prescribe them in an effort to avoid operating. The same goes for blowing into a balloon daily to unclog the eustachian tubes; even if Jimmy finds it amusing, it's not very effective. Decongestants, which are similarly ineffective, have more side effects than benefits [See: Decongestants].

Debunking Ear-Infection Myths

Contrary to popular belief:

- Allowing water into the ear in a bath or swimming pool will not cause a middle-ear infection. "Swimmer's ear" is a totally different condition that affects the outside skin of the ear canal [See: Below].
- Swimming with an ear infection is not a problem unless the eardrum is perforated [See: Perforated Ear Infections].
- There's no reason to cancel air travel if your child has an ear infection, unless the pain is intense [See: Air Travel].
- Allergies neither cause nor increase the chances of getting ear infections.
- Eliminating milk, wheat, or anything else from your child's diet won't minimize the chance of an ear infection.
- You can't treat or prevent simple ear infections with ear drops of any kind, including garlic oil. Drops don't pass through the eardrum, which seals the middle ear from the outside.

Ear Pulling

See also | **Ear Infections; Teething**

Many parents interpret ear pulling in an infant as a sign of pain caused by an insidious ear infection, when in fact it's simple exploration. Around four months of age, all babies start moving their hands around to test their new range of motion and to explore whatever happens to be sticking out. For Lucy, this includes her ears; for Jimmy, what sticks out are his ears and his penis (when he is naked). But I digress. It's true that ear pulling may signal general discomfort when teething pains start (around eight months of age). Whenever Lucy experiences throbbing in her gums, she will cry, touch her face, rub her eyes, and pull on her ears. This little display could convey the false impression that she is suffering because of her ears, rather than because of the erupting tooth. Pain medication will help her deal with the worst teething episodes. For the record, Jimmy's penis pulling is rarely a sign of discomfort.

Ear Tubes

Ear tubes are tiny hoses surgically inserted into the eardrum to drain accumulated ear fluid following recurrent ear infections. This insertion is a simple and safe outpatient operation done under general anesthesia. When indicated, the surgeon will perform it in conjunction with adenoid removal [**See:** Adenoids].

This operation has been overprescribed, however, and for many years it was almost fashionable to have tubes in the ear. But in fact, they should be inserted only when multiple ear infections have caused significant hearing loss, as demonstrated by a hearing test [**See:** Hearing Screening].

When indicated, the operation is very efficient. Hearing improves almost the same day, and the infections become much less frequent. If your child does fit the criteria for ear-tube placement, I recommend that you don't hesitate. The best time for the surgery is just before the winter, when ear infections are most prevalent.

There is a limitation that you should be aware of: As wonderful as these little tubes are, they only buy temporary relief. After six months or so, they become blocked and fall out. The procedure may then have to be repeated once or even several times until your child outgrows the ear infection stage at six to eight years of age.

Ear Wax

Many people feel that if it's brown and it's in their ear, it should come out immediately. The truth is that it's better not to dig it out. Ear wax protects the skin of the ear canal, muffles sound, and isn't dirty, despite its color. Attempting to scoop it out either pushes it in further or irritates the ear canal. Poking a cotton swab into Lucy's ear will only pack the wax in deeper, which can interfere with her hearing by forming a plug.

It's equally unnecessary to melt the wax with oil drops that contain hydrogen peroxide, as some doctors recommend. The notion that excessive ear wax causes hearing problems is doubly wrong. First, most people produce roughly the same amount of ear wax. Like water, however, ear wax seeks its own level, so the more you remove, the more the ear produces. Second, ear wax in itself doesn't cause hearing loss unless it is artificially packed in.

In short, clean away what you see on the outside, and leave alone what you don't see on the inside. If you don't know what's in there, you won't be tempted to dig it out.

Eczema

In predisposed babies, eczema generally starts around three to four months of age. The mildest and most common forms show up as dryness on the cheeks, torso, and limbs. Moderate forms look like windburn, cause the skin to look red and crusty, and occasionally lead to infection. Eczema is quite itchy and bothersome enough that even newborns will demonstrate amazing coordination in their efforts to scratch it. Unfortunately, the scratching worsens the condition and provokes a vicious cycle of irritation. In older children, eczema appears less on the face and more on the torso, belly, and extremities.

The course of the condition is unpredictable and very frustrating. It often waxes and wanes dramatically from one day or week to the next. Equally frustrating is the fact that flare-ups seem to happen independently of any triggering factor that you can put your finger on. Happily, eczema generally disappears with age, or at least the episodes become less intense and less frequent. Most kids completely outgrow it after their first birthday, and for those who don't, the outbreaks become less frequent and less intense until they outgrow it later.

Eczema typically runs in the family; usually, one or both parents had the condition as a child.

Causes

Eczema's triggering factors are so multiple and intertwined that you could drive yourself nuts trying to figure out what's causing it in your child. In my opinion, food allergies are the least likely cause, despite what you may have read. I have frequently seen parents eliminate different nutrients from a child's diet in misguided attempts to avoid or reduce eczema. These changes might appear effective at first, since the eczema will improve naturally, but it soon reappears as part of its normal cycle, even on the new diet.

Environmental factors are actually more important, especially in older children. Here are a few:

Soaps

Drying agents like soap or shampoo or, even worse, bubble baths certainly don't make things better [See: Soap]. Plain old water is the most soothing way to wash your child. Frequent soap-free baths won't trigger or worsen eczema, especially if a moisturizer is applied afterward.

Warm Weather

Exacerbates eczema, because sweat irritates skin.

Cold Weather

More precisely, dryness caused by heating systems in cold weather provokes irritation.

Mechanical Irritation

Washcloths, wool, or any abrasive material can also be irritating to the skin.

Viral Infections

Eczema frequently flares up during colds and flus. Distinguishing between a viral rash and a bout of eczema can pose a diagnostic challenge, but fortunately treatment is the same for both: Apply moisturizer.

Treatments

Moisturization

Eczema starts with dryness of the skin. This leads to irritation, which in turn causes itching, then scratching, and finally abrasions that can become infected. You can control the cycle of irritation by using a moisturizer. Any greasy ointment, even petroleum jelly, will trap moisture in the skin and prevent it from drying. You're going to need a lot of moisturizer, so there's no need to spend a fortune on a fancy formula. Apply it liberally every day (even twice daily, if necessary) to damp skin, because the added moisture makes a huge difference. The skin should feel greasy almost all day long when you're treating severe eczema.

Steroids

At times, no matter how diligently you have hydrated the skin, it will stubbornly remain irritated. That's when an anti-inflammatory prescribed by your doctor can help considerably. Steroid creams such as hydrocortisone have potent anti-irritant effects and work wonders for eczema, stopping the nastiest-looking outbreaks in a matter of days. They are available over the counter or in more potent prescription strengths. Apply the cream as directed and for the time prescribed by your doctor. This course of treatment will take at least a full week or even a little longer until the condition is completely cleared up.

People often apply steroids too sparingly or stop treatment as soon as the rash fades in intensity. Mistake! Since the irritation process has not been fully eradicated, the redness will reappear right away, prompting you to resume treatment. Ultimately, you will end up applying more than you would have if you had followed the directions.

Steroids can also be used safely on the face. The information inserts that come with these creams can certainly make you wary. It's true that the medicine can be absorbed through the skin into the bloodstream and that high levels can be toxic, but when used judiciously, steroid creams are perfectly safe and extremely effective.

Nonsteroidal Anti-Inflammatory Drugs (NSAIDs)

Drug companies have been working to develop new anti-irritant drugs that can be applied over prolonged periods of time and don't have the potential side effects of steroids. Introduced in the past two years and heavily pushed by their manufacturers, creams such as Protopic and Elidel are supposed to prevent the outbreaks, but their efficacy has not yet been proven. I've found their action limited. They can have undesirable side effects. Protopic in particular can cause a burning sensation.

Anti-Itch Medications

Anti-itch medications (antihistamines) make sense in theory: Decrease the scratching, and you'll stop the vicious cycle of eczema. But in practice, long-acting preparations such as Zyrtec have limited effects and undesirable side effects, while the short-acting drugs such as Benadryl work well but require frequent administration and cause drowsiness. I recommend you use the latter when the itching becomes very intense.

Toddler "Manicures"

There is one final nonpharmaceutical way to reduce the harmful effects of scratching: Trim Jimmy's nails.

In Summary

The best approach to eczema is to prevent outbreaks by moisturizing regularly and to treat the really bad episodes with steroids. Rest assured, age will bring relief.

Eggs

See also | **Feeding; Food Allergies**

For kids, eggs are fascinating objects, and they taste good too. But some adults don't share this taste or fascination: They are wary of allergic reactions or intolerance to eggs [**See:** Food Reactions]. Of course, eggs, like any food, can cause allergies in rare instances. However, if your child were allergic to eggs, the reaction would be immediate and intense at the first ingestion, which would warn you to avoid eggs in the future. Sensitivity to eggs is more common, but the effects (such as hives) are relatively mild, and may not recur the next time your child eats an egg.

When can you introduce eggs to the diet? Opinions differ: Some people advise steering clear of eggs before the one-year mark, while other folks are anti yolk. Both ideas are unfounded myths. I have learned from experience that an egg—the whole thing as it occurs in nature—is perfectly healthy and can be served as early as solid food is introduced, around six months. If Lucy turns out to be allergic to eggs, the timing of introduction won't make a difference, and delaying exposure won't prevent the allergy. As for egg sensitivities, they are rare and mild enough not to discourage you from sharing your brunch with her.

Eggs are excellent for older kids too. Given regularly, even once a day, they are a good source of protein and calories. They're high in cholesterol, but children, unlike adults, are active enough to use this form of fat as a source of calories without it clogging their arteries. That said, even kids shouldn't eat eggs too often. Any diet that relies too heavily on one food sacrifices variety and balance.

Eyes

Eyesight

What can Lucy see at birth? Not much, but enough to find her way to a nipple and take a look at its owner. Since she spends the better part of the day looking at the insides of her swollen eyelids while sleeping, she doesn't need more optic power. Her vision improves markedly over the first few weeks as the swelling goes down, and you'll notice her perking up and looking around.

Eye Color

Before six months, a newborn's eye pigments are still in flux. Light eyes may not be light forever. Initially, the iris is usually an indeterminate gray, and it's not until four to six months of age that the color becomes obvious. At that time, the white of the eye also loses its initial grayish hue and becomes whiter.

Red Spots

Newborns occasionally have small spots of blood in their eyes, marking where tiny vessels burst from increased pressure on the head during birth. After a month or two those spots disappear.

Trapped Lashes

If you notice what seems to be an eyelash stuck in Lucy's eye, it's probably just an illusion. Tears at the surface of the eye form a film, and a reflection at the edge of that film often resembles a stuck eyelash.

Nearsightedness (Myopia)

Jimmy is more likely to develop myopia, usually between six and ten years of age, if one or both of his parents is nearsighted. It's far from a foregone conclusion, though.

Watch for signs like squinting or, more simply, your child's own report that he or she can't see well. Once again, I am compelled to debunk a few myths: Complaints of headaches while concentrating on chalkboards or posters are not a reliable sign of decreased vision. Reading in the dark won't cause myopia, and neither will sitting close to the TV. Early detection of nearsightedness won't change the progression of the impairment, nor will wearing glasses. On the other hand, it will help Jimmy see the chalkboard and keep him from bumping into things.

Decreased Vision (Amblyopia)

Decreased vision (near and far) sometimes occurs in childhood, especially if there are associated conditions like lazy eye (eye deviation). Eye screening is not reliable before two years of age, and the degree of amblyopia remains difficult to assess until a child is old enough to offer a credible report.

Eye Blinking

Just like Bambi, young babies can develop a blinking habit as early as eight months. The first blinks are simply to test eyelid movement, but since Lucy looks awfully cute when she's giving you the eye, your attention may generate many more blinks. As darling as it looks, when the novelty has worn off, dismiss her blinking, and she too will cease to find it so amusing after a while.

Repetitive blinking can occur in older children as well, especially those with high-strung personalities (often high achievers). It becomes a bit of a tic, and as with every tic, your attention will reinforce it. Just ignore it and encourage non-competitive physical activity to reduce your child's tension, and the blinking will disappear [**See:** Tics].

Eye Crusting

Right After Birth

Abnormal tearing and eye discharge are usually caused by the antibiotic drops routinely applied by doctors right after the baby's birth. Designed to protect the newborn's eyes from any sexually transmitted germs that might be present in the mother, the drops also have an irritant side effect. This discharge quickly resolves on its own.

In Infants

Occasional crusting is usually due to the small size of infants' tear ducts or, more rarely, to an infection [**See:** Eye Tearing].

In Older Children

Occasional crusting, especially when accompanied by red eyes, is usually caused by an infection. Persistent crusting, however, typically indicates an allergic irritation of the eyes or a predisposition to inflammation. Warm soaks and antibiotic drops prescribed by your doctor will alleviate the condition when it flares up.

Eye Deviation (Lazy Eye)

The reason we have two eyes is not just because it looks nice but because seeing with two eyes affords superior vision. Each eye focuses on the same point from a slightly different angle. Muscles keep the eyes aligned, and then the brain combines the two perspectives to create depth perception.

Up to six to eight months, you can expect Lucy's eyes to cross now and then because of muscular awkwardness. If the eyes appear to stay crossed for extended periods during the day, this could be an impression caused by the shape of certain eyes whose inner eyelid is especially slanted, or it could signal a rare case of early "lazy eye." When in doubt, mention it to your doctor.

In some children, the eye muscles differ in length from one eye to the other. The brain still orders the eye to look at the correct angle, but when the muscles are strained, the eyes become lazy and don't obey; they wander in or out and appear crossed. Lazy eye is more common in toddlers, especially toward the end of the day, when the child is tired. Other early signs include squinting one eye in bright light or tearing. You may also be able to detect it in photos, where an assymetrical "redeye effect" will expose the uneven alignment. If you do notice lazy eye, bring it to your doctor's attention. Left to his own devices, a child will compensate by favoring one eye, which could compromise vision in the other over a prolonged period of time. Depending on the severity of the condition, an eye doctor will let the condition resolve itself or will prescribe a patch on the good eye for a few hours daily to force the lazy one to work. In rare cases where many months of patching have proved inefficient, the doctor may prescribe corrective surgery. Detected early, however, the condition is often fully corrected without surgery.

Eye Infections

Viral Conjunctivitis (Pinkeye)

Pinkeye usually refers to a common, self-limiting viral infection that affects the surface of the eyeball and causes tearing and red eyes for a few days. It can also produce a thick yellow or greenish discharge that dries into a crust and looks particularly dramatic in the morning, when the secretions have accumulated and glued the eye shut. Viral pinkeye can show up on its own or with a cold.

Contrary to common belief, pinkeye usually requires no treatment, because viral infections don't respond to antibiotic drops, which will just sting Jimmy's eye and increase the irritation. Your best bet to alleviate the discomfort is oral pain medication and numbing cold compresses. The condition usually resolves on its own after a couple of days.

Viral pinkeye is very contagious, and it can create havoc in nursery schools. Once one child has it, fifteen others get it within a few days. Hand washing has no preventive effect unless you can make Jimmy wash his hands every time he touches his face. Keeping him out of school won't really help, because the disease is very contagious even before symptoms become obvious, which means kids are spreading the virus before they even get sick.

Schools often require kids to be "treated" before they can be readmitted to classes, but the irony is that there is no efficient treatment for pinkeye.

Bacterial Conjunctivitis

If your little patient's symptoms are very dramatic, he may have bacterial pinkeye, in which case treatment is required. Bacterial conjunctivitis is much rarer than the viral version, but it produces more impressive symptoms. The whites of the eyes are quite red, the lids are conspicuously swollen, and the discharge is abundant throughout the day. This condition does require evaluation by a doctor, and, unlike viral conjunctivitis, it will respond to antibiotic drops.

Eyelids

Sties

When the base of an eyelash gets infected, it causes localized swelling, redness, and discomfort. The swelling may shut the eye almost completely. The sty usually lasts a few days, after which it pops spontaneously or decreases in size. Place a warm compress on the area to reduce discomfort and hasten healing, but I don't recommend antibiotic creams, which have little effect.

White Bumps

In rare cases, some kids have small white bumps at the margin of the eyelid. Known as *chalazions*, they can appear at any age, last for months or years, and require no treatment unless they are inside the eyelid and cause irritation during blinking. In this unusual event they should be removed.

Eye Tearing

See also | **Eye Infections**

If eye discharge persists for a few weeks, it may indicate clogged tear ducts. Babies are tiny, and so are their tear ducts. These little inlets, located at the lower inner corner of the eyes, are designed to reabsorb and recycle tears, but their small size predisposes them to obstruction. Such a blockage results in excessive tearing of the eyes and the intermittent formation of crust from inflammation. Blocked tear ducts aren't serious, but their symptoms can resemble those of an eye infection. The main difference is the severity: An infection produces much more prominent redness, discharge, and swelling than blocked ducts do.

You can treat clogged ducts by wiping off the crust with a warm compress whenever there's too much accumulation. Keep in mind that the crust does not bother Lucy. Massaging the tear ducts by rubbing the corners of the eyes won't open the ducts, and Lucy will hate it. The tearing and discharge at times can become intense, but this is still an inflammation, not an infection. As a result, antibiotic drops are rarely warranted and can even irritate the eye further. Some folks suggest applying breast milk to the eyes, but I think you should save it for better uses.

Most cases of obstructed tear ducts wax and wane over the first few months and disappear soon thereafter. If the condition persists to the end of the first year, it may require a simple surgical procedure to widen the ducts.

Persistent Tearing

Persistent tearing could be either an allergic irritation of the eye or clogged ducts persisting from infancy. Allergic conjunctivitis affects older children and is usually a seasonal response to pollen allergens. The eye tears constantly, and the child may also experience associated crusting, nasal congestion, and even rash. Rubbing an itchy eye may cause redness and swelling. Unfortunately, treatment options are limited. The non-steroid anti-inflammatory drops are not that efficient. Steroid drops should be used only in severe and stubborn cases. As with most allergies, it's often preferable to learn to live with mild symptoms than to risk the medicine's side effects.

Clogged Tear Ducts

According to the textbooks, clogged tear ducts that persist beyond the first birthday with prominent discharge and tearing may require a simple surgical procedure to open the inlet. In my experience, however, even later cases still stand a good chance of resolving on their own in the second year of life.

f

Family Bed

See also | **Cosleeping; Sleep**

For those of you who have never heard of a family bed, it's a king-size bed that the whole family plops into at night. (I might argue that it's a challenge to create a larger family when your family is in your bed, but that's not my point here.) Some parents are convinced of the emotional benefits of such arrangements. The families I see adhering to this philosophy are all happy and balanced. On the other hand, the families that are scattered into a queen-size bed and a few twin-size ones are also happy and balanced. My feeling is that frequent physical contact in the first few months is essential, whether you sleep with your kids or not, but after that kids quickly adjust to whatever routine you provide. The reverse may not be true: Some parents still need close contact with their kids until they are older, and this is perfectly fine, within reason, of course.

Fears

See also | **Nightmares and Night Terrors**

I** once saw a child who was terrified of the wind. His mother thought he had developed the fear from watching an episode of* **Winnie the Pooh** ***in which all the characters were blown away in a windstorm. Although the characters all seemed to enjoy it, her son refused to go out on windy days after watching this episode, which meant that both mother and child were confined at home. He became so fearful that he would not even peek out the window for fear of seeing tree leaves fluttering in the wind. In fact, most of their conversations had narrowed down to meteorological matters.

All children experience fears as early as the toddler stage. Jimmy may worry about wild animals, supernatural creatures, the dark, or things that should not be scary, such as the wind. Despite your best intentions, if you try too hard to allay his fears, you could unwittingly validate them. For example, if you dive under the bed to prove there are no monsters, you only emphasize the reality of his emotions, and he'll end up talking about monsters all day. Besides, you wouldn't look too good if you did find a monster down there, would you? Kidding aside, fears are perfectly normal in young children. Treat these fears in a controlled, dismissive manner by offering short and rational reassurance so they don't take on a huge significance in Jimmy's life and yours as well. Don't insist if Jimmy is not convinced by your explanations. He'll eventually realize by himself that what he is scared of is not that scary.

To the best of your ability, limit Jimmy's exposure to whatever he fears, but he'll most likely have to face the object of that fear at some point. For example, if he's afraid of the wind, like my little patient was, he'll go outside eventually, and when he realizes that he isn't being blown away, he'll overcome his apprehension. If he doesn't go out, he's only delaying that moment of awareness. Happily, these normal childhood fears always diminish and disappear, even if the process takes many months.

Febrile Convulsions

See also | **Fever; Flu; Roseola**

In predisposed children, a high fever can cause an irritation of the brain that produces febrile convulsions (also known as febrile seizures). Without any warning, Jimmy falls unconscious, his limbs shake, his eyes roll, and he foams at the mouth. The convulsion often takes you by surprise, because it can happen at the first onset of rising temperature. The seizure generally lasts for just a few seconds, which seem like an eternity, since Jimmy appears not to be breathing. He is, but the respiration is very shallow. When the convulsions stop, he falls into a deep sleep and feels boiling hot to the touch. Upon waking up a while later, he looks as if nothing has happened.

Any illness that causes a high fever, such as flu or roseola, can trigger these events. Febrile convulsions are more common in children from six months to six years, and they run in the family. As dramatic as they seem, they are not dangerous to the brain, either in the short or long term, but because they're called "seizures" they tend to generate excessive medical intervention. For starters, parents often panic and call an ambulance to rush the child to the emergency room. This almost always leads to unnecessary tests and sometimes even unwarranted hospitalization. While this overreaction is understandable, most doctors now advise parents to observe the episode at home while speaking to a medical professional on the telephone and address the cause of the fever later.

Febrile convulsions can resemble symptoms of meningitis, a very serious but fundamentally different condition. Whereas febrile convulsions are a short-lived irritation, meningitis is an infection of the brain that causes a child to become extremely sick gradually, so that by the time a seizure occurs, he is usually on the brink of coma. In febrile convulsions, the onset is sudden, and the recovery appears magical.

WHEN TO WORRY

- **If the shaking lasts longer than ten minutes.** Unless you looked at the clock when it started, don't rely on your impressions, because convulsions always *seem* to last forever.
- **If your child does not regain alertness after fifteen or twenty minutes.**
- **If there is no fever before or afterward.** This could point to a seizure disorder that has nothing to do with febrile convulsions, such as those caused by brain abnormalities.

If any of these situations occur, take your child to the hospital immediately.

WHEN NOT TO WORRY

- **If the convulsions happen while Jimmy has an illness** that causes high fever, such as flu, an ear infection, or roseola.
- **If the shaking lasts for less than ten minutes.**
- **If Jimmy gradually comes out of his sleep** and looks the same as before.

WHAT TO DO

- **Make sure Jimmy is lying flat during convulsions.** This makes breathing more comfortable.
- **Once the shaking has stopped and Jimmy is sleeping,** call your doctor to discuss the event and the treatment of the associated illness. You may be advised simply to keep him at home to rest.
- **You can give acetaminophen or ibuprofen to reduce the temperature** [**See:** Pain and Fever Medications].

WHAT NOT TO DO

- **Don't panic.** (This is the hardest part.)
- **Don't use a damp cloth to cool him off.** It won't shorten the period of shaking, and it will probably give him uncomfortable chills.

Prevention of Febrile Convulsions

If Jimmy is predisposed to febrile convulsions, using medication aggressively to lower the temperature has not proven effective in preventing the seizures. It's not the high temperature that causes the convulsions but rather a sensitivity in the brain to a rapid rise in temperature. In fact, if Jimmy has a high fever, the temperature will rise rapidly when the medication wears off, increasing the likelihood of seizure.

Recurrent Convulsions

If febrile convulsions occur once, there's a small chance that they'll recur during a future febrile illness until Jimmy outgrows the risk (at around six years of age). If you are in that situation, learn to manage the condition at home with the help of your doctor, and avoid the trauma of repetitive and unnecessary visits to the emergency room.

Feeding

***Y**ou were very excited to start feeding Lucy solid foods. Excited but scared, because so many allergies run in the family. You've already introduced the three grains in what you believe to be the proper order (barley, rice, and oats). You waited anxiously for a reaction, inspected the diapers carefully, and watched her skin for any suspicious rash. When nothing turned up, you boldly introduced fruits and vegetables, according to color and consistency. You cautiously stayed away from the forbidden ones: carrots for nitrates, oranges for their laxative properties, and strawberries because of allergies. After a while, your excitement about solids was lost amid all these rules and regulations, and you went to the baby jars, which seemed like less of a hassle.*

Some child-rearing books would have you believe that introducing your baby to solid foods is a risky scientific experiment. These books are full of frivolous warnings that could drive any parent crazy.

The reality is much different. When Lucy is ready (usually around six months), introducing solid food is very natural and straightforward. Unfortunately, too many parents approach this new phase with apprehension. This is the effect of clever marketing and lobbying by baby-food companies that try to sell processed foods by arguing for their superiority. But most of the myths are simply untrue. For example, you may hear that you should, after introducing a nutrient, wait three days before introducing another, in order to detect any reactions. This is unnecessary. Real food allergies are extremely rare, and their effects are very obvious. The allergic reaction would be immediate and fairly mild the first few times. If Lucy is predisposed to allergies, delaying or avoiding the introduction of certain foods won't prevent an eventual reaction, so it's better that you know early on. Sensitivity to foods is another phenomenon that shows up as a mild rash on the face or trunk within a few days or results in looser stools [See: Food Reactions]. It could be hard to pinpoint the offending substance if you're mixing foods, but it doesn't really matter, since these reactions are mild, short-lived, and may not even recur with the same exact food.

Before Six Months

Technically, Lucy doesn't need anything other than breast milk or formula until this age. Even after six months, calories from solid foods play a modest role, taking on additional importance only when she reaches eight to ten months of age.

In order to start eating solid foods, Lucy needs to be able to do three things. First, she has to sit up (until they become teenagers, it is hard for children to eat slumped over). Second, she must coordinate all the muscles involved in swallowing. It doesn't sound like much, but bringing the food from the front of the mouth to the back and then down the throat takes some real coordination. Last, but not least, she needs to be interested in eating.

The average baby fulfills these conditions around six months of age, although some do so earlier. Not long ago, parents used to spend hours under their doctors' directives trying to feed three-month-old babies spoonfuls of bland cereal. Now most doctors agree that an infant can thrive perfectly well with breast milk and/or formula for a good six months. This does not mean, of course, that you can't try a few little tastes of food here and there. Doing so makes for a fun-filled family moment. If you don't mind the mess, once in a while you can mash up a bit of what you're eating and put it on your finger, then let Lucy eat it off. You'll get a broad grin and probably some excited arm flailing. And who knows? She may actually eat some of it.

REAL QUESTIONS FROM REAL PARENTS

Why does my baby stare at me when I eat?

Your baby is always looking at you, no matter what you do.

Someone told me that my baby should start eating solids when she reaches twelve pounds. Is that true?
Some babies weigh twelve pounds at three months, others at one year. Weight has nothing to do with when you introduce solid foods. Eating is a developmental stage.

My baby is so big. Doesn't she need solid foods?
Big babies don't need to eat any sooner than small ones. And to tell you the truth, chubby babies tend to be a little less coordinated and sit up later, so they may not be able to eat solids until they reach their own comfort zone in terms of coordination.

Should I put cereals in the bottle?
You can, but there's no reason for the extra calories, and the starch content may provoke constipation [See: Cereals].

Would solid foods help my baby to sleep at night?
Sleeping at night has less to do with hunger and more to do with Lucy's capacity to soothe herself when she wakes up [See: Sleeping].

From Six to Eight Months

Around this age, Lucy is ready. She is able to sit upright better and has refined her swallowing technique. When the time comes to feed her solids, introduce them liberally. Purée any mild-tasting fruits and vegetables and offer them to her. Lucy will act surprised at first, but she'll grow accustomed to the new foods and let you know what she likes. Foods popular among babies include sweet potatoes, carrots, bananas, apples, squash, peas, green beans, and mangos. Harder fruits and vegetables should be strained, while softer ones can be puréed without cooking. Prepare meals without spices at first, but don't be shy about adding them a few weeks after this initial introduction.

How, When, What

How Much?

Lucy will take whatever she needs, from nothing to a whole bowl. It's also very easy to tell when to stop: Lucy pushes the spoon away or spits out the food. Conversely, as long as she keeps eating, there is no reason to stop feeding; let her tell you.

When?

Whenever it's convenient for both of you, but try to pick a time when Lucy is neither too hungry (she won't have the patience) nor too full (she won't have the interest).

How Often?

Start with once daily but increase to two or even three times a day, depending on Lucy's interest. The goal is three meals a day.

What?

Whichever fruits and vegetables she seems to fancy. Follow her cues, not some rigid list from a book. Feel free to mix and match in the same meal (or even the same dish). You can add a little cereal to thicken the purées that are too liquid, but there's no need for cereals alone; they are bland and bulky, and their iron benefits are overstated. Instead, use baby staples such as sweet potatoes, apples, and bananas, which all contain plenty of starch on their own [See: Cereals].

In What Order?

Start with fruits and vegetables. The idea that you should introduce vegetables before fruits to avoid creating a sweet tooth is just an unfounded myth. A carrot has virtually the same amount of sugar as an apple.

As Lucy's interest grows, you can mash up protein sources such as soft cheeses, yogurt, fish, or meat. Even at six or eight months, her little stomach can handle all of these. Again, waiting three days in between nutrients is overcautious. Food reactions are rare, so it's better to be a little more adventurous and deal with a mild reaction than it is to avoid a new food entirely for fear of an unlikely reaction.

How Soft?

At first, make the food pasty. As her ability to chew increases, you can introduce chunkier consistencies.

What Kind?

Homemade food is always fresher, tastier, and cheaper than jar foods. If you're concerned about organic ingredients, shop at a health food store.

REAL QUESTIONS FROM REAL PARENTS

Is there anything we should avoid?

Not really. Uncooked honey is not recommended in the first year because of the remote risk of botulism, but Lucy doesn't need it anyway. Processed sugars are not ideal either, although a lick of ice cream isn't the end of the world, and it will probably get you a standing ovation.

What if my baby doesn't have teeth yet?

Not only are teeth optional for Lucy at this point, but even if she had them, she wouldn't use them. The ones she has in front are meant to break hard foods which you're not giving her at this age.

What about choking?

Choking is not a hazard with mashed or puréed foods. If the food goes down the wrong pipe, Lucy will bring it right up by coughing, and she'll be a little more careful the next time [**See:** Choking].

How much is too much?

Trust Lucy to regulate her own appetite.

What should I do with regard to breast milk or formula?

Let Lucy adjust her own intake. The more solid food she eats, the less liquid nutrition she will require.

What about the nitrates in carrots and spinach?

A small amount of nitrates could be found in these vegetables if they were grown in a region with nitrate-rich soil. Nitrates can cause an extremely rare anemia in babies younger than three months, but at six months, when Lucy is first trying solid foods, the risk is negligible.

How about citrus?

Whatever mild citrus you can mash is fine: kiwi, for example. Lemons and oranges are impractical for this purpose, although some babies enjoy the acidity. Let Lucy decide. Initially, the acidity of some fruits may give her a brief case of the runs, but that will resolve itself rapidly.

What about berries?

Same as citrus: After their initial frowns, babies love berries. On occasion, berries may induce mild sensitivity reactions, including a slight rash on the face and body that lasts a day or two. If this happens, keep the offending fruit away for a month or so and then reintroduce it. The reaction may not recur. True allergies to berries are very rare.

Should I hold off on dairy foods?

Don't feed Lucy cow's milk in a bottle yet, but feel free to include cheese and yogurt in her diet. Dairy allergies are overstated and rare [**See:** Milk, Cow's], and lactose intolerance does not develop until late in childhood in predisposed children.

Introducing solids is straightforward and simple. Dismiss all the unnecessary warnings that you come across, ignore baseless anxieties, and join Lucy in this fabulous process of discovery.

From Eight to Ten Months

Now the fun really starts, as you introduce Lucy to new foods regularly. Three times a day, take whatever you are eating, put it in the food processor (or mash it up well with a fork), and feed it to her. I mean it: Short of hot pepper, feed her some of everything, no matter how spicy or bitter, no matter how "adult" you think it is. For the longest time, the accepted wisdom was that infants needed bland and tasteless diets. This just isn't true.

In all her senses, Lucy has flashy tastes: She prefers a red toy to a beige one, she'd rather listen to head-banging music than "The Four Seasons," she'd sooner touch something furry than a smooth surface, and at mealtime, she'd rather eat something spicy than bland mash from a jar. Spices are not only perfectly safe for infants but recommended. Garlic, salt, pepper, and other spices are encouraged (you're gonna see some funny surprised faces at first), but after that she'll be all over her funky new tastes. Some babies like lemons. Others go for liver. This age represents a precious window of opportunity to develop a palate for exotic flavors. Don't underestimate or shortchange her with bland food.

REAL QUESTIONS FROM REAL PARENTS

What if my baby is not interested in solids?

Some don't develop their interest until later on, and that's fine. The liquid diet has plenty of calories. Keep offering Lucy solid foods casually. Everyone ends up eating eventually.

What about finger foods?

By now Lucy can hold food by herself, and you should encourage her to do so, as long as it is something that won't break into hazardous chunks. Soft fruits are fine, as are biscuits or bread. But don't overdo the starch, as it will interfere with her appetite for healthier foods. These finger foods also tend to act as pacifiers, so try not to let Lucy have food unless she's hungry [**See:** Finger Foods].

What about salt?

Babies can handle salt as well as adults can, if not better, since their kidneys are brand-new.

What about milk?

You can give Lucy yogurt and soft cheeses, but cow, sheep, or goat's milk in a bottle is still off-limits until ten months [See: Milk, Cow's].

What about eggs?

Some people tell you to feed babies the whites; others, to feed them the yolks. They're both right; babies can eat both the white and the yolk. If a mild sensitivity reaction occurs, stay away from eggs altogether for a couple of weeks, then reintroduce them [See: Eggs].

What about juice and water?

Juice is hardly ever necessary. You can start giving a little water at mealtime or between meals in a bottle, or in a cup with your assistance.

I want to give my child a balanced diet, but I'm a vegetarian. Is meat necessary for babies?

Lucy should eat whatever you eat. If you don't eat meat she can follow the same diet, as long as she gets plenty of other sources of protein [See: Vegetarian Diet].

Do I have to process the food completely?

It depends on your child. Some babies can eat chunky foods early on, while others still have trouble chewing at ten months. Increase the consistency steadily, and pay attention to Lucy's response.

In Summary

In general, there's little that can go wrong with food introduction. You will notice that Lucy enjoys things you never thought she would, and mealtime will become a kind of adventure for the whole family.

From Ten Months to a Year

If you've followed the program described above, Lucy is probably eating almost everything by now. She's also attempting to feed herself, which you should encourage despite the mess. If she's on formula, you can stop it at this point and give her cow's milk (or any other milk) instead. There is no need to wait until one year—the "officially" recommended age—to graduate to milk, since you've probably given her dairy in the form of yogurt with no problem. If she's going to have trouble handling cow's milk, two months won't make a difference by this point. The amount of milk she needs will vary from almost none to four or five bottles a day, depending on her solid-food intake.

If Lucy is still not very interested in food, it could be that she simply isn't ready yet. Like every milestone, eating varies from one baby to another. But it could also be that your cooking is too bland or that you're relying too heavily on tasteless jar food. I have seen countless babies turn their heads away for this very reason. Feed her some of your food; it's tastier, fresher, and cheaper. Finally, if Lucy refuses to eat, it could be that you aren't giving her a chance to work up an appetite; don't be too quick to offer breast milk or formula.

After a Year

By this time, Jimmy should be eating everything you give him and doing it by himself. Encourage this autonomy; it's the best way to learn how to control his intake, and feeding him could come across as pressure. You will almost certainly notice variations: At some meals he'll clean his plate, and at others he'll leave almost everything. Respect his shifts in appetite.

Jimmy's schedule should coincide with yours: three meals a day and two snacks in between. The composition of the meals should also be the same as yours: more or less: a good, commonsensical diet. Don't count calories, ounces, or recommended daily allowances of vitamins.

As for milk, the amount will vary. Contrary to what experts thought years ago, there is no minimum intake for milk after one year, and some children just don't drink any. Milk is a good source of calcium, but so are yogurt, eggs, cheese, broccoli, and fish. Is there such a thing as too much milk? If you sense it's interfering with Jimmy's appetite for other foods, limit his access to two to three bottles daily, max [See: Milk, Cow's].

By now Jimmy can eat everything. He can even have shellfish, seafood, or raw fish, although most children don't really go for the oyster platter. Indeed, if he has a rare shellfish allergy, it's better that you find out early on. Limit processed sugars or juices that contain too much sugar, at least at home, where you have more control. Sugar reduces the appetite and fosters both bad eating habits and cavities. Slow sugars such as pasta should not be given in excess either, as kids rapidly develop a predilection to starch that can be hard to break.

At this point, you are probably very pleased with Jimmy's voracious appetite. Enjoy it while it lasts, because this will change in the next few months, when he discovers that he can get more desirable food by throwing what he finds undesirable on the floor [See: Picky Eating].

Feet

See also | **Sensory Integration; Shoes**

Pigeon Toes

In utero, a baby's feet are squeezed into a C shape with the soles turned inward. Sometimes this shape lingers after birth. For those with an interest in Latin, this condition is called *metatarsus adductus* or, more commonly, "pigeon toes." In the old days, foot specialists systematically braced these little feet. This is no longer a common practice, except in those rare occurrences where the deformation is very pronounced. For most kids, a daily ankle massage will help the foot achieve its normal position, though the adjustment may take many months.

Flat Feet

There are whole continents—Africa and Asia, to name two—where flat feet are the norm, and they don't seem to impair mobility among billions of people. Africa has consistently produced some of the finest distance runners in the world, and it seems silly to suggest that they'd run even faster with well-articulated arches. But that's exactly the kind of pro-arch propaganda that was rampant thirty years ago, when specialists routinely prescribed supplements and special shoes.

As it turns out, all toddlers have flat feet. Later on in childhood, the arch forms, but some children still have almost no arch. That's just the way it is: a matter of taste, perhaps, but not of medical importance.

Toe Walking

When some children take their first steps, they occasionally do so on the tips of their toes. In the vast majority, this walk disappears after a couple of months, but it sometimes lasts well into childhood. Toe walkers point their feet as they walk, mostly out of habit resulting from an unusually high muscle tone in the calf. But if you ask a toe walker to put his feet flat on the floor, he can. If the condition persists after a few months of walking, consult your doctor to evaluate whether the heel muscle is abnormally tight. Anecdotally, toe walking is often found in children with "sensory integration," high-IQ children who are especially sensitive to their environment [**See:** Sensory Integration].

Once your doctor has established that there's nothing wrong with the foot's anatomy, it becomes a matter of gently redirecting your child's behavior. As with all habits, the laissez-faire approach is best (ignore it or at least pretend to). The more attention you pay, the more you reinforce the behavior. Braces are prescribed sometimes, but I don't recommend them; they are inefficient and stigmatizing.

Most toe walkers will eventually walk on the soles of their feet, although it may take many years. Often, normal socializing is an incentive: In elementary school, the child will become self-conscious and try harder to lose the habit. In the rare instances where the condition lingers beyond the teen years, surgery can be performed to lengthen the Achilles tendon.

Fever

See also | **Febrile Convulsions; Thermometer**

Fever is good and bad. It's good because it warns you that something is going on in the body, and, since most viruses don't fare well in heat, it helps purge the illness. It's bad, obviously, because your kid is sick and uncomfortable. But as serious as a febrile illness may be, a fever in and of itself is not dangerous for the body and won't damage the brain, even in the rare event that it causes convulsions [**See:** Febrile Convulsions].

A normal temperature is between 97° and 99°F, a low-grade fever is around 100.5°F, a moderate fever is around 101.5°F, and a high fever is over 103°F. The margin of error is about half a degree, depending on how you take the temperature and the type of thermometer you use. There is also a wide variation in the amount of fever a child generates. The same illness will make some kids boiling hot, while it leaves other kids cold, so to speak.

In Newborns

For the first few days outside the womb, Lucy's temperature can fluctuate for no apparent reason. Her "thermostat" is not yet fully operational, because you performed temperature regulation for her in utero. Covering her with too many blankets can slightly raise her body temperature above 100.5°F (the official cutoff for a fever). In newborns, fever is rare and a poor indicator of serious illness. In fact, a drop in temperature below 97°F may signal an infection. Other signs, such as poor feeding or extreme sleepiness, indicate the severity of an illness better than a fever does. In any event, don't bother taking Lucy's temperature routinely when she's a newborn, only if she feels unusually warm or cold to your touch. You should promptly talk to your doctor about any fever or drop in temperature.

Before Three Months

Before three months of age, fever is still very rare. If Lucy feels warm to the touch and has a recorded temperature of more than 100.5°F, she definitely has a fever. At that age, fever could be the sign of a serious ailment and therefore must always be addressed, especially if she's sleepy or lacks appetite. Don't waste your time lowering her temperature with medication; take her to the doctor to determine the source of her fever.

After Three Months

When Jimmy has a fever, the most important question is not "How high is it?" but "Why is it there?" A child could have an uncomfortable but harmless flu with a temperature of 105°F or, alternatively, a much more threatening illness with a temperature of 101°F. Don't let yourself be falsely worried or reassured by the number on the thermometer.

WHEN **TO WORRY**

- **If Jimmy is very sleepy or sluggish** and remains that way when the fever drops after anti-fever medication.
- **If he has other symptoms,** like respiratory difficulty or repetitive vomiting.
- **If his fever persists over several days,** or subsides and returns.
- **If he drinks little fluid,** which could lead to dehydration.

WHEN **NOT TO WORRY**

- **If Jimmy is lucid and aware,** even in discomfort.
- **Even if you can't bring the fever down,** you shouldn't necessarily worry; some flus and viruses produce fevers that medications can barely touch. This is not a reliable sign of an illness's severity.
- **If the fever disappears after a few days.**

WHAT **TO DO**

- **Lower Jimmy's temperature** with either acetaminophen or ibuprofen or even both, more to alleviate discomfort than to get a better reading on the thermometer. If his discomfort is pronounced, don't be stingy; use the highest recommended dose for his age, and repeat as often as needed [**See:** Pain and Fever Medications].
- **If you have any doubt as to the origin of the fever** or the need for treatment, address the issue with your doctor.

WHAT NOT TO DO

- **Don't take Jimmy's temperature over and over again.** You know he has a fever. It will go up and down until the illness resolves.
- **Don't use cool baths or an alcohol rub.** These strategies date from prehistory, and they just create chills and discomfort. Medications are much more effective.

REAL QUESTIONS FROM REAL PARENTS

How high is too high?

I know a high fever is nerve-wracking. Nevertheless, it doesn't necessarily spell doom. Readings can even reach over 105°F with fairly short-lived viral illnesses. Of course, you'll want to discuss any fever over 101.5°F with your doctor to determine what course to take.

Why is his little heart racing?

Because it's supposed to race. When the body is warm, a reflex mechanism speeds up the heart to help expel heat. The more the blood circulates, the more heat is reduced.

Why is he breathing so fast?

For the same reason. Heat is dissipated in the breath.

What if he has a seizure?

High fevers can cause febrile convulsions in predisposed children. These look scary, but they're not dangerous. No matter what you may hear, you can't prevent them by giving fever medication constantly.

When should I lower the temperature?

Only if Jimmy is uncomfortable. Otherwise, let the fever follow its course while you monitor the symptoms. This way, you'll be able to gauge the progression of the illness rather than obscure the symptoms by suppressing them. Fever serves a purpose: The elevated temperature makes Jimmy's body a much less friendly environment for a virus. Also, the fever has a hidden advantage: It knocks him out so that he'll rest instead of run around under the influence of Tylenol.

Is it true that I have to keep my child inside for twenty-four hours after a fever?

I'm not sure who made up this rule. Most diseases are contagious before the onset of fever rather than afterward. You'll be surprised by how quickly kids bounce back after an illness. The next day, if Jimmy is up to it, let him play or go to school.

Fifth's Disease

Fifth's disease, so named because it used to be the fifth most common childhood condition (after measles, mumps, rubella, and chicken pox), is a mild contagious viral illness that affects children and sometimes adults. After about two weeks of incubation, a rash suddenly breaks out on the cheeks. In fact, it's commonly known as "slapped cheeks," which dates back to the time when kids were routinely disciplined that way. The rash can progress down the trunk to the extremities and usually lasts as long as a week or two before fading. Some days it will look worse than others. Like all rashes, it is most evident when blood flow to the skin increases, as it does during a bath or while crying, for example. Other symptoms may include fever, headache, sore throat, and itching. In rare cases, Fifth's disease may cause temporary swelling and redness of the joints. Since it is viral in nature, there is no treatment for Fifth's disease but time and relief of discomfort. Unless Jimmy feels lousy, he does not have to be out of school, because the illness takes so long to resolve and almost every kid around him probably has it anyway, thanks to the nature of viral maladies in schoolyards.

Fifth's disease is a potential concern for pregnant mothers. The virus that causes it can also induce miscarriage or severe fetal anemia if contracted in the early stages of pregnancy. Fortunately, this is rare, since most adults have acquired a natural immunity from previous exposure in childhood. In any event, avoiding contact is almost impossible, because the illness is so widespread, and those with the disease are contagious before symptoms appear.

Finger Foods

Around eight months of age, if Lucy grows tired of chewing on her own fingers, you can give her finger foods. Pieces of soft fruit, cereal, bagels, cheese sticks—anything that she can hold in her hands and that will dissolve into a paste is suitable. Lucy will chew them into an unattractive mash that will dribble onto her bib, and she may even eat some of it. There are a few things to watch for with regard to finger foods. First, the high starch levels could provoke constipation. Second, if Lucy grows too fond of finger foods, she might lose her appetite for healthier foods. Finally, there's the issue of food-as-pacifier: Once you find out that Lucy's fussiness eases when she's chewing on her biscuit, you may be tempted to give her another one every time she is cross.

Flu

See also | **Colds; Ear Infections**

Every year, the influenza virus makes millions of people miserable. You can catch it in summer, but it's more common in winter, probably less because of the weather than because people are inside more and in closer quarters. The flu starts with a sudden onset of high fever, headaches, and muscle pain, sometimes accompanied by nasal discharge and cough. In younger children, the fever is less prominent, and upper respiratory symptoms are more pronounced. The flu virus evolves constantly, and the severity of the illness varies with the virulence of the yearly strain. Some years, flu is no big deal; in others, it's a significant public health concern.

Flu lasts three to five days, after which time the fever should be down or gone and the other symptoms greatly diminished. Occasionally, the fever will disappear and return for a day before subsiding completely. Some controversial anti-flu medications for adults have been introduced, but these have not yet been approved for young children.

Complications from flu are fairly rare, although they do exist. Ear infections are the most typical and are usually accompanied by a persistent or worsening fever and discomfort. An older child will point to his ear and tip you off to an ear infection. Ear infections usually do not require antibiotic treatment unless they fail to improve within a couple of days. [See: Ear Infections].

A rarer complication is pneumonia, which shows up as a tenacious fever and causes a decline in the general condition. Instead of improving, Jimmy looks sicker and sicker. His appetite decreases. He may even have a productive cough and some difficulty breathing. This constellation of symptoms should prompt you to seek medical attention.

Flu Vaccine

The flu vaccine is not that effective. It's a pain in the butt and a headache as well, since it has to be given every year by injection. The protection depends on the yearly strain, but keep in mind that even if Jimmy gets the vaccine there is a very good chance he'll get the flu anyway. Since flu symptoms are milder in children, I don't recommend routine immunization unless there is an underlying chronic condition such as asthma that might make a flu rougher going. A new nasal-spray vaccine has just been released. It's less painful than an injection, but it's too early to tell if it's more effective.

Fluoride

See also | **Cavities; Dentist; Tap Water; Toothbrushing**

Dentists have long claimed that fluoride is an essential element for healthy teeth. For thirty years, toothpaste and tap water in many states have been supplemented with fluoride to prevent cavities, and over that time there has been a steady decrease in tooth decay. However, there is no conclusive evidence to show whether this improvement is due mainly to water fluoridation or to better hygiene and nutrition.

What everyone does agree on is that too much fluoride is detrimental. In excess it can actually stain or damage teeth. Fluoride supplementation is not currently recommended for babies under six months of age. From six months on, the amount in tap water suffices if Lucy drinks water and you live in an area where the water is fluorinated. If not, your doctor will prescribe vitamin drops that contain fluoride or recommend bottled waters that are specifically reinforced with the element.

When children start brushing their teeth, they get plenty of fluoride from toothpaste and therefore no longer require supplementation. Be careful that Jimmy doesn't overdose on fluoride by eating your toothpaste as if it were candy. That is why you should buy him a children's formulation, which will have the appropriate fluoride concentration.

Fontanel

The fontanel is the soft spot on top of Lucy's head. Everyone in the family is afraid to press on it, except her brother Jimmy. The fontanel is part of a fascinating skeletal process. In order to facilitate the passage of the baby's head through the delivery canal, the skull is made up of several bones that are attached loosely together; after birth, this design allows the brain and skull to grow. Between these bones there are actually two soft spots: a large one on top and a less obvious one in the back. The top one varies in size from large to almost nonexistent. Lucy's soft spot becomes more noticeable when she cries, which increases pressure on her brain and makes her spot bulge. If she gets a fever, you can see the fontanel pulsate as her blood flow increases. When Lucy sleeps, pressure diminishes, and it becomes slightly depressed.

Fontanels close at different times. The rear one usually disappears by her third month, and the one on top remains more or less until her first birthday. Generally, the larger the spot, the longer it takes to close. As far as the fragility of the fontanel, you can let Jimmy touch it; a strong membrane protects this mysterious area, and incidental pressure won't hurt.

Food Reactions

See also | **Feeding; Milk, Cow's; Wheat**

Food Allergies

Food allergies and sensitivities are significantly overdiagnosed. Most kids don't have any of these and never will. I have attempted to group the different reactions to foods in an effort to clear away the myths.

First of all, let's define our terms. True food allergy, or anaphylaxis, is not a simple matter of a child reporting itching or an upset stomach. In anaphylactic reaction to foods—the most common being to nuts and shellfish—Jimmy immediately turns red and suffers a swelling in the throat that can impede breathing. Fortunately, these true allergies are rare. They usually show up at the first introduction of the offending food, and they can be triggered by the smallest amounts. In fact, anaphylactic reactions can occur before a child has even eaten the food. For example, an adult who has eaten peanuts and still retains trace elements on his hand can induce anaphylaxis merely by touching a highly allergic baby's mouth. While this first reaction is generally a mild redness on the face, each reintroduction of the allergen will produce a stronger reaction, eventually triggering respiratory involvement. Kids can be allergic to many different nutrients, such as milk, or to medications, such as antibiotics.

Anaphylactic reactions are predetermined in an individual and cannot be prevented. And just because one person in your family has a severe food allergy doesn't mean that your baby will. Determining true food allergy is tricky. Blood tests are relatively unreliable. Before a dangerous food has been ingested, the baby's blood has not yet produced any of the specific markers that indicate an allergy. In addition, these tests often misfire with false positives, leading you to label harmless foods as potential anaphylactic culprits. I've seen too many lab reports that claim high levels of allergy for a specific nutrient, despite the fact that the child has been happily eating the alleged allergen for years. These inaccurate tests can drive parents to limit their children's diet too drastically. Skin tests are a little more accurate but impractical.

The best way to know if Lucy is allergic to a particular food, believe it or not, is to assume she is not. If she turns out to have an allergy, you'll see an intense rash, possibly accompanied by difficulty breathing, very soon after the ingestion. Even with a pronounced food allergy, severe reactions rarely occur upon first ingestion, but they're still unpleasant enough for you to recognize them and take the warning. The first time around, the rash will subside rapidly, and the breathing should be only slightly impaired, but if the reaction appears very intense—or if Lucy is struggling to breathe—rush her to the hospital. Conversely, if Lucy eats some peanut butter and sails on through, there is a near-certain chance that she is not allergic to peanuts.

If Lucy does have one of these rare severe reactions, you (and soon enough she) will become an expert at reading food labels in order to avoid the allergen even in trace amounts. You will also have to carry an epinephrine-filled syringe with you at all times. Anyone involved in her care should know how to handle and administer this medication; you can use an orange as a practice patient.

Food Sensitivity

A "food sensitivity" is a mild allergy caused by a certain type of food. Sensitivities are also quite rare, and the reactions they cause are all over the map: They are usually delayed, can occur once or many times, and may appear for the first time at widely different ages. Fortunately, they're usually limited to hives and redness around the mouth. For example, Lucy might get a rash for a day or so the first time she eats a strawberry. The tricky thing about food sensitivities is that the offending foods are less obvious and therefore harder to identify than serious allergens. On the other hand, food sensitivities tend to diminish with time, unlike allergies and anaphylactic reactions, which tend to get worse. This category includes the mild rashes commonly seen with fruits (such as berries), chocolate, and eggs before three years of age.

There is no test for food sensitivities; simply avoid the food that caused the reaction for a few months, then reintroduce it periodically until Lucy can tolerate it.

Food Intolerance

Food intolerance occurs when, owing to a digestive enzymatic disorder, Jimmy doesn't digest certain foods properly. Allergy is not the culprit. For example, lactose-intolerant kids don't have the enzyme necessary to digest a milk protein properly [**See:** Milk, Cow's]. Wheat intolerance is another example [**See:** Wheat].

The symptoms associated with food intolerance vary widely in severity. Some children show no symptoms at all, while others suffer from chronic diarrhea, bloating, and belly cramps. The diagnosis is usually cumbersome, and the only treatment is to avoid the offending substance, which can also be quite cumbersome.

Formula

See also | **Feeding; Milk, Cow's**

Once considered healthier than breast milk, formulas are now seen as a second-rate option for infant nutrition. Neither assessment is really fair. Formulas are a fine choice too. If you plan to use them, either as a sole source of nutrition or in combination with breast milk, this is what you need to know.

All baby formulas contain the same basic nutrients in the exact same ratio. This is not by chance but by law. In fact, to be called formula, a substance must meet strict FDA requirements by replicating the amounts of fat, sugar, protein, vitamins, and other elements naturally present in breast milk. The amount of iron varies from formula to formula [**See:** Below for more iron in formula]. The proteins in formula come from diverse sources, generally cow's milk, soy milk, or a lactose-free milk, but all sources provide the same nutrition.

Formulas are sold as a powder or reconstituted liquid. The latter is just a more expensive version of the former mixed with sterile water and packaged in a can. If you're using a powder, you simply reconstitute it following the directions on the can by using tap water, which, in many states adds the appropriate quantities of fluoride [**See:** Fluoride]. As for boiling or even filtering the water, it's largely unnecessary, as most tap water is not contaminated and therefore perfectly safe for babies.

Every so often, formula companies trumpet the addition of a "super element" such as a lipid; the text on the side of the box stops just short of suggesting that this magical ingredient will guarantee Lucy admission to an elite university. None of these "super elements" has a proven benefit, apart from increasing the company's sales.

REAL QUESTIONS FROM REAL PARENTS

Why are there so many kinds of formula?
Don't let yourself be confused by the diversity. Just as with detergents, the variety is mostly a matter of marketing.

Which one should I use?
I recommend the cheaper one. It's just as good as the others and only cheaper because the company is keeping its marketing costs down.

Liquid or powder?

Powders are much more convenient. But follow the directions on the can carefully; incorrect concentrations may pose a serious hazard for newborns.

Iron or no iron?

Every formula contains the recommended amount of iron, but some are further supplemented. A little extra iron doesn't hurt, although I feel that the benefits are overemphasized. The extra iron could also cause constipation, so if you notice hard stools, switch back to a low-iron formula [See: Iron].

How do I know if my baby is allergic to a milk-based formula?

Again, allergy to—or, more accurately, intolerance to—formula is much rarer than people think. Some signs to watch for are vomiting or extreme diarrhea, poor weight gain, or blood in the stool, in which case your doctor will recommend a soy or lactose-free formula. Be aware that crying is unlikely to be a sign of allergy or intolerance. The same goes for spitting up or vomiting, which are more likely normal or caused by overfeeding or reflux.

Do I have to stay with the same brand?

Absolutely not. Hospitals receive lucrative incentives to provide you with a specific brand's free sample just after delivery, under the assumption that you'll probably stick with it. Exercise your consumer freedom and switch brands at will. In the rare instance that your baby has a proven intolerance to one kind of formula (those based on soy or cow's milk), that will of course limit your options.

Why are there so many chemicals in formula?

Formulas synthesize a natural substance, but there are chemicals in all substances. If the FDA ran amok and required mothers to identify all the ingredients in breast milk, you'd see chemicals in that list too.

Are there any organic formulas?

At present, there are none for infants. One is available for toddlers, but by that age they don't need it.

What about predigested formulas and those antireflux formulas for fussy babies?

Predigested formulas should be reserved for babies who have real digestive problems, as some premature babies do. All too often, these types of formulas are used when they're not warranted—for a crying baby, say—and they don't solve the problem. They do solve another problem, which is what to do with your money; even though they have the same nutritional content, they can cost up to twice as much.

The antireflux formulas are even less defensible [**See:** Reflux]. Like predigested formulas, these tend to be a crutch for parents and doctors who don't want to investigate the cause of a baby's fussiness. As far as I'm concerned, these products are a rip-off. Reflux is a mechanical problem rather than a nutritional one, and special formulas won't affect it at all.

How long can I safely use formula in the bottle if my baby doesn't finish it at first?

Two to three hours, at least. When Lucy breast-feeds, the nipple always has a small amount of remnant milk on top, which gets contaminated. When she returns to the nipple, this is the first breast milk she encounters, and it doesn't make her sick. Use the same reasoning to assess the formula's freshness.

How long should I keep the baby on formula?

I recommend switching babies away from formula to milk at ten months, when they can handle cow's milk or an equivalent. The next-step formulas, which are targeted at babies over a year old, are another product of marketing: They have no real nutritional advantage at that point in Lucy's life and are quite expensive.

g

Gas

See also | **Colic**

The first thing people tell you about babies is that they're cute. The second thing is that they're flatulent. Everyone has a theory on gas: It's related to colic or pain or too much food or too little food. For the most part, these theories reflect superstition rather than medicine.

Gas is produced in a mechanical chain of events. Whether or not you're a baby, your intestines naturally produce gas as a by-product of digestion. The more Lucy eats, the more gas she ingests and produces. And like most babies, she fusses and cries, which not only makes her swallow more air, but also prompts her to raise her legs to her stomach and cramp her abdominal muscles. The result? Increased belly pressure and the release of gas. After passing gas, Lucy generally stops crying, either from surprise or relief.

While observing this chain of events, you might be led to believe that the release of gas relieved her belly pain. But actually, the coincidence of crying and muscle contraction caused the release of gas. If you massage Lucy's belly or pump her legs in order to help her evacuate more gas, you may succeed, but you'll unfortunately agitate her further. She'll cry more and therefore swallow more air and pass more gas. And if you assume she's crying because she's hungry when she's not, feeding her will give her a full belly, increase her digestion and its byproducts, and thus make her cry even more. See the cycle?

As for those antigas concoctions, ranging from gripe water to simethicone drops to chamomile tea, they're deceiving. Since they're all sweet, Lucy won't mind their taste, and for a while you may think they're working miracles. Until she passes gas again. Faced with a cranky baby, it's much healthier for the whole family to avoid medications that have virtually no effect and to understand that the problem with the baby simply resides in being a baby [**See:** Colic]. For the first couple of months, our little creatures are none too happy to be outside, and they let you know it by crying, kicking, and incidentally farting.

My theory bears repeating: Lucy has gas because she cries; she doesn't cry because she has gas. Gas is not a sign of discomfort but rather an ever-present condition that has become associated with discomfort as a result of a misunderstanding.

Goat's Milk

See also | **Milk, Cow's**

Goat's milk has always had the reputation in alternative circles of being healthier than cow's milk. It is leaner, which may be an advantage for adults but not for children, who can handle the fat and need the calories. Other than that, its composition is largely the same. Goat's milk is harder to find and more expensive. There is a vogue suggesting that newborns can be fed goat's milk because of its chemical similarity to breast milk. This is not recommended, at least not for very young children. If you buy goat's milk for an older child, buy the pasteurized kind. Fresh goat's milk is associated with specific bacterial infections that could be harmful.

As for allergies, goat's milk is not suitable if a child is allergic to cow's milk, because of cross-reactivity.

Growing Pains

See also | **Joint Pain**

The growing pains people always talk about occur commonly in children six years of age and older, and they manifest as nonspecific tenderness in the lower legs, typically in the evening or at night. If the pain occurs without limping, redness, or swelling, and if it comes and goes over the course of a few months, then it qualifies as growing pains.

As with all vague complaints in children, you shouldn't give them overt attention. If, for example, you give Jimmy a half-hour calf massage, you'll find that the growing pains themselves grow as he figures out how to use them for his benefit. Instead, use occasional pain medication and get him back to bed quickly.

Growth Charts

See also | **Height; Size; Weight Concerns**

Growth percentiles have been calculated for American babies by simple statistics: Researchers measured large numbers of children and determined an average. If Jimmy is in the sixtieth percentile in weight, he is heavier than sixty out of every hundred kids. But be careful about reading too much into these percentiles, which have little to do with nutrition and usually reflect simple differences in morphology; they are largely useless in predicting future size.

It's slightly more useful to compare weight and height percentiles in order to detect overweight and underweight children or at least early warning signs. For example, a child who is in the thirtieth percentile for height and seventieth percentile for weight might be overweight. But numbers are only numbers; when in doubt, look at the kid himself.

Charts and percentiles are also useful in monitoring head growth. Charting the head circumference can flag those rare conditions where head size is abnormally large, which may indicate excess fluid in the brain [**See:** Head Shape].

Growth charts may look scientific, but they are far from precise. In general, their flaw is that they assume steady growth: According to these charts, skinny babies stay thin through later life. Mother Nature doesn't always work that way; skinny babies can plump up, and plump babies can thin out.

Growth Spurts and Appetite

See also | **Growth Charts**

During infancy and childhood, there are periods during which the appetite increases. These are part of the normal fluctuation and don't necessarily correlate to growth spurts. Similarly, a low appetite doesn't mean the child isn't growing; it could be caused by teething or a low-grade cold, or simply be a period of no appetite to be followed by a voracious one.

Gums

See also | **Teeth; Teething**

In Infants

Infants' gums can have multiple little bumps: some white, some purplish, none of clinical significance. An amateur tooth hunter can easily confuse these bumps with new teeth about to bust through, so you'll need to inspect carefully before you claim Lucy is cutting a tooth.

Another condition you may encounter in Lucy's mouth is thrush, a mild fungal infection wherein white curdlike deposits appear on the gums, inner cheeks, and tongue [**See:** Thrush].

Many books and Web sites devoted to child care tell you to clean infants' gums carefully with gauze pads. They also give beautiful lectures on why oral hygiene is very important for babies. But none of them tell you what you accomplish by rubbing the gums. Sorry, I can't answer that question either, since I don't see any benefit to it. And the kids? Babies *hate* having their gums rubbed with gauze. So until somebody gives me a valid reason, I'll continue to advise parents: Leave those gums alone.

In Children

Canker sores are circular white lesions in the mouth or on the tongue. They can be painful, but they don't produce a fever. Lucy may get one or several, but they probably won't last longer than four days. If she finds eating difficult, try cold foods and liquids, which may go down more easily. In extreme cases, pain medication may be required.

Many childhood illnesses affect the gums with blisters and sores, the most common of which are the Coxsackie viruses and oral herpes [**See:** Coxsackie; Herpes of the Mouth]. These lesions can be even more painful than canker sores and can interfere with eating or drinking.

Hair

Some babies are born with it and some without. All of them get hair eventually, although it could, in some extreme cases, take a couple of years. Those who have it at birth may lose it in the first few months—or not. It really varies from one baby to another, and there is no way to predict who will and who won't have hair. Lucy is likely to lose at least the hair on the back of her head from the constant and repetitive friction against her bedsheets. In either case, lost hair will regrow after a few months.

Hand Washing

The habit of washing your hands each time you handle a newborn is both unrealistic and unnecessary. When you're changing a diaper, you don't wash your hands after each and every step. For that matter, the diaper itself isn't sterile. And hand washing is completely ineffective at preventing the spread of those airborne viruses that cause colds and flus. There is one exception: If you have a boil on your skin or any communicable infection, such as a fever blister on your mouth, then you should wash before any contact with Lucy.

Having said that, hand washing has at least the benefit of dissuading people from handling newborns too much. This is just as well, since Lucy doesn't particularly want to be passed like a hot potato from one cooing admirer to the next.

Headaches

Headaches become a source of concern when children are old enough to complain about them. This is not to say that they don't experience them before they can talk about them, but preverbal kids can only produce general crying and screaming rather than anything more specific. Headaches can occur with illnesses or without. They can be occasional or recurrent. Here's a quick guide on how to distinguish the severity of headaches.

Headaches with Fever

When headaches occur with a fever, meningitis, although extremely rare, should be in the back of your mind. Watch vigilantly for the symptoms: intense pain, vomiting, and trouble moving the neck. Pain medication won't help much.

Flu headaches show up differently and with less dramatic symptoms than do headaches associated with meningitis. Generally, there's no vomiting, and while Jimmy may suffer general muscle pain, moving his neck hurts no more than anything else does. Pain medication will make his headache disappear for at least a couple of hours.

Sinus headaches, which are rare in young children, can occur with sinus infections, but they tend to be localized in the forehead area.

Occasional Headaches with No Fever

These are common enough, and most of them are not serious. They are usually the result of an associated illness; strep throat, for example, can produce headaches without fever. The same goes for colds. The headache will improve as the illness does.

Recurrent Headaches

Children commonly complain of headaches that last several days or recur frequently over time. The older the child, the more common the problem. In general, such headaches could be due to neck tension, which decreases the blood flow to the head, or to migraine. Eyestrain headaches occur much less often than people think, and it is questionable whether this can even be a cause.

WHEN **TO WORRY**

- **If the headache occurs every day**
- **If the headache increases in intensity** as the days go by
- **If the headache is present** when Jimmy wakes up
- **If he is vomiting or has difficulty moving his neck**
- **If he is less than five years of age**
- **If there are vision problems** such as double vision
- **If the headache is resistant to medication**

These signs could point to a rare occurrence of intracranial growth, such as a brain tumor. Seek medical attention if your child suffers any of the above symptoms.

WHEN **NOT TO WORRY**

- **If the headache is easily relieved with pain medication**
- **If the headache has no particular schedule**
- **If there are no other symptoms**
- **If the headache comes and goes,** sometimes for months, without worsening
- **If it does not impede daily activity**

Once you have established that Jimmy experiences plain but recurrent tension headaches, give him occasional pain medication. Lying down for a moment in a quiet, darkened room is an excellent way to relieve tension headaches. It may even help your own headaches.

Psychological Headaches

It all started when you had a problem at work, and you developed a splitting headache. Recently, Jimmy's been pointing to his head at different times of the day, some days on, some days off. Once it was so bad he cried. You wondered if it was from his habit of sitting too close to the TV, but on the contrary that seems to relieve him. Strangely, when you massage his feet he improves.

Kids are experts at noticing when complaints bring special care. If Jimmy's headaches yield head massages, trips from class to the nurse, or opportunities to watch a movie, he'll learn to point at his head and frown whenever he needs a little extra pampering.

A strain in the family can cause psychological headaches. I also see children who emulate a frequently complaining parent. If you think Jimmy's headaches are psychological rather than physiological, don't give him too much attention. Simply tell him to go lie down and wait until he feels better. If his headaches persist despite these measures, keep a diary and note their duration and intensity as well as the effectiveness of various relief strategies. This record will help your doctor determine the next level of intervention.

Head Banging

Toddlers often bang their heads against walls, doors, or furniture, horrifying their parents in the process. In a way, that's the point: While the first few times are accidental, the behavior quickly evolves into an attention-getting tactic. You have two strategies for dealing with head banging: Either put padding on all the walls of your house and ignore it, or just ignore it. I recommend the latter. After two or three episodes, Jimmy will realize that head banging hurts and isn't much fun. And when it provokes no reaction, he'll find it even less enticing. If, on the other hand, you try to dissuade him, he'll bang his head even more.

Head Injury

In cases of head injury, the problem isn't so much Jimmy's skull as his brain. In other words, while many bumps and knocks may look dramatic, Jimmy will just shake them off and move on. When the blow is particularly strong, the concern is, of course, to assess the risk of intracranial bleeding. A head X ray has limited value, in that it only reveals the skull. A CT scan is much more accurate for showing a brain injury, although a slow intracranial bleed could fail to appear early on, which would falsely reassure you. Again, assuming Jimmy is fine after the fall, the best and only way to assess potential brain damage is to carefully observe his behavior for the next day or so. Trauma-related changes are usually visible within a few hours following the injury, but they could take up to a few days to appear.

In Infants

Despite all the warnings, infants frequently fall from changing tables, couches, or infant carriers during split seconds of inattention. It is very rare that these falls cause brain injuries, but it does happen.

WHEN TO WORRY

- **If the fall was from a height of more than three feet,** especially onto a hard floor
- **If Lucy has a bump on her head,** which in a baby could point to a significant impact
- **If she has lost consciousness**
- **If she is very drowsy after the fall** and can't stay awake at a time when she is supposed to be
- **If she is very irritable after the initial crying fit**
- **If she looks very pale**
- **If she seems uncomfortable in her sleep**
- **If she loses appetite after the fall**
- **If she vomits several times**

Any of these symptoms require immediate medical attention.

Contrary to what people think, changes in pupil size are a late sign of complications and therefore not a reliable early indicator.

WHEN NOT TO WORRY

- **If Lucy's energy level remains the same after the fall**
- **If she falls asleep peacefully** and comfortably after crying and you can wake her at least once
- **If she keeps a normal color**
- **As scary as it may look,** a baby's tumble from a table or a bed less than three feet high rarely causes head injuries

WHAT TO DO

- **Watch Lucy closely in the hours following the fall.**
- **If it's nighttime, let her sleep next to you,** and watch that she is sleeping peacefully and comfortably as usual, without any moaning, grunting, or vomiting.
- **Check at least once during the night** to make sure she is wakeable and responsive.

WHAT NOT TO DO

- **Don't try to keep Lucy awake when she's sleepy** or wake her up if it's sleeping time. If you do, you'll disrupt her sleeping pattern, and any judgments you make about her alertness or mood will be based on faulty information.

In Children

If Jimmy falls, it shouldn't be too difficult to assess the severity of his injury, since he can tell you what hurts and how.

WHEN TO WORRY

- **If Jimmy loses consciousness after the fall**
- **If he is drowsy and slurs his words after the fall**
- **If he vomits several times,** especially if it worsens as time progresses
- **If he has a headache that increases in intensity**
- **If he seems disoriented or walks unsteadily**
- **If he falls into restless sleep**

Any of these signs would require immediate medical attention.

Changes in pupil size are a late sign of complications and therefore not a reliable indicator.

WHEN NOT TO WORRY

- **If Jimmy cries right away**
- **If he falls into a peaceful sleep**
- **If he acts normally after the fall**
- **If he vomits once or twice after the event but quickly stops** (The jolt to the head, even if it's not serious, can provoke this reaction.)
- **If he has a bump on his head.** While this is worrisome in the case of a very small infant, in an older child, a hematoma on the scalp is in itself not indicative of a brain injury.

WHAT TO DO

- **Watch Jimmy more closely for the next day.**
- **If there's a bump, apply an ice pack for a few minutes if he lets you.** If he won't, don't add to his distress, because it won't make much difference in the swelling. Otherwise, no bump, no ice.

- **Let him take a nap or fall asleep if it's nighttime,** and watch him to be sure that his sleep is peaceful.

If any of the serious signs described above occur, take him to the hospital immediately.

WHAT **NOT TO DO**

- **Don't keep him from going to sleep.** A fall and the intense crying that follows can be draining. Not only is it hard to prevent sleep, it's more important to observe the quality of sleep after a fall.
- **Don't give headache medication more than once;** it could mask discomfort and provide false reassurance.

Head Shape

See also | **Neck**

Here are the common issues covering infants' heads.

Head Size

Head size varies from kid to kid. During regular visits to the doctor, the head circumference is measured to monitor the growth [**See:** Growth Charts]. If Lucy has a very small or a very large head in comparison to her body, look at your own; you may discover that it's a family trait.

Big Bump on the Head

In a newborn, you may feel a soft bump on the head. Pressure against the pelvic bone during delivery sometimes causes bleeding in the scalp. This bump can be quite large and take a couple of weeks to disappear. It can even cause the baby to be jaundiced in the first few days [**See:** Jaundice].

Small Bumps on the Head

If you run your hand over Lucy's or Jimmy's skull, you'll feel multiple bumps and ridges. The bumps are little lymph nodes that are normal on a child's skull, while the ridges are the intersection of the bones of the skull. So, now you can enjoy petting your kid's head without any worries.

Flattening of the Head

Because babies spend most of their time lying on their backs, their skulls, which are softer than adults' heads, can flatten temporarily. This is usually a mild condition that reverses as the head grows. In rare cases, the skull flattens more significantly on one side, which leads the baby to lie on it more often, further increasing the flattening. Babies who have large heads and *torticolis* (a tendency to bend the head to one side) are more likely to be affected, as are premature babies.

Your concern over a flat head is understandable, but rest assured it is purely aesthetic. Even severe flattening has no effect on the brain, and in most cases the condition will completely resolve on its own. That said, positioning Lucy can minimize further flattening. Prop her up with foam cushions so she's resting on the side that is not flat. Place mobiles or other toys on the opposite side of the crib to attract her gaze [**See:** Crib Paraphernalia]. If torticolis is a factor, a gentle neck massage will loosen the muscles [**See:** Neck Tilting].

Ordinarily, treatment ends with these simple positioning measures. Even significant flattening becomes barely noticeable with age and a full head of hair. In extreme cases, some doctors use helmets to reshape the skull, but such treatments are expensive, and I have not found convincing evidence that they are efficient.

Hearing Screening

In Newborns

Hearing screenings are performed routinely on newborns at the hospital to detect rare instances of congenital deafness. If Lucy passes the test, it means she can hear. But even if she fails, it doesn't necessarily mean she can't. These tests are difficult to perform accurately in a noisy nursery setting. Your doctor will repeat the test in better circumstances. There is also the old-fashioned way to know whether Lucy can hear: Just clap your hands loudly and see if she blinks or if she turns her head toward you. And in the weeks to come, you should also notice her responding to your voice.

In Older Children

Hearing screenings should be performed at every regular visit after infancy. The older and more cooperative the child, the more reliable the test will be. But accuracy is limited before three years. Hearing tests are performed even more frequently on children who have recurrent ear infections with ear fluid trapped behind the eardrum, in order to monitor hearing loss [See: Ear Infections].

Height

While predicting Jimmy's height is hardly an exact science, the height of the parents and prevailing trends in both families can provide some insight. If everybody in your family is under five feet tall, it's unlikely that he'll play in the NBA. But some kids of tall parents are unusually small and vice versa.

When a child is unusually small, parents sometimes worry about a hormonal deficiency. This is extremely rare and can be ruled out with a simple X ray of the wrist to evaluate the "bone age." If that test is normal, a growth-hormone deficiency is extremely unlikely. Extensive athletic training has also, at times, been implicated in stunting a child's growth, but the link isn't clear. In the vast majority of cases, the best bet is to wait and see.

Herpes of the Mouth

See also | **Coxsackie; Gums**

Oral infection with the herpes virus produces a painful febrile condition for young children. It starts with aching sores inside and around the mouth, and it makes Jimmy miserable for a few days. Eating and drinking become uncomfortable ordeals, and combined with varying degrees of fever, his lack of fluid intake may lead to dehydration. In about five days, the lesions become crusty and slowly disappear. The virus will stay dormant in the area, however, but can be reactivated later—even a few years down the line—as a single fever blister that lasts a few days on the lip.

Oral herpes is acquired from direct contact (like kissing) with an adult whose active fever blister represents the reactivation of some childhood virus. It cannot be caught from indirect contact with an adult who has genital herpes lesions; this is a different virus that can only be transmitted sexually.

Pain medication is the key to treatment [**See:** Pain and Fever Medications]. If Jimmy spits up his medicine because of the sores, you might have to resort to acetaminophen suppositories. In addition, an antibiotic cream on the lesions around the mouth will prevent secondary bacterial infections. In terms of prevention, there is little you can do, partly because the virus is contagious even before the fever blister appears and partly because it's hard to prevent kissing.

Hiccups

Hiccups, or *singletuss*, are nothing more than a contraction of a baby's diaphragm as a result of immaturity. During the first months of Lucy's life, hiccups come and go, no matter which folk remedy you practice: sips of water, the football hold, or trying to make her laugh to restore regular breathing. By definition, the last trick you try is the one that works; when the hiccups disappear, you attribute the relief to the final strategy you attempted. In truth, the relief matters more for you than for Lucy, who is unfazed by her hiccups.

Hip Dislocation

During initial examinations, your pediatrician will aggressively twist your newborn's hips to detect congenital hip dislocation. This is a rare malformation in which a child is born with the thighbone out of the hip socket. If the thighbone develops in such a way, the consequences can be so serious as to impede walking. With early detection, however, doctors can treat this efficiently and avoid serious crippling. If indeed there is a dislocation, further tests will be ordered to visualize the bone, and placing the hips in a harness for the first couple months of life will correct the abnormality.

Hitting

See also | **Discipline and Boundaries**

Take a look at a pair of kittens playing together. They hit and bite each other, and what does the mother cat do about it? Absolutely nothing. Why? Because hitting and biting are perfectly natural behaviors for kittens. Toddlers are the same way. They are naturally aggressive, at least up to a point, and attempting to parent all violent behavior out of existence and program Jimmy into a flower-power frame of mind could backfire. How? Well, positive or negative attention reinforces the behavior. This is especially true when kids go through phases where they hit those close to them, whether mommies or little sisters.

From a practical point of view, I recommend that you treat hitting as you would any other inappropriate behavior. If it's just a little tap, let it go. If it's a big whack, then treat it as a disciplinary issue. Rather than launching into a long lecture on respect, say "Don't hit your sister" and put Jimmy in his crib for a couple of minutes. Let him vent his frustration there by crying, thrashing, and doing whatever else he can think of. After a couple of minutes, remove him from the crib and put him down by himself with no extra affection, no lecture, and no demonstration. Don't look for an apology; Jimmy's not sorry, and it's not because he's evil but because he didn't mean any harm.

Occasional hitting should disappear within the third year of age. If it doesn't, I suggest you visit us at our discipline booth, under "D."

Hives

See also | **Food Reactions; Medicine Allergies**

Hives are itchy red blotches that occur in reaction to food ingestion or external contact with an irritant. Most hives break out within a few minutes, although they sometimes take a few days to appear. Once in effect, the blotches wax and wane during the day and last about a week. Normally, hives are not accompanied by breathing difficulties. If they are, that could signal a real allergic reaction that should be treated as a potential emergency.

Hives are often grouped with allergies, and while this is somewhat justified, hives are much more difficult to track back to an allergen. They can occur erratically: You could eat the same food for years without a reaction and then suddenly develop hives. Even if you identify a hive-producing food, repetitive contact will not necessarily trigger a subsequent reaction.

The itching that hives cause can be severe enough to drive Jimmy absolutely crazy. You can control it with short-acting antihistamines such as Benadryl, which are the most efficient option and can be taken as often as every six hours, in spite of their side effects; a little drowsiness is much more bearable than the infernal itching. If Jimmy isn't itching, he doesn't need any antihistamines. When hives last longer or are more intense, your doctor may prescribe a short course of oral steroids, which will reduce the intensity and duration of the episode.

Hives are notoriously mysterious. If you're lucky, you may be able to trace their origin to a new laundry detergent or food, though you'll often end up scratching your head while Jimmy's scratching his arm. Don't spend too much time trying to put your finger on the trigger so to speak. Consider allergy testing only if the episodes recur again and again.

Humidifiers

See also | **Colds**

There's nothing wrong with dry air, even if it has a reputation for being harsh on the skin and mucous membranes. On the other hand, there are few proven benefits of humidified air. It doesn't soothe the airways, and it won't necessarily help breathing during a cold or an asthma attack. (One exception is croup, a condition that humidified air helps considerably.) On the other hand, when air is too humid it provides a perfect culture medium for molds, bacteria, and allergens. For those reasons, I don't encourage humidifiers. If you insist on having one, they come in different sizes and prices, depending on factors such as noise level and their alleged ability to limit mold production. Whether the moist air is cold or warm makes no difference, since it ends up taking on the room's own temperature.

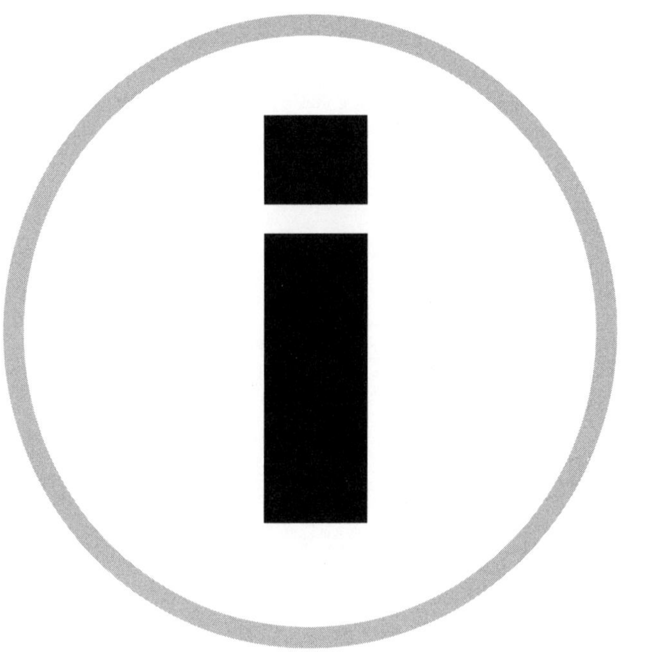

Ice Packs

See also | **Head Injury**

y youngest child, Fanny, has a habit of going to the school nurse for every little boo-boo. Fanny likes to complain about the service: "All the nurse gives me is an ice pack."

The ice pack is a small miracle cure for bumps and bruises. The cold temperature penetrates the skin and contracts the blood vessels, thus slightly limiting the swelling and numbing the pain. For best results, use it in the first ten minutes after injury. After that, it doesn't do much good, so if Jimmy refuses to let you put ice on him, don't chase after him with it. And if he doesn't want it at all for whatever reason, don't worry; ice packs are nice little miracles but not indispensable.

Illness Management

Throughout the book, I have discussed specific illnesses. Here are some general guidelines for dealing with sick children, no matter what has lain them low.

Fluid During Illness

The adage "lots of rest and lots of fluid" is one of the most stubborn in folk medicine. While it's true that a high fever or vomiting can bring on dehydration, insisting that your child gulp down gallons of water won't really make a lot of difference in the course of an illness. Make sure Lucy's not dehydrated, especially if she's got a stomach bug, but beyond that, don't worry about "flushing out toxins," a process which I suspect is more psychologically beneficial for the parents than physiologically useful for the baby.

Rest During Illness

How much should Jimmy rest when he's ill? Let him regulate the amount of rest he needs on his own. Take the flu, for example: An important part of the healing process involves sleeping extra hours and sweating it out. If you give him antifever medication to bring his temperature down, he'll end up bouncing around instead of resting, sweating, and recovering.

Rest After Illness

How long should Jimmy rest after an illness? It depends. Some parents believe additional rest will help replenish the child's energy. In fact, it can be more like house arrest, actually prolonging a low-energy phase in which Jimmy mopes around and watches TV all day, thus perpetuating the impression that he needs more rest. My advice: As soon as his energy begins to return, encourage Jimmy to resume his normal activities.

Regression After Illness

You are naturally more attentive to a sick child. You carry Jimmy around the house, rock him to bed at night, cuddle him, make special meals, and sing special songs. But what about when the illness ends? After you've sat in first class, it's hard to go back to coach. You may find that even a fully recovered child continues to demand special treatment.

Babying your baby for too long after an illness can backfire over time. Sleeping patterns are among the earliest victims of illness: Dozens of parents have told me that their baby was a perfect sleeper until he had a cold and that since then he's been all out of sorts at night and for naps. My advice is to reset Jimmy's expectations as soon as the illness disappears, and return him to the schedule he was used to before his illness. This may cause some discontent, but that too will pass, and soon enough Jimmy will be back to his happy self.

Loss of Appetite During Illness

In the midst of a flu, cold, or ear infection, Jimmy loses his appetite. A couple of days later, his ribs are showing. Worse, after the illness vanishes, he's still not eating. This is normal. It will take a few extra days for his appetite to return, but soon enough he'll be asking for seconds. If you pressure a newly healthy child with food, your efforts could turn him into a picky eater.

Immunization

By any standard, immunizations are a blessing. A generation ago, childhood diseases such as whooping cough caused serious respiratory illnesses in babies and even death. Today, many such killers are history.

But vaccines are a victim of their own success. They work so well that they have virtually obliterated the dangerous diseases they thwart. As a result, the focus has shifted from their benefits to their side effects, which range from mild to serious. This has led some people to question the wisdom of vaccines in general. For starters, let me assure you that vaccines are safe. To be approved, they have to meet strict FDA criteria for safety and efficacy. This process requires years and years of research and trials before release, and even after a vaccine's release, safety and efficacy are constantly monitored in the several million kids that are vaccinated yearly. We doctors are required by law to report any unusual side effects. In short, the process for testing and monitoring the safety of vaccines is quite comprehensive.

Mild Side Effects

By far the most common side effect of vaccinations is the few seconds of crying after an injection. But there are others.

Pain

Injections hurt. Any doctor or nurse who tells Lucy that it feels like a little pinch is lying. These shots sting, not so much from the needle piercing the skin as from the fluid entering the muscle. Some fluids hurt more than others: The DPT vaccine, for example, hurts much more than the polio vaccine, even after the initial needle prick. The little pinch doesn't last long, though. After a few seconds, Lucy forgets why she was crying, especially if she is distracted or fed. Before the shot, oral pain medication is largely ineffective (though it may be helpful after), and local anesthetic creams are pointless, as they numb the skin but not the muscle, which is where the fluid hurts the most.

For younger kids, breast feeding during vaccination won't decrease the pain, and it may even increase yours if Lucy bites your nipple. For older children, the anticipation is worse than the pain itself. Don't spend a week preparing Jimmy for the shot. During the injection, hold him gently against you instead of pinning him down. A pleasant sensation can offset painful ones, so you may want to give Jimmy his lollipop ahead of time. Seeing you in a calm, quiet mood will also help him.

Inflammation

In the hours and days following the injection, Lucy's arm may be sore and red, especially after certain vaccines. Here, pain medication works wonderfully; repeat as often as necessary. This irritation should resolve within a few days, but it could turn into a painless hard ball the size of a nut that remains under the skin for a couple of months. In rare cases, the redness may persist or worsen, which could indicate infection and require medical attention.

Fever

Fever, despite what you may have heard, is a rare side effect of vaccinations. If it's going to occur, it usually starts the night after the shot or the next day and is evidence of the immune reaction the vaccine has caused. With live attenuated vaccines like the MMR (measles, mumps, and rubella), the fever appears ten days after the shot, along with a mild rash on the torso. Fever from vaccines lasts twenty-four hours or less. Acetaminophen and ibuprofen should be used more for the discomfort than for the fever itself.

Serious Side Effects

As far as serious side effects go, if you were to read the full warning label on a Tylenol bottle, you'd never take one again. The same is true with vaccines. Full disclosure of all possible outcomes includes many horrible scenarios—among them severe allergic reactions and death—but these are tremendously unlikely.

REAL QUESTIONS FROM REAL PARENTS

Is it safe to pump all these drugs into such a small baby at one time?

This is an understandable emotional concern but not a valid scientific one. These vaccines have been thoroughly studied and designed to be safe for very young children. The physical size of your baby is not an issue.

Isn't four shots too many?

Of great parental concern, administering this large a number of shots has been studied extensively and judged to be perfectly fine. Still, in my office, I try to limit it to two shots per session to reduce the cumulative side effects and decrease the emotional strain on the parents.

What about the combination of vaccines?

Vaccine combinations have proved to be safe and efficient. As a matter of fact, research is now focusing on ways to further combine vaccines, thereby decreasing the number of injections.

i

What about thimerosal?

Thimerosal, a mercury derivative, is no longer used in children's vaccines. A few years ago, infinitesimal amounts of it were used in vaccines to prevent contamination in multiple-dose vials. For a while, and in spite of all tangible evidence, some people feared that even these small amounts might contribute to mental illnesses like autism. Since then, thimerosal's use in vaccines has been discontinued, not because of any findings of toxicity but because vaccines are now stored in individual doses, and contamination is no longer an issue.

My child has a bad cold. Can he still get his vaccines while he has it?

Colds do not interfere with the effectiveness of vaccines, and vaccines do not make colds worse. If the cold is producing discomfort, a shot may make it a little worse, but pain medication will take care of it.

Are there other types of more natural immunizations?

"Natural" immunizations simply don't exist.

I breast-feed my baby and she hasn't had much contact with the outside world. Why does she need these immunizations?

Breast feeding is a good way to build up some immunities, but it is in no way an effective alternative to immunization. Unless you keep Lucy in a glass bubble, you can't avoid contact with the outside world.

The Controversy over Vaccines

In the media and on the Internet you'll find hundreds of experts that exaggerate or invent side effects, arguing that immunization is part of a worldwide pharmaceutical conspiracy. Very few of these claims have a scientific foundation, but the literature has certainly made people wary of injecting anything they don't fully trust into their new baby. My simplistic theory is that any antivaccination theory, no matter how irrational, appeals to the vaccine-hating child in all of us, because as kids we all tried to hide under the table, but we ended up getting our shots anyway.

Having said that, if you choose to delay immunization or skip vaccines altogether, you aren't putting your baby at a huge risk, simply because most of these diseases have been more or less eradicated, and most other people do vaccinate their children. But more or less eradicated doesn't mean entirely eradicated. There are still slight medical dangers. In addition, there are social and community pressures, since most schools require immunization. And the idea of delaying the vaccinations until the child is older and thus more docile is a flawed idea; giving shots to older children is, if anything, more difficult.

In the end, collective immunization is the only way to defeat a disease, and I recommend the full battery of standard vaccines. However, I find that many parents, despite all my explanations, are still apprehensive about immunizations and want to delay or avoid them. My approach is to discuss the issue and to respect their decision even if I don't share their point of view. I also attempt to give them a realistic idea of the risks involved in delaying vaccinations. You will find this below, with a brief discussion of each specific vaccine as well as how necessary they are for school entrance requirements.

Immunizations (Disease by Disease):

As noted, most states require many vaccinations for school admission, and many more vaccinations are recommended. At present, four are required in all fifty states: the DTP (diphtheria-tetanus-pertussis) vaccine, the MMR (measles-mumps-rubella) vaccine, the polio vaccine, and the Hib (Haemophilus influenza b) vaccine. Here's an overview of these and others.

Mandatory

Diphtheria-Tetanus-Pertussis

The DTP vaccine is a cocktail that handles three different diseases. The diphtheria virus, whose symptoms include a bad sore throat and heart problems, has almost disappeared. Tetanus is better known as lockjaw; unlike most other diseases, it's not communicated by one person to another but lies dormant in the soil or on rusty nails. Pertussis, or whooping cough, causes a terrible cough and sometimes a pneumonia that is dangerous for babies and young children. It has almost disappeared, but we still see a few outbreaks in small pockets of the United States.

Years ago, this combination vaccine was less efficient and had significant side effects. These days it's much improved and better tolerated. In fact, in the future, even more diseases will be folded into this vaccine, such as the polio and hepatitis B vaccines (this is already done in Europe).

If you do: The DTP vaccine requires five doses, starting in infants and continuing in toddlers, followed by boosters throughout life every ten years. It is mandatory for school admission. Side effects vary with age. Infants may experience a little discomfort and possibly even fever for the first twenty-four hours. In toddlers, it can produce a local reaction, with arm swelling and redness that can be impressive but that decreases in a few days. In older children it makes the shoulder and arm hurt temporarily and sometimes causes swelling.

If you don't: Diphtheria has been almost completely eradicated. Tetanus is always a risk with a deep soiled cut, but since babies and young infants rarely incur such wounds, the risk is small (and even with a cut, tetanus can be treated by the injection of tetanus immune particles that will limit the development of the illness). Pertussis still carries a significant risk because it flares up in outbreaks around the country every once in a while.

Measles-Mumps-Rubella

This is another combination vaccine that handles three diseases. Measles, a very unpleasant flulike illness with a rash and rare serious complications, has been eradicated almost entirely, thanks to immunization. Mumps and rubella are mild diseases with potentially serious complications: Mumps can cause sterility in boys, and rubella can cause birth defects in the fetuses of infected mothers. These latter consequences constitute the primary reasons to immunize. At this point, the three diseases are almost nonexistent in the United States.

The MMR vaccine is very safe, but of all the immunizations, it gets the worst press. Unlike most of the other vaccines, it is a live attenuated vaccine, which means that the viral component has been modified so that it's nonvirulent. Still, the notion of a live virus makes many people uncomfortable. In addition, a deeply flawed but well-publicized study some years ago proposed a controversial association between the MMR virus and autism. In all likelihood, this is simple coincidence: If a child is autistic, the condition usually becomes evident in the second year, which is also the time when MMR is administered. The media were eager to report this flawed study but not as good about publicizing the numerous serious studies that invalidate the linkage. Finally, the combination of the three vaccines is erroneously perceived as toxic by parents who worry about loading up their kids with drugs and biological agents. Regrettably, people have been turning away from MMR in fear, thus giving these diseases a chance to return.

If you do: MMR has two doses, one at the toddler stage and one before kindergarten. You probably won't see any side effects. If you do, they may consist of a rash on the body and a moderate fever that, unlike the side effects of other vaccines, occurs about ten days after the administration and lasts for one or two days. These are due to a miniature case of measles induced by the attenuated virus.

If you don't: Measles, mumps, and rubella are currently only a remote possibility, though that may well change if the current trend against the MMR immunization persists. Giving the vaccines separately is no longer an option in the United States, as the manufacturer has discontinued all single-entity vaccines, owing to decreased demand.

Polio

Polio represents one of immunization's most impressive successes. Once a fairly common disease that terrified generations of parents, it has almost been eradicated worldwide. When the polio vaccine was introduced by Jonas Salk a half-century ago, it was an attenuated form of the polio virus given orally on a piece of sugar. The attenuated virus could vaccinate the entire family; those who came into contact with the immunized child were, in effect, catching the vaccine rather than the virus. But a decade or so ago, doctors became worried about the extremely rare risk that people might contract the disease from the attenuated virus. By the end of the nineties, the immunization process was revised, and a dead-virus vaccine has been used ever since. If the worldwide effort to eradicate the disease continues as successfully, the polio vaccination will be discontinued altogether as the disease vanishes into extinction.

If you do: The polio vaccine is given by injection to infants and toddlers. It produces no major side effects and is one of the less painful shots.

If you don't: The disease has been eradicated in the United States, but travel to developing nations carries a slight risk, and cases have been reported as close as the Caribbean.

Haemophilus influenza b

This dreadful bacteria once caused brain infections in children as well as a severe swollen throat infection that could result in suffocation. It has been almost eradicated through vaccine. Hib is one of the least controversial immunizations: It is not live, and it has very few side effects. It can be given in combination with the hepatitis B vaccine, and it's mandatory for school admission.

If you do: The vaccine is injected into the muscle of infants and toddlers. Redness at the site is the most frequent side effect.

If you don't: The risk is currently quite low because of the vaccine's great efficacy at keeping these bacteria at bay, but it's still a remote possibility.

Mostly Mandatory

Hepatitis B

Since Lucy is not at risk for IV drug use or promiscuous sexual behavior, there's little chance she'll contract hepatitis B now. Still, there is a good reason to give her this vaccine. Hepatitis B is a terrible condition. It causes jaundice, produces debilitating liver illness, and it can kill you quickly or slowly. The vaccine is efficient and creates lifelong immunity, so if we give it to every newborn for the next twenty years, we can eliminate the disease entirely (and with it, any need for the immunization). Another reason to give it early on is that hepatitis B requires three boosters a few months apart for the immunity to develop. When do people see doctors that frequently? When they're babies, of course. Sometimes the vaccine is even given just after birth in the hospital, though I'm not sure why. Early vaccination is not detrimental, but it creates a false sense of urgency and anxiety in a new parent.

If you do: This immunization comprises three doses, all administered within the first year. It is mandatory for school admission in most states, and older children who were not required to get it as babies must get it before starting classes.

If you don't: If you decide to put off the hepatitis B vaccine, you're not creating any substantial risk for hepatitis B until Jimmy is much older. But it's not necessarily any easier to give an immunization then; dragging a wily teenager to the doctor three times—for shots, no less—may prove a daunting task.

Chicken Pox (Varicella) [**See also:** Chicken Pox]

Since this relatively new vaccine was introduced, we've seen a dramatic decrease in the number of cases. Yet some parents still don't see the wisdom of vaccinating for a disease that is relatively harmless in most children. Varicella is not as harmless as it seems. Those little poxes are uncomfortable, especially on the eyeball and on or inside the genitals. The poxes can also get infected, and in highly rare cases can lead to the flesh-eating bacteria so popular in tabloid newspapers. And then there are the extreme cases, which can lead to pneumonia, neurological complications, and even death. Vaccinating against chicken pox early in life decreases the chances that Lucy will contract this disease, which is unpleasant at a young age, more severe in older kids, and potentially debilitating for adults.

The chicken pox vaccine is a live attenuated virus that is safe and efficient, though not as efficient as other vaccines; a vaccinated person can still get chicken pox, but if he or she does, it's almost always a mild case. The immunity decreases over time (unlike the actual postdisease immunity, which is permanent), so future boosters may be added to the vaccine regimen. The chicken pox immunization is becoming increasingly mandatory for school admission.

If you do: So far, the vaccine is given once in toddlers. Side effects, which are rare and minimal, may include a few poxes on the body.

If you don't: Chicken pox remains, for infants and toddlers at least, a mild illness in general. But as the vaccine becomes more common, the virus becomes rarer and therefore harder to come in contact with even if you want to. If Lucy doesn't catch it as a young tot, she'll eventually have to be vaccinated later, because the severity of the actual illness increases with age.

Recommended

Pneumococcal Vaccine

This is the most recent addition to the immunization schedule. Known as the "ear-infection vaccine," it technically prevents a rare form of meningitis that is particular to young children, and to a lesser degree it also decreases the occurrence of some pneumonias and ear infections. There has been no controversy surrounding this vaccine so far; it is very safe and well tolerated. It is not yet mandatory for school admission.

If you do: It is given in several doses before the second birthday. The most common side effect is temporary redness at the site.

If you don't: The disease is rare and even rarer now that we give the vaccine, but it's not yet fully eradicated.

Others

Hepatitis A

Doctors increasingly recommend this shot, although it's more of a comfort vaccine. Hepatitis A is a very mild disease in children that has flulike symptoms or none at all. In adults it is more tiring, with jaundice and fatigue that can last for weeks. Hepatitis A is most prevalent in countries with poor hygiene and contaminated food. You may consider this vaccine if you travel abroad, more for yourself and your peace of mind than for your child's health [**See:** Travel in Exotic Places].

Flu Vaccine

By far the most problematic of immunizations, the flu vaccine has to be given every year, and even then it doesn't work all that well. The protection rate fluctuates between 30 and 60 percent, depending on the year's virus (the vaccine must be reformulated each year to immunize against the newest strain of the virus). Because of its relatively limited effectiveness, it should be reserved for kids who cannot afford to get the flu, such as asthmatics or children with other chronic conditions. A new nasal-spray vaccine has just been approved; it's too early to say if it's more efficient.

Impetigo

Any time the skin is disrupted, it can become infected. When the infection comes specifically from a staphylococcus germ, the resulting condition is called *impetigo*. It consists of red, crusty lesions that occur in clusters. Itchiness follows, and scratching spreads the impetigo from one place to another.

A classic example of impetigo can occur when Lucy has a cold; if you have her blow her nose too frequently, the abrasion from the rubbing may get infected and cause impetigo. Impetigo has a bad reputation, but it's hardly leprosy. While it's mildly contagious among children, it's no reason to keep a kid out of school.

You can treat impetigo with frequent application of topical over-the-counter antibiotics and by keeping the nails short to limit spreading. If the infection is intense or worsens considerably, you should take your child to the doctor, who will decide if oral antibiotics are necessary.

Iron

See also | **Formula; Screening Tests**

Ever since Popeye started shilling for spinach, iron has been synonymous with health and strength. This has some medical foundation; iron allows the red blood cells to carry oxygen to the body's tissues. A deficiency results in anemia, which is characterized by pallid skin and fatigue.

These days, though, iron is everywhere. Pregnant mothers take supplements. Formulas are reinforced with iron. Babies are fed iron-rich cereals. I think this iron overkill is silly. A balanced diet provides plenty of iron, not only from red meat but also from broccoli, chicken, chocolate, potato skins, beans, peas, and of course spinach. Doctors generally screen babies for iron deficiency around the first birthday.

Still not sure Jimmy's getting enough iron? Here's a simple test. Take a look at his cheeks and fingertips. If they're pink and he has normal energy, his iron levels are almost certainly fine.

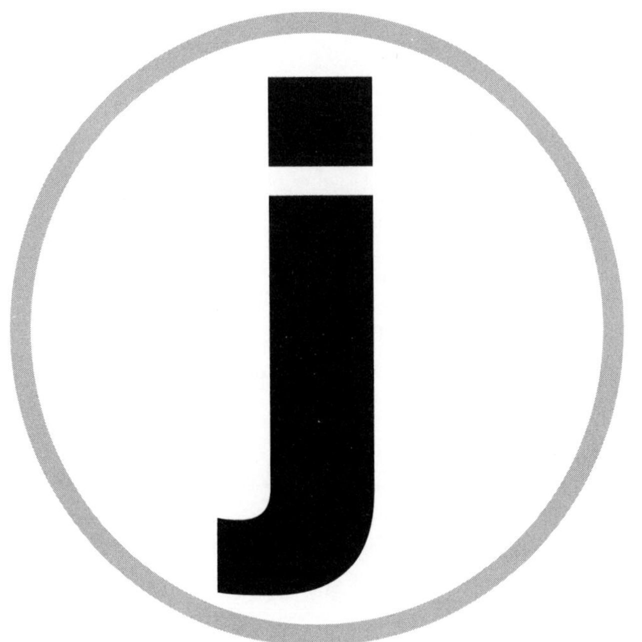
j

Jaundice

Jaundice, the condition of having yellowish skin, is not a rare occurrence in newborns. In fact, it's common, so common that most of the alarm it causes doctors and parents of jaundiced babies is unwarranted.

The scientific mechanism of jaundice is simple. Life in the womb requires about a third more red blood cells than adults have in order to transport oxygen from the mother's blood. With a baby's first breath, those extra red blood cells are destroyed. Their hemoglobin content is shed into the bloodstream and eliminated in the form of a yellow compound called *bilirubin*, which the infant slowly excretes via urine and stools. While this process is happening, however, some of the bilirubin seeps from the bloodstream into the skin tissues, including the whites of the eyes.

In some newborns, the condition is more pronounced. Certain factors may exacerbate the process. For example, when a mother and her baby have different blood types, the postpartum destruction of red blood cells could be greater, resulting in higher amounts of bilirubin and hence a rather dramatically yellow baby. Also, a large hematoma on the scalp caused during delivery can predispose to jaundice, because as it heals, the blood it contains is processed into the bloodstream as bilirubin [**See:** Head Shape].

This temporary accumulation of moderate bilirubin levels is usually harmless. Most of the concern about jaundice results from the fact that extremely high levels of bilirubin can be toxic, notably to the brain. This condition, however, is extremely rare and completely different from most cases of infant jaundice [**See:** Below]. Moderately jaundiced babies can be treated in the first few weeks of life with ultraviolet lamps. Similar to the ones in your local tanning salon, these lamps convert excess bilirubin into a less toxic compound. The treatment has no side effects other than the temporary difficulty of maternal separation.

Practically speaking, I'd say that at least a third of all newborns exhibit some kind of yellow tinge. Mild jaundice tends to appear on the second day, peaks around the fifth day, and then slowly decreases over time. It may still be detectable around week six.

WHEN TO WORRY

- **In its most severe form, jaundice develops intensely very early on,** after just a few hours of life, and peaks around three to five days with a striking yellow skin color.
- **In rare cases, pronounced jaundice may also indicate infection.** Babies thus afflicted are extremely sleepy and feed sluggishly rather than waking up active and ravenous after long periods of sleep, as healthy newborns do.

If this describes your child, have your doctor evaluate the condition; he may recommend treatment with ultraviolet light.

WHEN NOT TO WORRY

- **If Lucy feeds like a typical newborn,** which means erratically: sometimes actively and sometimes sleepily
- **If she's active like a regular newborn,** which means sleeping a lot but waking up alert
- **When her jaundice does not markedly increase in the first five days**

Once you've established that Lucy has only moderate jaundice:

WHAT TO DO

- **Continue feeding her the same way you have been.**
- **Monitor her color,** her feeding ability, and her activity level.

WHAT NOT TO DO

- **Don't wake Lucy to feed at set intervals.** There is only so much you can feed her, and following her normal schedule will be more efficient.
- **There's no need to make her sunbathe on the windowsill.** The amount of UV in sunshine is negligible (unless you live in Australia), and Lucy would much rather be snugly swaddled than left uncovered.
- **Don't stop breast feeding.** Many mothers are erroneously advised to do so to reduce bilirubin levels, and they switch to formula as a result. While it's true that breast milk can marginally increase bilirubin levels, "breast-feeding jaundice" has never been found harmful for a newborn, and it will go away by itself. And what you think will be a short hiatus from breast feeding could well be its end, since returning to the breast after having the bottle will be difficult for babies who must learn to latch on all over again.

▶ **Don't let the inevitable remarks get to you.** People will probably comment that your baby looks a little yellow, with an anxious catch in their voice, most likely because they don't know that moderate levels are harmless.

Not long ago, doctors typically monitored and treated even those newborns with moderate bilirubin levels simply as a precaution against rare toxic effects. While there is no doubt that threatening levels should be monitored and treated aggressively, recent scientific evidence shows that moderate levels are safe. Unfortunately, malpractice anxiety still motivates many doctors to overtreat jaundice even now, a situation that has led to the unnecessary isolation of newborns in incubators for a few days, along with formula feeding by nurses and parents ridden with anxiety.

Joint Pains

See also | **Growing Pains; Limping**

If Jimmy injures one of his joints, address any swelling with your doctor. If there is no swelling or deformity, you can let him rest, monitor his pain, and then reassess the next day. He should avoid using the affected limb if it is painful. If the pain is still intense, an X ray will probably be necessary. If Jimmy has not injured himself and there is swelling or pain in the joint, he'll also need medical evaluation, especially if he has an associated fever, which could indicate a joint infection.

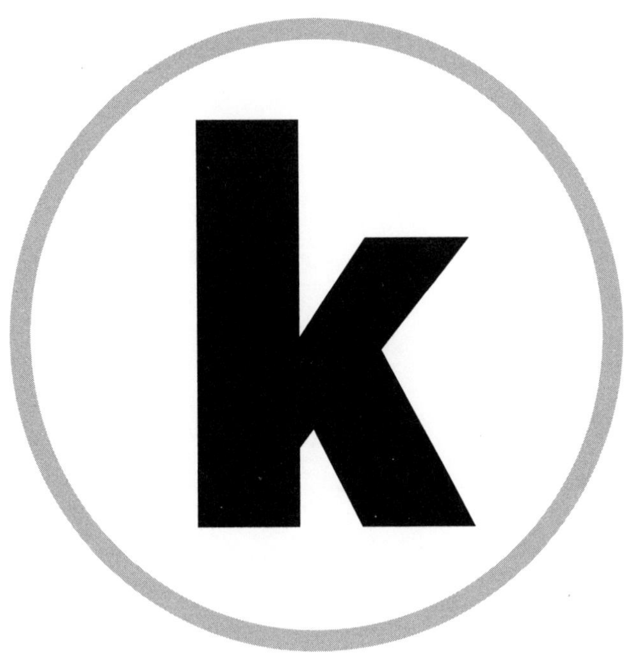

KNOCK KNEES

Knock Knees

Knock knees, a condition characterized by a turning in of the knees, are relatively common in children, especially in toddlers who have very flexible ligaments. This condition usually disappears as a child gets older, although it sometimes persists into childhood and even adulthood as a normal variant. Being overweight can accentuate the condition by increasing the load on the legs and worsening their angulation, so this is another good reason to keep your child within normal weight parameters.

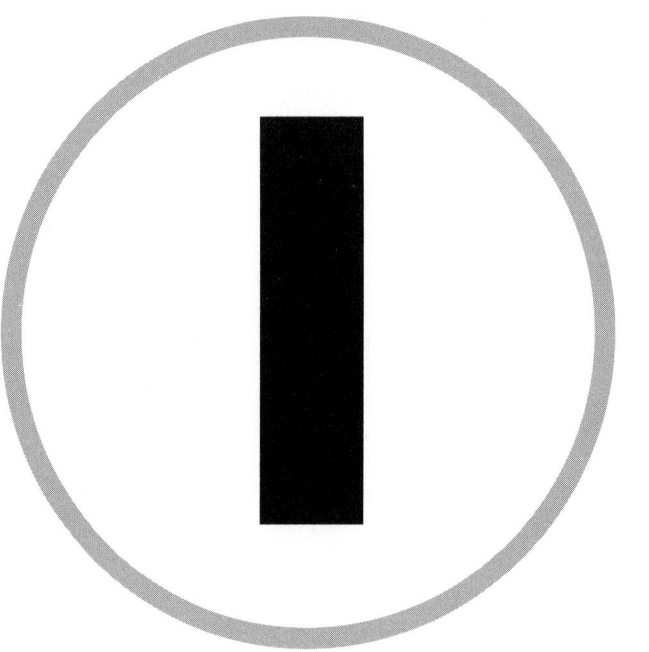

Language Acquisition and Late Talking

Einstein did not speak until he was four. Even if Jimmy doesn't become a prominent nuclear physicist, he may also pick up language slowly. Children acquire speech at different ages, and there is no magic point at which Jimmy will utter his first words or first sentences. Parents often worry needlessly about late talkers.

Generally, children start saying a couple of two-syllable words between the ages of ten and twelve months. These words don't mean much, or they could mean many things. "Dada" represents daddy, but it could also be the cat, the TV, and any number of household items. Even if there are only a few of these quasi-nonsense words, they represent an important milestone. They tell you that Jimmy can hear and reproduce sounds. This is the basis of language acquisition. Though these first words occur at twelve months on average, they can come as late as twenty-four months. After his first breakthrough, Jimmy slowly builds a vocabulary. On average—and this is only a rough guideline—he will have a firm command of five words by fifteen months and a few dozen words by eighteen months.

If Jimmy begins talking late, it is most likely the result of one of three scenarios:

1 | He doesn't hear well. Does he respond to your voice or to music? If you have any doubt, your doctor will perform a hearing test. Hearing deficits are usually caused by an accumulation of ear fluid following recurrent ear infections. If that's the case, ear tubes will probably be indicated [**See:** Ear Infections and Ear Tubes].

2 | He is mentally delayed. Some children suffer from nonspecific mental delay and are therefore compromised in many areas: fine and gross motor coordination, and cognitive and emotional development. This would already have been evident. Other forms of mental retardation specific to language show up as a child's inability to relate even to the people closest to him. At the end of the spectrum is autism; these children are oblivious to the people around them [**See:** Autism].

3 | He's just a late talker. This covers the majority of cases, and as a parent you can usually diagnose this by exclusion: If Jimmy does not have a hearing impairment and isn't mentally delayed, then he is most likely a late talker. Language acquisition depends on a specific part of the brain that develops differently from child to child.

WHEN TO WORRY

- **If you suspect that Jimmy does not hear well**
- **If he can hear but doesn't seem to understand what you say**
- **If he does not establish eye contact** and engages in self-stimulating repetitive activities (like turning in circles)
- **If, instead of seeing slow progress,** you see no progress or if you even see regression in language acquisition
- **If his language consists more of repetitive,** imitative words than spontaneous, even nonsensical words

WHEN NOT TO WORRY

- **If Jimmy is receptive to language** and responds to simple sentences like "Bring me your shoes"
- **If you see slow but steady progress**
- **If he interacts and shows marked interest in others**
- **If he listens to you while you're reading**
- **If he points to things**

WHAT TO DO

Like any other milestone, language acquisition varies greatly. One kid will walk at ten months, while another takes timid steps at eighteen months. But at three years both kids will be walking the same way, and training the late walkers won't get them on their feet any earlier if the brain hasn't yet decided it's ready. Once you've established that Jimmy is simply a late talker, you should speak and read normally to him, as if he is capable of carrying on a conversation. When the part of his brain that commands language does mature, he won't stop talking.

WHAT NOT TO DO

- **Don't coach him to talk.**
- **Don't make him repeat things.**
- **Don't attempt amateur speech therapy.** A late talker will talk when the language section of his brain has matured, not because he's been taught how to.

REAL QUESTIONS FROM REAL PARENTS

Do boys speak later than girls?
On average, girls begin talking about a month earlier than boys. No biggie!

My child learned a few words and then stopped speaking altogether. What happened?
This is very common. Children often develop erratically: two steps forward and one step back. Within a couple of weeks the momentum should pick up, and word acquisition will recommence. If the slowdown persists, however, consider with your doctor the possibilities of language delay or a hearing deficit.

Does being in a multilingual environment delay language acquisition?
Learning two languages simultaneously may delay language acquisition by a few months. However, the advantages of acquiring fluency in another language are enormous, since we pick up languages so much faster as children. If your mother tongue is not English and your child is a late talker, I still recommend that you use your native language. [See: Multilingual Education].

Lead Poisoning

Lead toxicity is primarily of concern in young kids because it can affect brain development. As soon as they start crawling around, infants and toddlers are especially at risk of eating lead in the form of paint chips, which are small and colorful, or of licking windowsills. If you're an aficionado of *This Old House*, lead poisoning should be in the back of your mind, especially if your own home predates the late seventies, the period when lead was banned from paint. Other sources of lead, such as exhaust emissions, water pipes, and contaminated soil are much less responsible for lead toxicity. Lead toxicity usually produces no immediate symptoms, but it can later cause impairments ranging from learning disabilities to behavioral problems and even brain damage, depending on the severity of the ingestion.

In most states, children's lead levels are tested at least once at the year mark and possibly more, depending on the number of old houses in the area. If there's an additional suspicion of lead ingestion, testing is done accordingly.

Lead levels up to ten are normal. A slightly elevated number (approaching twenty) would require you to attempt to identify and remove the lead sources in the environment and retest the blood three months later. For lead levels of forty-five or above, treatment is given as an oral medication or intravenously for severe poisoning.

Legs

As fathers, we have the manly role of toughening up the baby. To this end, you rock Lucy, throw her into the air, and perform other manly tricks, all to her delight. One of your tricks is to make her walk by moving her legs forward for the amusement of the whole family. But amusement quickly turns to aggravation, and when Lucy and her mom are both screaming at you, you may feel a little less manly. . . .

Bouncing Legs

Babies' legs are stronger than you might think. Even in her first week, bearing weight won't harm Lucy's legs, unless she were to do it for hours. As far as bouncing chairs, saucer-shaped baby holders, door-frame swings, and the like—all of these are fun for both you and the baby once Lucy has developed enough upper-body strength to keep her head up (around six months). They're also fine on the legs. Babies love the bouncing, and you can snatch a few moments for yourself until you have to come up with the next activity.

Bowed Legs

I don't know of any babies with straight legs. They all have slight bowing, and some have a little more than others. But their legs always straighten with age, although some adults keep a slight residual bowing, which is of no concern, especially if you're a cowboy. Many years ago, when babies were put in walkers for hours at a time as early as six months, accentuated bowing of the legs did result and sometimes even persisted [**See:** Walkers].

Lice

***T**he school nurse has just called you at work to come and pick Jimmy up at school immediately. With a somber voice, she informs you that he has lice. There's silence on both ends of the line. The implication, you think, is that you're not running a clean household. When you arrive at school, the nurse appears in her crisp white outfit, walks you over to Jimmy, and shows you the little white eggs in his hair, along with the tiny six-legged creatures leaping off his head.*

Not Quite the Eleventh Plague

The particular pest you are dealing with is the head louse, a bloodsucking insect that thrives only on the human scalp and can hop but cannot fly. Here are the essential facts you need to know:

- Lice infestations are a common occurrence among children in *any community setting*, from that small elite nursery school to your overcrowded public school.
- Lice do not show up or spread because of poor hygiene, nor do they prefer one type of hair over another. If your child gets them, you've done nothing wrong! Anyone who has hair can get lice.
- Lice are not noisy guests; the itching is minimal.
- Lice do not live more than forty-eight hours if they can't feed on somebody's head. This means you do *not* have to wash every single fabric item you own, from curtains to doilies to the party clothes at the back of your closet.
- The diagnosis of lice can only be made by finding the six-legged little bugs in the scalp. The eggs they lay (called *nits*) are only suggestive of infection. Tiny, milky white, and shaped like grapes, they nestle at the base of the hair shaft. (The dead ones are loosely attached to the hair, away from the scalp.) At first, they'll be hard to differentiate from dandruff flakes, but after you've extracted a few and examined them, I guarantee that you will become an expert louse detective. The worst news? Virtually every kid will get lice at some point. But you will get rid of them, and here's how.

Search and Destroy

Talk about sticky little creeps. While a single application of antilice shampoo was once all you needed to get rid of these bloodsuckers, in recent years the louse has become increasingly resistant to topical medications.

Currently, in my opinion, the best way to a louse-free head is bug busting the nits by hand—just like our cousins the monkeys do it—in combination with lice shampoo. Removing nits manually, one by one, is a tedious and time-consuming process, but it works.

WHAT TO DO

- **Sit Jimmy down in front of a favorite video.** Wet his head, then part the hair into many small sections.
- **Working section by section,** slide the nits off with your fingers or with a fine comb sold specifically for this purpose. A magnifying glass may help.
- **Dispose of the nits and lice in the sink.**
- **At the end of the first session,** use an over-the-counter antilice lotion such as Nix.
- **Repeat the process a week later.** Note, however, that because these shampoos dry the scalp, they may provoke mild itching, a symptom that could lead you to believe the lice are still thriving. And the flakiness caused by the drying can make surviving nits harder to hunt down.
- **Wash only the clothes and linens** that have been used for the past few days.

Other Treatment Options

- If you and Jimmy don't mind the military look, a crew cut may hasten an end to this plague, if only because much shorter hair makes it easier to spot and remove those elusive nits.
- Some people (including my wife) swear by rubbing petroleum jelly or tea tree oil onto the scalp, covering the head with a plastic bag overnight, then washing the hair the next morning. The operating principle here is that you're smothering the lice in grease. There are no data to support this strategy, and the grease is hard to remove from the hair and scalp.
- Antilice shampoos and lotions other than those sold over the counter are available by prescription from your doctor, but they are not much more effective and present more inconvenience. Malathion, for example, a medication to which lice appear less resistant, is stinky and flammable, must be left on overnight, and can irritate the scalp. I recommend using the prescription lotions only when the lice infection is stubborn and you've exhausted the other treatment methods described above.

Persistent Lice

Be prepared to fight several battles in your war against lice. Jimmy's lice could be members of a resistant faction, or his head could become reinfested, since half the school has lice anyway. When a lice epidemic is declared, it will last a few months, unless the principal declares a state of emergency, closes the school for two weeks, and ensures that every kid's head is inspected and treated.

Also, be aware that what seems like persisting lice may not be. Nits on the head don't necessarily indicate infestation, especially if they're just dead nits that sit away from the hair shaft. Dandruff flakes may also look like nits. Persistent or recurrent infections can only be diagnosed with a live bug sighting. In any case, if Jimmy catches lice again, or has a resistant strain, don't be the elephant scared of the little mouse. You've got to fight. In the name of victory, go back to the beginning of the chapter.

Limping

See also | **Joint Pains**

Obviously, Jimmy may limp as a result of a limb injury. If the limp is severe, especially if there is swelling, you should go to the doctor for X rays. But limping can also occur with no evident injury. One common cause in toddlers is a condition called *toxic synovitis*. In this case, Jimmy would wake up one day and refuse to put weight on his foot despite the fact that there is no obvious swelling on the leg and that he feels no pain if you press anywhere on it. Toxic synovitis may sound frightening, but it's simply a temporary inflammation of the hip joint that frequently follows a cold or another viral illness. There is usually no fever, and it disappears quickly. The next day or so, Jimmy will walk normally again. If the pain persists, or if fever and swelling occur in any leg joint, take him to the doctor.

Lyme Disease

Tick bites, especially from deer ticks, are of special concern in the northeastern United States, because deer ticks are known carriers of Lyme disease. This malady starts with a rash on the skin that appears, on average, ten days after the tick bite. If unnoticed and untreated, the illness can progress into a wide range of other symptoms, such as fever and joint pain.

In endemic regions, a recent increase in awareness of the disease has in some cases spilled over into hysteria, resulting in countless unnecessary prescriptions and blood tests, not to mention anxiety. There are a few salient points to remember about Lyme disease. First, only deer ticks transmit the disease. Second, even if a deer tick is infected with Lyme disease, the probability of getting the illness after a bite is low, unless the tick has remained on the skin for more than a day. Third, the disease is treatable with a simple antibiotic, especially when diagnosed early.

Prevention

If you find a tick on Jimmy's skin, just remove it, either with tweezers or by scraping it off with a blade or a credit card. You don't need a doctor to take it off. No matter how precise you are, it's almost impossible not to leave a little bit of the tick in the skin. These suckers don't let go easily. That's okay, though, because the part of the tick that's left in the skin doesn't increase the chance of transferring Lyme disease; for that, the tick has to be alive and actively sucking blood. Don't dig deeper to remove that last bit; it will eventually disintegrate, just like a splinter, and digging around could cause an infection.

Once you've removed the tick, throw it out; there's no need to analyze it. The lab could tell you whether or not it's a deer tick, but your course will be the same in either case. A simple tick bite warrants neither preventive antibiotic treatment nor blood tests, which are unreliable [See: Below].

After the tick is out, observe the site of the bite for any changes. In the early days you may see an inflammatory reaction that resolves quickly, like any insect bite. If the spot becomes infected, you'll see spreading redness and pain; this local infection can be treated with an over-the-counter antibiotic cream. If the characteristic Lyme disease rash were to develop, it would only appear one to three weeks later. It is circular and red, and the center gradually clears, forming what looks like a bull's-eye with a red and scaly edge. Lyme rashes vary in intensity and appearance, so any redness that appears after a few days in a spot where you removed a tick is suspect and requires medical attention.

With treatment, Lyme disease is easily cured, and the rash wanes within a week. Most cases that progress to a more severe or chronic infection do so because people either didn't notice the rash or dismissed it. So the keys to prevention in heavily infested areas are careful daily inspections, along with insect repellents and full clothing coverage.

Blood tests for Lyme are notoriously inaccurate and may give you a sense of false security or a false alarm. They should be used in the case of a diagnostic challenge. Yearly blood tests to detect Lyme infection despite the absence of any symptoms are especially unhelpful. In addition, a recently introduced Lyme vaccine was discontinued almost immediately due to lack of efficacy.

MASSAGE
MASTURBATION
MEDICINE ALLERGIES
MEDICINE CABINETS
MERCURY
MILK, COW'S
MOLD
MOLES
MONONUCLEOSIS
MULTILINGUAL ENVIRONMENT
MUSCLE TONE

Massage

See also | **Colic**

The authors of several modern baby books recommend many different methods for infant massage, some of which are illustrated with elaborate diagrams and employ magical oils and unguents. I suggest you keep it simple. Everybody enjoys a little rubdown, but Lucy may wonder what's going on when you start chanting mantras amid exotic scents. Also, as idyllic as your massage is, it may lead to sensory overload and more fussiness in an already overstimulated newborn with a cranky disposition.

Short of this scenario, newborn massage, i.e., touching and caressing Lucy gently, is sweet. You may even be doing it now without realizing. As for the illustrations, if you're like me and don't get them, make up your own technique.

Masturbation

See also | **Penis; Vagina**

In public or in front of grandma, Jimmy's masturbation is embarrassing for everybody but Jimmy, who finds it pleasurable. Childhood genital exploration is a perfectly normal developmental stage that you should not discourage as long as it is done where appropriate. It begins as early as the end of the second year. But before Jimmy turns three or four and gets a feel for social pressures, he won't understand why he can't do it whenever he wants. If it happens in public, just distract him with another activity without offering an extensive lecture. When he's older he'll naturally seek privacy for this activity. Masturbation can cause irritation in both girls and boys. For Jimmy, let him explore the fine line that lies between pain and pleasure as he discovers that too much yanking will hurt him. As for your little girl, keep her nails short, and apply a little Vaseline on the outside of the vagina if it becomes irritated.

Medicine Allergies

Just like foods, medications can induce allergies, with antibiotics being among the main culprits. And just like foods, most reactions are mild, especially the first time a medication is administered. A typical allergic reaction will show up as welts and itching a few days into the treatment. When the medication is discontinued or replaced with a substitute, the eruption fades within a couple of days. The itching can be controlled with antihistamines. Such an outbreak doesn't necessarily mean a severe allergy. It could simply be a sensitivity and may not even recur if the medicine is readministered again later. In practice, however, we would rarely attempt another dose, since alternatives to most medications exist.

An intense reaction with breathing difficulty indicates a severe medicine allergy that requires careful subsequent avoidance of the problem drug. Fortunately, such severe reactions are quite rare. If one of the parents is allergic to a specific drug, the child's risk is only slightly higher. If the drug is needed, your doctor will still prescribe it but will have you monitor Jimmy closely for early signs of sensitivity.

Medicine Cabinets

Besides pain medication, I can't think of anything you should stockpile at home. You can get most products for your kids fresh from the drugstore when you need them. Even keeping Ipecac, a medication that induces vomiting in case of poisoning, is controversial [See: Poison]. And by limiting the potential dangers in your medicine cabinet, you'll be reducing the chances of poisoning.

Mercury

See also | **Immunization**

Mercury is a chemical element normally found in nature. High concentrations can be toxic for the brain, especially for children, because their nervous systems are still developing.

Most mercury has been eliminated from the daily life of children. Broken thermometers used to be a common source of poisoning, but they no longer contain mercury. These days, our greatest exposure to mercury is fish, which accumulate the chemical as a result of environmental pollution and industrial waste. Although the exact levels of mercury toxicity are not well known, the Food and Drug Administration advises pregnant women against eating large quantities of big fish such as tuna and swordfish, which are more prone to contain mercury.

Many of the parents I see express concern about mercury content in the vaccines we use. Their fears are based on the fact that thimerosal, a mercury derivative, was used many years ago to prevent contamination in vaccines. It was removed from most vaccines four or five years ago, not because it was detrimental but because it is no longer needed.

Milk, Cow's

Why should a toddler drink cow's milk? The answer is simple: Why not? It tastes good, and it provides calories, fat, protein, vitamins, and calcium. And since children are accustomed to either breast milk or formula, they tend to remain fond of milk into late childhood and even adulthood.

But milk is not a necessity. Contrary to what pediatricians advised years ago, there is no minimum amount of milk that a toddler must drink. A balanced diet, especially if it includes other dairy products, contains all the nutrients present in milk. So if Jimmy isn't crazy about it, don't force it on him. As an alternative, you can also try goat's milk or fortified soy milk or rice milk, all of which have good nutritional value.

That takes care of the too-little-milk problem. But how much is too much? Some kids chug milk like it's going out of style. The rule of thumb here is simple: If Jimmy still has an appetite for solid food, his high milk intake isn't a problem. But when picky eaters fill up on milk as a substitute for solids, you need to reduce their milk intake to help them develop appetites.

Milk Myths

- "Milk increases mucus production": This ingrained popular myth does not make much sense on a physiological basis, since milk—like all nutrients—is digested and broken down by the intestine into the bloodstream, not into the nose. This misconception may be based on the fact that milk and mucus have roughly the same texture. The only reason to avoid milk during viral illnesses is that it can be a little heavy on the tummy and may induce vomiting, especially in young children.
- "Milk predisposes children to infection." This one may be left over from the prepasteurization era. These days, there's no correlation between milk intake and infections.
- "If a mother drinks milk while nursing, her baby will be cranky." Some mothers swear this is true, but it has no scientific basis. Breast milk is manufactured in the mammary glands from the mother's blood. By the time it reaches the baby, the milk the mother drank has been processed, so even if Lucy happens to be milk-intolerant she won't be affected.

Milk Intolerance

Milk intolerance is the inability to digest lactose, a sugar found in cow's milk [**See:** Food Reactions]. The problem, which is relatively common, is caused by a deficiency of lactase, the enzyme that digests lactose. In most people, the intolerance is partial: The body can digest small amounts of milk, but larger amounts produce symptoms such as gas, diarrhea, and cramping. Lactose intolerance is more common in African Americans and Asians. Symptoms generally start in toddlerhood and last through life, but the lactose intolerant usually learn to avoid large amounts of milk and stay symptom free. No treatment currently exists, besides taking lactase supplements or drinking lactase-enhanced milk products.

Contrary to what you may hear, lactose intolerance is extremely rare in infants. To further complicate matters, the diagnosis can be confusing in formula-fed infants. If Lucy is producing diarrhea or streaks of blood in the stools and they disappear after you switch her to a milk-free formula, milk intolerance still might not be the culprit; the problem could be caused by the temporary immaturity of her intestines. Intolerance is even more unlikely if Lucy cries and has gas. Babies cry. Babies have gas with or without lactose [See: Gas].

Breastfed babies are even less likely to show signs of milk intolerance. Breast milk does not contain lactose, and its nutrients remain the same, whether the mother drinks milk or not.

REAL QUESTIONS FROM REAL PARENTS

Every time my child drinks milk, she gets diarrhea. What should I do?
As I said above, it may be due to intolerance. Or not. Toddlers often go through periods of runny stools, either because of mild viral infections or sometimes for no discernible reason at all. Stop the milk, see if the stools harden, then reintroduce the milk and see if they loosen up again. If you find a correlation, you'll have to decrease or stop milk altogether.

When should we introduce cow's milk?
Although most books recommend twelve months, I find that when kids are on formula, ten months is perfectly fine. At this age their little stomachs are able to handle cow's milk, and it's cheaper than formula. For breast-feeding babies, there's no reason to switch until you decide to wean or to cut back on nursing.

How should we switch to milk?
Just pick a day and give the kid milk. You could mix it with formula for a day or two, but since milk tastes better, you generally won't need to.

What if my baby is not interested?
You can offer a substitute form of milk (soy, rice, goat) if you want, or you can let the whole matter drop. As I said, milk is not mandatory.

Fat-free, low-fat, or whole milk?
According to common wisdom, you should switch kids to low-fat milk at two years of age. This rule was much more relevant in the old days, when kids drank huge amounts of milk. Since they ingest more reasonable quantities these days, whole milk's high fat content is less of an issue; in fact, it's actually a good source of calories for children (though not for adults). If you're concerned about fat, don't lose sight of the real enemies: pizza, hot dogs, chips, and fast food.

Milk has received some bad publicity recently. For a couple of generations, the eminent Dr. Spock promoted the calcium benefits of milk in creating strong bones, but in his most recent edition he pooh-poohed moo juice as unhealthy, impure, and the cause of many diseases. The dairy industry is scrambling to reestablish milk as a vital part of any diet, not just for kids but for adults too. The reality, of course, lies between the two positions. Milk is neither a lifesaver nor a devil in disguise, but a reasonable source of nutrition that may not be right for everybody.

Mold

Increasingly, indoor molds are being recognized as a triggering factor of allergic reactions. Mold grows in damp environments: near water leaks in basements, in humid corners of old houses, in bathrooms that never quite dry out. Humidifiers can also disperse mold if not cleaned properly. If Jimmy suffers from unexplained nasal allergies and has constantly tearing eyes, nasal secretions, and an itchy nose, he could be reacting to mold in your house. The same goes for unexplained recurring episodes of hives and asthma.

That said, don't jump to conclusions too quickly. These respiratory symptoms could simply be due to a recurring cold [**See:** Colds]. Unfortunately, proving the allergic connection will be difficult, since skin tests for mold aren't very reliable. If you suspect mold allergy, look for humid, moldy spots in your house and clean them up as best as you can.

Moles

Take a moment to inspect yourself. You probably have hundreds of small moles all over you that you've acquired throughout your lifetime. You'll start noticing them on your child's skin as early as age two. Their numbers increase with sun exposure, and regular sunscreen protection can apparently limit their proliferation. Small moles rarely undergo potentially cancerous transformations, and if they do, it usually happens later in life. On the other hand, very large moles, especially those with hair on them, bear a more significant risk of cancerous transformation and should be evaluated regularly by a dermatologist.

Mononucleosis

See also | **Strep Throat**

"Mono" (short for mononucleosis) is a viral illness that resembles strep throat and affects children after two years of age, although symptoms are worse in older kids. It is contagious through saliva, hence its nickname, "the kissing disease." Some children, especially young ones, get very mild cases or have no symptoms at all, while in others it is quite intense and lasts for weeks. Most adults are immunized by a bout in childhood. Mono's incubation period can last for several weeks, and then symptoms start with a painful sore throat, swollen tonsils, and a fever that can be in the 104°F range. A generalized rash on the whole body may appear for a few days. Suspicion of mono arises when symptoms suggest a strep throat infection, but the strep test your doctor performs comes back negative. Blood tests are somewhat unreliable and only of value if the diagnosis is unclear.

There is no treatment for mono except rest as needed. Fatigue can persist for weeks, especially in teenagers. The spleen may become enlarged and even rupture if subjected to a blow. For this reason, participation in violent sports should be avoided for up to a month after the illness has been diagnosed.

Multilingual Environment

See also | **Language Acquisition and Late Talking**

As an expatriate Frenchman who learned English as an adult, I am a big believer in giving kids the advantage of bilingualism. If you're raising Lucy to speak two languages, start speaking your maternal tongue to her as early as the newborn stage. This will help you communicate with her in the most spontaneous and natural way. Later, you'll be happy she can chat with grandma and grandpa in their own language. Don't worry about the English; she'll pick it up when she starts socializing.

Switching from one language to another may be a little confusing for Lucy, but most bilingual kids acquire both tongues simultaneously at the same point that their monolingual peers are mastering just one. For late talkers, this exercise may delay language acquisition a little, but stick with it! The benefit of having two languages outweighs the disadvantage of lagging a few weeks before talking. In either case, be careful not to mix languages within one sentence or conversation, because this may confuse someone who's just starting to understand them both.

I wish I had practiced what I preach with my own kids. I only spoke French with the first one, and she's managed to keep some of it. By the time the two youngest showed up, I'd become lazy. Now I pay Veronique (their charming French teacher) thirty dollars an hour each week to instill in them the rudiments of Voltaire's tongue.

Muscle Tone

Some dancers are very toned; they perform the high jumps and leaps. Others work closer to the ground and provide the beautiful pauses in a routine. Both are needed for a show.

Babies are the same: Some have extremely tight, conditioned muscles, while others are, simply put, mushier. The toned ones tend to be smaller and leaner, while those with lower muscle tone are generally plumper. This is difference can generate unnecessary concern: Softer kids hold their heads upright a little later than others, they sit up a little later, they walk later, and so on. Because of these apparent delays, doctors subject them to unnecessary tests and interventions, such as physical therapy and special exercise. In most cases, this is unnecessary; babies with normal low muscle tone will develop at their own pace. This is different from "congenital hypotoniae," a serious condition that is marked by extremely low muscle tone and severely delayed milestones, and requires extensive physical therapy.

NAILS

NAPPING

NASAL ASPIRATOR

NECK LUMPS

NECK PAIN

NECK RASH

NECK TILTING

NIGHTMARES AND NIGHT TERRORS

NIPPLE CONFUSION

NOISE TOLERANCE

NOSEBLEEDS

NOSE BLOWING

NOSES, BROKEN

NURSEMAID'S ELBOW

Nails

Nail Clipping

Lucy's long fingernails can cause small scratches on the face, both yours and her own. To prevent scratches, you can trim them with baby nail clippers if you have good eyesight and motor skills. The difficulty lies in gauging exactly where the tiny nail ends and the finger begins, which makes this simple task a risky business. If you do clip the finger accidentally, it will bleed profusely because of the abundant blood vessels. Other than clipping, you can file the nails down if you have patience or even bite them if your teeth are sharp enough. I don't recommend putting Lucy's hands in mittens, which will deprive her of her sense of touch and interfere with the important activity of sucking on her hands.

Nail Shape

Babies and toddlers always have oddly shaped nails. They can be flat or even slanted upward, especially on the big toe. As kids grow up, their nails take on normal shapes.

Ingrown Nails

Ingrown nails are common on the hands and feet of babies, but the nails rarely dig deep enough into the skin to cause significant infection, as they do in adults. A minor infection, such as a small area of redness and yellow pus on the side of a nail, will usually resolve on its own. You can help it along by soaking in warm water and by applying antibiotic cream and then wrapping it in an adhesive bandage a few times daily. If it worsens, bring it to your pediatrician's attention.

As children grow older and their nails harden, ingrown nails can cause infection more swiftly. You'll see red swelling with some pus at the edge. Treat the condition with warm soaks and antibiotic creams. If the infection worsens, a draining incision along with an oral antibiotic may be necessary; consult your doctor.

White Spots

Contrary to popular belief, white spots on fingernails do not indicate a calcium deficiency. They represent normal variations in pigmentation.

Nail Biting

Children who are sensitive to tense situations are also prone to biting their nails. This is not a sign of emotional imbalance. Often, one of the child's parents had (or still has) the habit. Just like thumb sucking or any other tic, nail biting should be ignored. Reminding Jimmy to stop chewing on his nails, pulling his hands away from his mouth, or getting mad only reminds him that he is doing it and, for that matter, getting attention from it. Nail biting generally decreases or disappears on its own if you manage not to make it a big deal, although the age at which that happens varies greatly.

Napping

See also | **Sleep**

During nap time, it's no longer clear who is putting whom to sleep. Is it the back rub you gave Lucy for a half hour that helped her fall asleep, or was it Lucy's cooing that soothed you? Before her eighth month, naps were like clockwork: ten in the morning and two in the afternoon, an hour each, no interruption. Lucy was always in good enough spirits for her music class at 11:30; she could always clap her hands on the beat, more or less, with a smile and energy. Now, every day is different, and nothing can be planned. God forbid if Lucy misses her morning snooze; she might start throwing things and screaming in the middle of music class. And then, two minutes after you leave, she's passed out in the stroller. What happened to your calm, napping baby?

Infants

Many parents' lives revolve around their baby's nap schedule. Up to six months, Lucy will sleep like a kitten without any pattern. After that age, you'll see some regularity in her schedule. But the amount of napping still varies greatly. Some babies sleep three to four hours at a stretch or take two naps daily, while others won't sleep at all during the day. My advice is that you go about your business and not enforce naps too strictly. If she's tired, Lucy will find a way to sleep, whether at home in her crib or outside in a stroller, a car seat, or in your arms.

If you find yourself performing a half-hour soothing routine and tiptoeing out of the room before Lucy's naps, you may want to change your strategy, more for your benefit than for hers. Of course this is not a problem if you enjoy the closeness of the moment and have the time to spare. But keep in mind that rubbing her back or forehead is just a soothing habit. Nappers who don't want to nap on their own usually don't want to go to sleep on their own at night either and also wake up throughout the night. Deal with nap issues just as you deal with nighttime sleep issues [See: Sleep].

In Toddlers

In order to better understand napping, you have to visualize the different states of wakefulness in an older infant. Jimmy begins his day happy and giggly, and then gradually becomes more active. At the peak of his activity, one of two things occurs: Either he cools down and takes a snooze on his own, or he continues to push the envelope of activity beyond the pale, a sign that he needs rebooting. When he reaches that point, lay him down in his crib. If he sleeps willingly or cries himself to sleep after a few minutes, that's good. When he wakes up, you'll find a rejuvenated Jimmy. If he cries for just ten to fifteen minutes but doesn't sleep, that's good too. Take him out of the crib. Crying relieves just as much tension as sleeping does. If he has calmed down, resume your day: singing, playing, learning to walk, and so forth. If he's still all over the place, put him back in the crib for another ten minutes. Repeat until he is calmer or asleep.

That said, all children have different sleep requirements. As early as eight months, some kids are happy to bounce around all day without any nap. If yours is one of them, you may be the one who needs the nap.

Nasal Aspirator

See also | **Colds**

As a child, I often stared at the bulb syringe lying on the night table next to my crib. Ironically, one reason for my fascination was that it resembled my pacifier, which I really enjoyed. But I feared the moment when the syringe would actually be put to use. My parents felt they had to suck up some of my nasal secretions periodically, which they would discard with pride and relief while I was catching my breath. Boy, did I hate that thing in my nose. The worst part was when they'd pour saltwater in my nostrils, trying to loosen the

mucus in preparation for the aspirator. To this very day, I can still remember the taste. As I got older, I developed a technique of sustained resistance until my parents finally gave up the fight.

Who invented these diabolical bulb syringes? Nasal secretions occur naturally and increase in response to viral irritation. Most of the mucus is secreted at the back of the nose and ingested into the stomach, unless it's brought up and spat out. What you see leaking from the nose is only the tip of the iceberg.

Nasal aspirators are worthless even when Lucy has a full-blown cold. First of all, kids hate them. Second, using one is like emptying a swimming pool with a tablespoon: You can go and suck out a little mucus, but ten minutes later you'll just have to do it all over again. Worse, the aspirator will occasionally injure the nasal membranes.

Nasal saline drops are equally dubious. They push secretions down the airway, creating lots of gurgling. Of course you want to help, but this situation happens to be one in which the best help is to refrain from doing anything. A baby can be both snotty and beautiful.

Neck Lumps

If you rub Lucy's neck, you'll feel some pea-sized lumps within the muscle. These so-called *lymph glands* or *lymph nodes* are a normal part of our immune system, designed to kill germs and then process them. Whenever there's a germ attack in the area, the lymph glands close to the site swell up and become much more noticeable for a few months. As long as these lumps are small and painless and move under your finger, you can ignore them, although they will be there for a few months. In rare cases, these lymph nodes can become red, enlarged, and tender when infected by the very germs they're supposed to destroy. Your doctor will treat the condition with an oral antibiotic.

Neck Pain

See also | **Headaches**

The same things that give you a stiff neck—cold or sudden movement—can trigger one in your child. Jimmy's stiff neck hurts just as much as yours does, and it makes him hold his neck at an angle just like you do. Pain medication, repeated as needed, will help considerably, but kids usually don't go for heating pads.

Neck pain should last no more than a couple of days. If it persists or if it's accompanied by significant fever over 102°F, it raises the suspicion of meningitis, a rare but serious infection of the brain. If your child is suffering from lingering neck pain and fever, call your doctor.

Neck Rash

See also | **Skin Condition in Infants**

Because newborns have no neck to speak of, the area between the torso and the face can become very sweaty and aggravated. This moist irritation of the skin can also affect other creases or folds, such as the armpits or the area behind the ears. This type of rash is not painful. Some people advise applying cornstarch to dry the affected areas, but I don't; it's not particularly effective, and it makes the skin look caky. In more impressive forms (where you see extensive redness and moisture), this damp area can be colonized by a fungus, which loves humid places. In that case, apply an antifungal cream such as Lotrimin twice daily until the rash clears. But the definitive treatment is for Lucy to grow a neck. That'll take a few months.

Neck Tilting

Torticolis, or tilting of the neck, describes a situation in which a baby's head leans more to one side than the other. It's caused either by a heavy head that naturally falls toward a preferred side or by slightly tense muscles on one side of the neck. This tilted-neck condition is often associated with flattening of the head because it will make the baby tend to rest on the same side of the skull [**See:** Head Shape]. Torticolis will improve with a daily gentle neck massage to loosen up the muscles; in more pronounced cases a physical therapist may have to monitor its progress. Generally, after six to eight months, the baby has strong head support, and the neck straightens out.

Nightmares and Night Terrors

See also | **Fears; Sleep**

When Jimmy wakes up screaming from a sound sleep and tells you what just happened in his dream, it's a nightmare. When Lucy suddenly stands up in her crib screaming at the top of her lungs with her eyes wide open, but is still asleep and oblivious to your presence, it's a night terror.

In the first case, you can reassure Jimmy that Snow White wasn't in any danger, but in the second, the Evil Queen keeps coming after the future princess, even though you're right there in the bedroom trying to comfort her. Both nightmares and night terrors are perfectly normal between the ages of three to six. These nocturnal fantasies can be exacerbated by anything that stimulates a child's imagination; that video that seemed so cute to you may have taken root in Jimmy's mind and grown into a truly frightening scenario.

The first few times Jimmy has a nightmare, it will terrify you as much as it does him. Comfort him, but put him back to bed quickly. Avoid discussing the dream too much at the moment and even in the morning; focusing on it will only validate his fears and make the dream recur. If he insists on talking about it, explain to Jimmy in simple words that it was just a dream, which has nothing to do with reality.

When Lucy has night terrors, hold her if she lets you, but don't wake her up. You'll only create more drama. When her dream is over she'll lie down suddenly and enter her next sleep cycle, happy as a clam.

Be aware that a child who was sleeping without any issues can become a problematic sleeper if you make too big a fuss over nightmares. If you turn on the light, bring milk and cookies, and play soothing music, you'll see nightmares occurring every night. And if you systematically bring Jimmy to your bed, you'll be surprised at how quickly he gets used to the new routine.

Nipple Confusion

The most confusing thing about nipple confusion is the name. After birth, give Lucy a bottle five times in a row, and she'll only want to suck on a bottle. She won't be confused at all; the rubber nipple is much easier than the human one. That's why it's preferable to stick to your own nipple while nursing. If, for any number of reasons, you have to give her a bottle, you may lose a small battle, but you won't necessarily have lost the war. You can reintroduce breast feeding, though it may be a bit of a struggle. The only way to do so is to nurse naturally instead of using a confusing supplemental nursing system that will only teach her how to nurse from a tube. Please refer to the Breast-Feeding Problems chapter if you experience latching difficulties. Conversely, once Lucy is accustomed to your breast, she'll be confused if you give her a bottle [**See:** Bottle Refusal].

Noise Tolerance

During Lucy's first few months, you may be apprehensive about bringing her into noisy public places for fear of damaging her hearing. Rest assured, what is bearable for you is even more so for her. Lucy doesn't hear as well as you do, and young babies have an interesting feature called *suppression*: a shutoff mechanism that makes the baby completely oblivious to excessive stimulation. That's why you often see babies sleeping peacefully in a room full of loud people.

Nosebleeds

Nosebleeds can be alarming; they look like a torrent of blood and seem like they'll never stop. In reality, they're generally a harmless side effect of nosepicking. Some children are more prone to nosebleeds because their nasal blood vessels are slightly brittle. Warm weather and dry air are also contributing factors. After Jimmy has one nosebleed, you'll probably see a few more. The blood dries into a crust, which stanches the bleeding, but the crust is brittle, itchy, and bothersome, so kids pick at it, as they would a scab. Result? More bleeding.

To stop a nosebleed, pinch Jimmy's nostrils at the base for at least five minutes and tilt the head slightly forward. Rest assured, even if the bleeding starts when Jimmy is asleep at night and you don't perform this maneuver, it will still stop on its own. Moisturizing the nostrils with petroleum jelly so they become less itchy can decrease the frequency of these episodes. If nosebleeds occur very frequently and are profuse, especially before a child is coordinated enough to pick his nose, you may want to bring it to the attention of your doctor.

Nose Blowing

I once heard another doctor tell a parent that his child could get sinusitis if he didn't learn how to blow his nose! I don't know where he got that idea. While mastering the hanky helps an older kid keep his nose clean for aesthetic purposes and comfort, it does little for the littlest ones, and it may irritate the tender skin under the nose. If you really can't stand looking at mucus, gently wipe it off until Jimmy can do so on his own.

Noses, Broken

Before they are teenagers, children don't really have a nose to break; the cartilage that gives the nose its shape is too soft for any real damage. This isn't to say that a blow to the nose can't cause conspicuous swelling or a black-and-blue area from a ruptured blood vessel. Applying ice for the first few minutes will somewhat limit the swelling, which can take a good week to go down.

Nursemaid's Elbow

Jimmy and his nursemaid are walking down the street hand in hand. He suddenly stops short while she keeps walking, and his arm gets yanked. He starts crying, and the horrified nurse notices the arm hanging limply by his side. "Broken bone!" says the nurse. "Nursemaid's elbow," says the doctor, as he magically pops Jimmy's elbow back into place with a single twist of the forearm.

This is a textbook case of nursemaid's elbow, a condition that occurs in children under five in which the elbow tendon becomes slightly dislocated. This mild injury can happen when someone pulls Jimmy's arm or plays roughly with him.

After a brief period of crying, Jimmy won't be in pain, as long as he doesn't move his joint; he'll just walk around with his arm hanging by his side. There is usually no swelling or discoloration. Your doctor can perform a simple maneuver—flexing the forearm while turning the hand toward the body—and the elbow will generally pop right back into place. A few minutes later, Jimmy will be using his arm as if nothing happened. Even without this maneuver there's a very good chance that Jimmy will eventually flex his arm and pop the elbow back into place on his own. If he gets nursemaid's elbow in the evening, and there's no swelling or pain, you can just put him to bed and you'll probably see him using his arm normally in the morning. If not, you'll have to take him to the doctor.

Nursemaid's elbow tends to recur in children who are prone to it. If your child fits this profile, you may want to have your doctor teach you how to do the simple repair maneuver so that you don't have to pay him a visit each time it happens. And you can just forget about playing 1,2,3—Jump! and hanging Jimmy by his arms until he grows up.

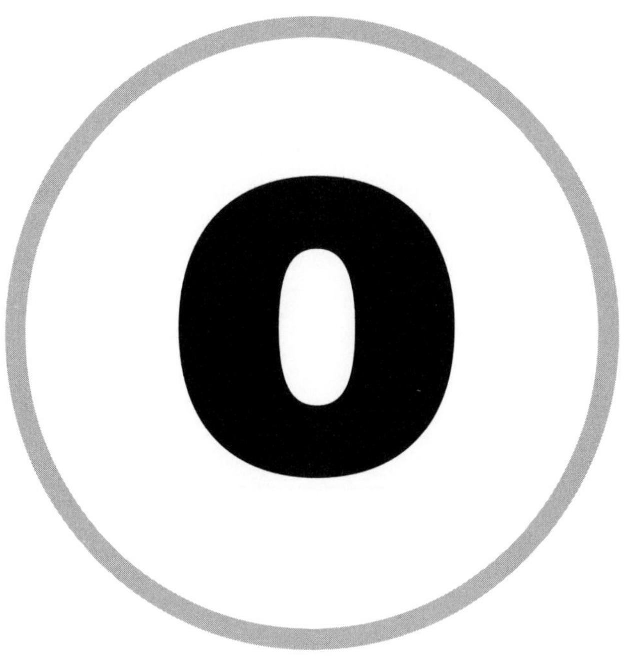

OUTSIDE WITH A BABY

OVERWEIGHT

Outside with a Baby

When can you take your new baby outside? At one month? At two months? At eight pounds? After the vaccines? The answer is simple: as soon as you'd like. People propagate many myths or superstitions concerning the dangers of taking a newborn outside. Although there hasn't been a conclusive study on the topic, you can resolve the issue with a bit of common sense.

Unless you install a hospital-grade air-filtering system in your home and outfit everybody in sterile space suits, the germs Lucy encounters at home are more or less the same as those she'll face in the outside world. In addition, if you ever leave the house or if you have visitors at home, plenty of germs will contaminate Lucy's surroundings. Small babies don't require a germ-free environment. Lucy may be little, but she has a strong immune system—far hardier than some people imagine. She also doesn't have to receive all her shots before being taken out, since most of the diseases against which we immunize are kept at bay in the general population by these same vaccines. So don't sacrifice your own desire for the outside world because of fear of contamination. Restaurants, malls, airplanes, parks—they're all fine places to take your new baby.

Overweight

See also | **Weight Concerns**

In infants, "overweight" represents a physiological predisposition, not a nutritional disorder. If your baby is chunky, the first thing to do is to ask your mom how big you were as a baby; you'll probably find that your baby looks just like you used to.

Keep in mind that, concerning XL babies, it's virtually impossible to overfeed an infant for the simple reason that if you do, the food comes right back up at you. Feed your Large baby on demand, just as if she were a Small or a Medium. As with all kids, beware of offering food as a pacifier, and do not provide a diet that leans too heavily on carbohydrates, because these habits could predispose her to heaviness later in life.

Here are a few other considerations about big babies:

- First of all, contrary to what you may hear, if Lucy is oversized, she doesn't need to eat solid foods any earlier than her peers do.
- When you do start introducing solid food (around six months), don't restrict her intake, even if she has a good appetite.
- Larger babies tend to be slightly less coordinated and will sit up later. They usually lose their chub when they start running around.

As for the comments, you'll be proud of all the "oohs" and "aahhs" Lucy generates at first, but you'll soon grow tired of hearing people say "How old is she? She's huge!"

Toddlers can also come in size XL, but as soon as their mobility increases, virtually all of them become leaner (despite that characteristic prominent belly). Whatever Jimmy's size and food inclinations, limit the sugars and fats he eats, like sugared cereals, juices, sodas, raisins, candies, cookies, pasta, pizzas, fast foods, chips, crackers, bread, ice cream, etc.

The best way to prevent your child from becoming overweight is to set good eating habits and limit the availability of fattening foods at home. That way, the struggle to limit access is much reduced, though you can still bend the rules on occasion, like at birthday parties and when you eat out.

When Jimmy is asserting his independence (around fifteen to eighteen months of age), resist the temptation to alleviate his frustrations with food or to offer things that taste better to him, so he does not become a picky eater [See: Picky Eating].

In Children

Some children are genetically predisposed to becoming overweight. But if yours is skinny now, don't be smug. A five-year-old kid who eats a fattening diet could be skin and bones, while another on the same regimen will be overweight. But that difference may not last into their teenage years; even the super-skinny child runs a good chance of becoming overweight if he sticks with the fattening foods.

In the vast majority of cases, children become overweight not because of hormonal issues but because of entrenched nutritional and psychological habits that take root at a very young age. One primary reason is the early introduction of sugar to the diet, as described above.

If Jimmy is overweight, the most helpful approach is nutritional counseling that provides a detailed diet, coupled with bimonthly weighings. The goal is to limit access to fattening foods, especially sodas, fast food, pizza, chips, and cookies. If you don't keep them at home, there won't be any temptation. Substitute low-fat foods such as fruits, vegetables, skim-milk cheese, meat, fish, or tofu. Encouraging exercise and limiting TV or videogames will also help; think of an hour of TV as an hour of gaining weight.

Of course, much of this is easier said than done. Making fattening foods unavailable is just half the solution. The other half is dealing with a child who is very unhappy and doesn't understand why he can't eat the things he's always eaten. Handling his moods will require determination, a willingness to set limits, and patience [**See:** Discipline and Boundaries].

PACIFIERS

PAIN AND FEVER MEDICATIONS

PEANUT BUTTER

PENIS

PETS

PICKY EATING

PINWORMS

PNEUMONIA

POISONING

POSTPARTUM LETDOWN

PREMATURITY

PRENATAL CLASSES

PUMPING MILK

Pacifiers

See also | **Thumb Sucking**

Rather than bore you with lengthy psychological theories on why babies like to suck on pacifiers, I will instead offer a few practical observations. For starters, some babies systematically spit them out; if yours does, don't waste your time reading this entry or skip to THUMB SUCKING, if that applies. For those babies who take them, pacifiers are a welcome but optional source of comfort.

Pacifiers and . . .

Nursing

Let's first address an enduring myth. Contrary to popular belief, pacifiers do not interfere with nursing; babies are smart enough to recognize that nothing comes out of them: no milk, no formula, nada. In fact, when it comes to oral-comfort issues, a pacifier is more convenient than your finger (which can be tiring) or your breast (which can be tiring and lead to overfeeding).

Addiction

Don't be afraid you'll make a pacifier addict out of Lucy. This was an issue in the old days when feeding on a rigid schedule used to deprive a baby of sucking, but now this is less of a problem. However, the type of pacifier can contribute to dependence. I always recommend the old-fashioned round type, because it's harder to keep in the mouth and will fall out right after Lucy falls asleep, thus reducing dependency. The improved "orthodontic" pacifier is so perfectly molded to her mouth that it can become an integral part of her anatomy. Finally, at around three to four months, the urge to suck decreases, and Lucy can satisfy her sucking desires with her own hand or thumb. At this point, if you make the pacifier less available, Lucy will gradually lose interest in it without any weaning process.

Language

Past a few months of age, if Lucy keeps a pacifier in her mouth for a good part of the day, it can interfere with vocalization, cooing, and chattering. The same interference at the toddler stage can delay language acquisition. Physical concerns relating to malformations of the jaw and teeth are much less of a concern, since a pacifier is too soft to modify the anatomy of Lucy's mouth.

Weaning

If, for whatever reasons, you have let Jimmy keep his pacifier for too long, you're probably wondering how to get rid of this little piece of rubber to which he seems so addicted. It's simple: When you've decided that the fateful moment has come for him to kiss his pacifier good-bye, just throw it away. If he asks for his "dummy" (as the English call it), play dumb yourself and pretend you don't know what he's talking about. He'll whine the first day, and by the third he'll have forgotten about it. If the pacifier mysteriously reappears, you'll have an even bigger problem on your hands, because he'll figure out how to get it back: whining.

Pain and Fever Medications

The difference between acetaminophen (Tylenol) and ibuprofen (Advil, Motrin) is the same as the difference between Coke and Pepsi: not much. Both medications will relieve moderate pain and lower almost any fever. They come in liquids and chewable pills, but only Tylenol comes in suppository form. Since acetaminophen and ibuprofen are different chemicals, you can alternate between them or even use them together. The side effects are almost nonexistent with appropriate doses. Both medicines can be given on an empty stomach since kids are not prone to acidity. Neither medication will treat a runny nose or congestion, unless it's marketed as a cold remedy, in which case it's supplemented with some additional undesirable decongestants, which I don't recommend. We no longer give aspirin to kids for fear of a very rare but serious side effect on the brain called Reye's syndrome.

If Jimmy is experiencing pain or discomfort from a fever, be sure to give him the correct dosage for his age and weight (or even a tiny bit more), or else you won't see the medicine's miraculous healing effects. You can safely repeat the acetaminophen dose every four hours; every six with ibuprofen. If needed, you can safely administer them several days in a row in the recommended doses, as long as you have addressed the cause of Jimmy's discomfort or fever.

As wonderful as both of these medications are, they should be used sparingly, not because they don't work or have side effects, but because they can either suppress symptoms that help an illness run its course or make it trickier to follow the course of an illness. Fever, for example, helps get rid of viruses and may also be an indication that the illness is worsening.

Peanut Butter

See also | **Food Reactions; Picky Eating**

Many kids literally live on PBJ (the technical term for peanut butter and jelly). Yet this American icon is not as ideal as you may think. In addition to a substantial amount of healthy proteins, peanut butter also contains a lot of fat, which, combined with the sugar of the bread and the jelly, amounts to a lot of calories. Finally, PBJ is all too often used to ensure that Jimmy "at least has something in his tummy," at the expense of other valuable nutrients, and becomes a synonym for lunch.

Parents often wonder when to start giving kids peanut butter. Don't let a fear of allergies guide this decision; if Jimmy is allergic to peanuts, delaying the introduction makes no difference; he'll develop the reaction no matter how old he is when he first tastes a peanut. In many ways, it's better that you know early on. That said, I suggest you encourage other nutrients like meat, fish, fruits, and vegetables.

Penis

See also | **Circumcision; Masturbation; Washing**

Penis Care

Penises are pretty much maintenance free, whether circumcised or uncircumcised. Doctors used to recommend pulling and retracting the foreskin to clean the penis and detach the skin. This is both painful and unnecessary; the white stuff that accumulates under the foreskin is not dirt but rather a coating substance with the lovely name of *smegma*. Since smegma is a natural secretion from the skin of the penis, there is no reason to remove it. Even if you did, more would appear. Just clean Jimmy's penis as you would clean his foot or hand: use plenty of water. Aggressive cleaning or retracting, of course, will create redness or irritation.

Red Penis

Apart from the natural swelling boys witness in their penises, they may also experience occasional redness and additional swelling due to irritation. In infants, you can probably blame diaper rash, but in older kids who have shed their diapers, masturbation is usually to blame. In either case, the condition resolves on its own after a couple of days. When masturbation is the culprit, the pain of irritation discourages further exploration . . . for a while. If the swelling and redness persist beyond a couple of days or worsens, have a doctor examine the area for possible infection.

Tight Foreskin

In some uncircumcised kids the foreskin is very tight and seems like it will never retract. This condition, called *phimosis*, is a normal anatomical variant. Years ago, doctors would routinely recommend that parents yank the skin down to free the penis, or even have the kid circumcised. Forceful retraction is still practiced, despite medical evidence that it is not just futile but harmful. If you pull on it, the skin around the head can become inflamed and swollen, and the tight foreskin can even strangle the head of the penis. If Jimmy happens to have a tight foreskin, leave it alone. He'll eventually loosen it up with masturbation in his own time and on his own terms.

No Penis

In chubby infants and toddlers, the penis can sometimes be buried in the pubic fat. Press on the fat, and the penis will pop out. This baby fat will eventually disappear, revealing the precious attributes that were hiding under Jimmy's too, too solid flesh.

Pets

In general, pets are at greater risk from kids than the other way around. Kids can learn positive values from caring for and playing with animals, such as responsibility and respect for living things that aren't parents, siblings, or peers. Try to teach Jimmy not to tug on the cat's tail or drop things on the dog for fun. Bites and scratches, whether provoked or unprovoked, represent the primary danger to children from household pets. We've all heard the myths about cats sleeping on babies' heads and smothering them. Not only is such a bizarre occurrence very unlikely, I could not find a single documented case in the literature. Usually, the less the cat sees the baby, the happier that cat will be.

Pet allergies are rare, even with a known predisposition (if, say, one or both parents are known to be allergic). They usually require a few years of exposure to develop, so they aren't a concern for parents of young babies. If such allergies do show up, they're obvious, producing teary eyes, sneezing, rashes, and even asthmatic reactions. If this happens, you may consider removing the pet from the home. You also have less extreme options: antidander shampoo for the pet, high-quality air filters, and even antiallergy shots to desensitize Jimmy. Note that there are hypoallergenic dogs such as poodles, which shed no fur or dander and are thus ideal for allergic households.

Picky Eating

See also | **Discipline and Boundaries; Feeding; Finger Foods**

You were so thrilled that Jimmy was a great eater. He used to devour everything, from seafood salad and vegetable soups to beef stew and even avocado. When he turned fifteen months old, though, his eating habits took an unexpected turn. Out of the blue one day, instead of gulping down his lunch as usual, he eyed his plate a moment and then swept the entire lunch onto the floor. No matter how you pleaded, he wouldn't reconsider his decision not to eat lunch. You tasted the food to make sure it wasn't spoiled. You ate, humming with pleasure, to show how you liked it and how he would too if only he tasted a teeny-weeny bit of it. You tried other dishes. No luck. Jimmy found it all quite entertaining.

Now, the only thing he'll touch is plain pasta, potato croquettes, pizza, and hot dogs, and only if served in front of his favorite TV show, and all subject to a meticulous inspection for hidden vegetables. What's with Jimmy all of a sudden?

Welcome to the assertive stage of development, the moment when kids discover that options exist. They strive to demonstrate their individuality by exerting their own choices, thereby limiting yours. This assertiveness manifests itself in several different ways. Try, for instance, to dress Jimmy in a jacket of the "wrong" color and you could end up in a serious wrestling contest: From his two-foot-high perspective, the "right" jacket is the red one.

The discovery of a panorama of options goes hand in hand with a desire to actively reproduce pleasant sensations (e.g., ice cream) and avoid those that seem unpleasant (e.g., spinach). Prior to this age, Jimmy is undiscriminating in his tastes. Nor does he realize that he could potentially get something even "better" with a little fussing, so he pretty much eats whatever is placed in front of him. Unfortunately, this easygoing attitude is short-lived. Like Jimmy, most toddlers come to frown upon the very same foods they once ate happily and without complaint.

Jimmy's motivations do not necessarily reflect strong, lasting convictions. His day-to-day choices are often determined by transient, arbitrary notions about, say, colors and textures, notions that could turn on a dime. Toddlers can be made more amenable than they appear, as I will explain in a moment. But first, let's ask Jimmy "Why on earth would you turn down this beautifully balanced, nutritious meal that your mother cooked for you with love and devotion?"

"I want something sweeter."

Jimmy has developed his preferences, and sweets and their derivatives are at the top of his list. The propensity for sweet tastes originates early: I don't know many infants who don't go for seconds when teased with ice cream. This is not to say that Jimmy's insatiable sweet tooth is set in stone from the start; I often observe that when parents have been very "sugar-conscious" from the beginning, their children show less interest in sweet foods later.

Jimmy's new food inclinations include "fast" and "slow" sugars. "Fast" (or "simple") sugars are a major constituent of juices, fruits, and any food containing processed sugar. The term "fast" describes how they're rapidly metabolized; it has nothing to do with how fast they go down. "Slow" (or "complex") sugars are the main component of pasta, bread, rice, potatoes, and cereals. (They get digested more slowly than simple sugars.) Hence Jimmy's predilection for "white foods." He may refuse broccoli, not because he really dislikes it but because it's just not sweet enough for him.

"What else you got?"

Jimmy will try this approach to find out if you are ready and willing to give him something more palatable when he pushes his food away.

"Too green."

Color plays a role in food rejection. Green is often perceived as unappealing by our little creatures, so they shamelessly spit out iron-packed vegetables such as spinach, broccoli, and green beans. Certain mealtimes may recall gory scenes from your favorite teenage horror movie.

"Too mushy."

Food texture may also trigger refusal. Although there are no universal rules here, most children prefer crunchy food.

"And what if I don't eat?"

For exploratory purposes, Jimmy may clamp his mouth shut when confronted with tomatoes, just to see what your reaction will be. For one thing, he truly enjoys watching you play "airplane."

"Too much pressure."

Jimmy may perceive your sudden interest in his nutritional intake as pressure. Pressure can range from gentle suggestion to outright insistence. Even your ecstatic praises when Jimmy polishes his plate could turn mealtime into a performance at which he must succeed. Parents who themselves were pressured to eat as children tend to be more anxious when their own children refuse food, which in turn produces even more pressure.

WHAT **TO DO**

The best reasons for a toddler to eat are hunger and pleasure. The worst is to please Mommy and Daddy. Healthy eating habits should be introduced at an early age. Unfortunately, too many of our kids become pasta-pizza-hot-dog eaters, and those bad habits tend to persist with age. Here is my recommended mealtime strategy:

▶ **For breakfast, lunch, and dinner,** try to give him the same foods you eat. There is no need to analyze the contents of these meals as if you were a scientist. Use good common sense to create a varied diet that will take care of all his nutritional requirements. In general, a meal should be a balanced combination of different food groups: a protein source, such as meat, fish, tofu, or egg; a starch, such as pasta, rice, or cereal; and some fruits and vegetables. Serve a glass of water for his beverage; there's nothing wrong with water, and it doesn't stain. Serve the food in courses, one after another or all at once, whichever you prefer.

- **Now sit back and relax, or even better join in.** Mealtime is not only about nutrition; it's also a precious opportunity for family bonding. Let him feed himself. He'll eat whatever he needs. That may mean nothing, half of it, the whole thing, or even seconds!
- **If he eats nothing, simply remove the plate,** take him out of the high chair, and go on to the next activity. This is particularly easy when the food goes overboard. If he eats half his meal, do the same thing.
- **If he cleans the plate, you scored!** But don't slather him with praise.
- **If he asks for more, oblige by adding a little more of everything.** Here again, no big party is needed to celebrate your victory.
- **Between meals,** serve light snacks such as fruit and crackers with milk or water.
- **If you're at home,** make snack time a sit-down, fun event.

WHAT **NOT TO DO**

- **Don't ask Jimmy to take a few more bites for Mommy,** Daddy, or anyone else.
- **Don't invent ingenious tricks to get more food in.**
- **Don't use the TV** or any other distraction to increase his intake.
- **Don't spoon-feed him when he can feed himself.** This will introduce pressure and interfere with his own regulation of hunger and satiety.
- **Don't empty the fridge to find a food he might prefer.** At the next meal he'll be waiting for that nice display again. And that display will end up including the usual suspects; pasta, pizza, hot dogs, or peanut butter and jelly sandwiches.
- **Don't serve the meal a half hour later if Jimmy changes his mind.** This is not the Hilton. The next food service will be the scheduled snack two hours later, even if your customer acts a little disgruntled by banging on the fridge, which you should treat as an inappropriate behavior [See: Discipline and Bounderies].
- **Don't continuously dispense snacks** (crackers, chips, goldfish, fruit rolls, and the like). The same goes for numerous bottles of juice and milk. When mealtime arrives, Jimmy won't understand why you just sat him down in front of all that food when he isn't hungry.
- **Don't give vitamin tablets to replace the nutrients found in fruits and vegetables.** Vitamins are commonly added to many packaged foods, including junk food, so even with a so-so diet, vitamin deficiency is unlikely. And, no, they won't increase his appetite.

- **Don't give him highly caloric shakes from a can.** He won't take them, and if he does he'll have less appetite for real food.

In Summary

By now I'm sure you get my point. When you see the early signs of a picky eater, don't be afraid to let Jimmy get a little hungry. Don't insist, don't suggest, don't bribe, and don't replace what he won't eat with what he will. He won't starve by missing a couple of meals. Hunger will be a strong incentive to try those ugly string beans, which he actually may end up liking. With this approach, you'll become one of those parents who brags: "This kid gulps down everything we put in front of him." No need to expand on how it happened.

Pinworms

These tiny organisms crawl along the anal margin and produce lots of itching, especially at night. Most common in school-age children, they're transmitted by direct contact, usually via the fingernails. The itching can drive your child crazy, and in girls it can cause irritation all the way to the vagina.

The diagnosis is made by looking at the anal margin, which will be quite irritated. You may even catch a glimpse of these tiny white wriggling creatures, which also sometimes turn up in the stool.

Your doctor will treat pinworms with two pills taken a week apart. Before that pill takes action, the itching can be alleviated with an antihistamine like Benadryl. Don't go crazy disinfecting every piece of clothing and linen in the house; pinworms don't live long outside the body.

If the itching reappears after treatment, the whole family may have to be treated to prevent the recurrence of pinworms; even if adults rarely show symptoms, they can be carriers.

Pneumonia

See also | **Cough; Flu**

Pneumonia is an infection of the lungs caused by a virus or bacteria. The viral type is milder and often goes undetected. The bacterial type, which can be a flu complication, is more serious but less common. Symptoms vary widely. A high fever is almost always present and persists for many days. When pneumonia follows the flu, the fever may drop initially or even disappear and then reappear. Respiratory difficulties beyond simple nasal congestion are also typical, as are low energy and paleness. If your child presents these symptoms, take him to the doctor, who may order a chest X ray to confirm the diagnosis. Contrary to popular belief, pneumonia does not always provoke coughing; in many cases, the child is too weak to cough. And a nasty cough without any other symptoms is rarely a sign of pneumonia.

Bacterial pneumonia is treated with antibiotics, sometimes in the hospital. Improvement usually occurs within a few days of beginning treatment. The viral variety resolves on its own in about the same time frame.

Walking Pneumonia

This term refers to a specific type of bacterial pneumonia (chlamydia, though not the same as the sexually transmitted disease) that behaves more like a viral pneumonia. It usually affects children over five and peaks in adolescence. The relatively mild symptoms look just like those of a flu, consisting of a sore throat, cough, and fever. If the illness persists and the flu diagnosis is called into question, an X ray may show a pneumonia that is far more impressive than the actual discomfort it's causing.

Unlike other types of pneumonia, walking pneumonia does not affect breathing or vastly restrict activity, thus the name. Doctors treat the condition with antibiotics, and the disease is moderately contagious. Walking pneumonia is frequently overdiagnosed; people who have an especially bad cough that lingers or a flu that can't be shaken are often treated unnecessarily for a touch of "walking pneumonia," when in fact they are likely suffering from a viral illness.

Poison

Dial 1-800-222-1222 for the Poison Control hotline. No matter where you live, this is the first number to call if you suspect poisoning. The answering party will guide you on what to do next. Ipecac—a medication that induces vomiting in case of poisoning—should only be administered after you've consulted with Poison Control, because it's contraindicated if certain poisons have been ingested. Plus, in the twenty minutes Ipecac takes to act, you could already be at the hospital if the ingestion warrants emptying the stomach.

As a rule, you should set up your house to reduce the chance of having to call Poison Control. Any medication, even something as common as acetaminophen, can be toxic or fatal for kids if the dose is high enough. Keep the minimum amount of medicines in your home, and put the ones you absolutely can't live without well out of reach. As for cleaning products, that space under the sink is entirely too accessible for tiny inquisitive people. Keep those harsh chemicals far out of reach, and put a good solid latch or lock on the cabinet where you keep them.

Postpartum Letdown

See also | **Breast Feeding and Medication**

For my beloved wife Jeannie and myself, the births of our kids were the happiest moments of our lives. I think it's safe to assume that most people feel the same way. So why do I see so many mothers bursting into tears at the two-week visit for no apparent reason? Let's face it: Having a baby is self-inflicted physical and psychological abuse. They suck on you, they keep you awake, they play with your nerves, they sleep when you want them to play, they cry when you think they should be happy, and the more you want to make them happy, the crankier they get.

A couple of years ago, I was amused to read that scientists are actively searching for the hormonal substance in the mother's brain that helps her tolerate all that abuse, because without it, mankind would have ceased to exist long ago. Imagine how many uses people would find for that substance if it were synthesized!

Seriously, having a baby is draining, both emotionally and physically, and before you adjust fully to your new life, you might experience a letdown moment (sometimes known as *postpartum depression*), typically after a week or two. If you feel spent, tired, and weepy, you could also feel guilty that you don't feel happy and fulfilled. You are all of those things, but you're also very tired. My advice is to sleep when Lucy sleeps, lay off work for a while, take time to chill out, and only think from one day to the next. Accept that Lucy is having her own letdown as well; she was much cozier inside you, and she needs a couple of weeks to adapt to her new environment. Be like her: Cry if you need to. There is a light at the end of the tunnel, and you'll reach that light of joy and contentment very soon.

Having said that, mothers who tend toward depression will experience a rougher bout of postpartum letdown. If this describes you, talk to your doctor about taking or resuming medications.

Prematurity

Lucy was premature, and she stayed at the hospital in an incubator, hooked up to all kinds of machinery. It's been a long and difficult journey, but thanks to the wonders of medicine, she's just come home.

Care of a Premature Baby

By the time Lucy makes it back to your house, she is most likely healthy and should be treated as such. Give her the white-glove treatment if you wish, but you needn't use the rubber ones. As with regular newborns, you can take her outside, have visitors, and let her play with siblings. Feed her on demand, don't weigh her obsessively, and don't count or measure temperatures, feedings, and stools. Just enjoy her as a normal baby, which she is. In terms of routine care, the first doctor visits may be more frequent to monitor weight gain. Immunizations generally start at two months after birth and follow the same schedule as those of full-term babies.

Nursing a Premature Baby

Moderately premature babies are able to nurse, but despite scientific evidence showing that nursing offers clear benefits for "preemies," doctors and nurses don't always encourage it. They are most concerned with strictly controlling the amount ingested. As a result, the average graduate of the neonatal intensive care unit is bottle-fed formula or pumped milk. At home, you'll have to take one of three paths:

Continue with Formula

This is the easiest option but not necessarily the best. Breast milk has significant nutritional benefits and will help create immunities. On the other hand, reintroducing nursing may be hard work, and you may not feel up to the challenge [**See:** Breast Feeding vs. Formula].

Feed Pumped Breast Milk Through a Bottle

For mothers who pumped their milk while the baby was in the hospital, this is a cumbersome though feasible option. Bear in mind that most of breast milk's physiological benefits in terms of immunogenic protection are achieved within the first couple of months. Since this method lacks the primary advantage of bonding at the breast, the stress of pumping may soon outweigh its benefits [**See:** Pumping Milk].

Go Back to Nursing

There is a chance that Lucy will go back to the breast. It depends on the degree of bottle addiction, the length of her ICU stay, and whether or not she was given a chance to nurse some of the time. If you choose this option, attempt to put Lucy at your breast for each feeding. Initially, she may not know what to do with your nipple and may be quite upset. If so, take a break and reattempt a few minutes later. After twenty minutes of this nursing workout, you should offer bottle supplementation with either breast milk or formula. Then, over the next few days, decrease the number of times you supplement with formula. She will get hungrier and more interested in nursing from the breast. Within seven to ten (probably frustrating) days, you may well be able to fully reintroduce breast feeding. If it's a fiasco, you always have the previous two options [**See:** Breast Feeding Problems].

Premature Babies and Development

The difference in physical development between a preemie and a full-term newborn of the same age varies with the level of prematurity. By six to eight months, most preemies born after thirty-two weeks of gestation achieve the developmental milestones that are normal for their age. Catching up in terms of height and weight may take longer, but by two years of age, most preemies have caught up with their full-term peers.

Prenatal Classes

I find that instead of being reassuring and informative, prenatal classes often create anxieties. Lamaze and Bradley classes can make you apprehensive by detailing every possible hurdle and pitfall, especially when it comes to breast feeding. The information they offer is often too specific or technical. On the positive side, prenatal classes form natural support groups where you can meet other expectant couples. This can be a big help, especially the first time around.

The bottom line is that if you decide to give birth naturally, it will hurt. Anesthesia is no panacea either; it may not take, and if it does it can make you push less efficiently and, incidentally, cause a serious headache that lasts for days afterward. If you breathe deeply it'll hurt a little less and you'll push better. Learning to breathe through intense pain is not a trivial affair, however, and mothers report to me that prenatal yoga is very helpful for developing that skill.

Pumping Milk

This section covers the many reasons to pump milk. Before discussing how and why, let's take care of what to do with pumped milk. You can store it in the fridge for a good twenty-four hours and in the freezer almost indefinitely. Just as with formula, you can give Lucy the rest of an unfinished bottle that remains at room temperature for a couple of hours.

To Stimulate Breast Milk

Contrary to what you may have heard, it's ludicrous to pump milk in the first few days after delivery in order to stimulate your production. This is the moment to let nature take its own course. Watching the few pitiful drops of colostrum that you painfully extract could make you assume that you don't have enough milk, but that's not accurate. Lucy is a much more efficient extractor than the pump. Also, when you offer her your breast she won't understand why, since you've depleted her food supply. Sure, you could follow up by giving her pumped milk in a bottle, but next time she'll remember how compliant the rubber nipple was in comparison to yours. You'll end up chasing your tail and become discouraged.

When Daddy Helps

Having papa participate in Lucy's feeding is an excellent idea if she's bottle feeding. If you're nursing and want to share feedings, pumping breast milk is a good idea in theory, but in practice it's often inefficient. The time spent pumping, storing, and supervising could simply be used to get the actual feeding out of the way. Also, in the first few days of feeding, pumping interferes with natural production and disrupts the breast-feeding schedule. If you want to feed pumped breast milk, do it after you've established a steady breast-feeding pattern, which usually takes a good ten days. And remember, feeding a few ounces of formula here and there for convenience isn't the end of the world.

Because Nursing Is Too Hard

Some mothers choose to feed their babies pumped breast milk with a bottle because they've been unable to breast-feed successfully. I doubt they enjoy the double hassle of first pumping and then bottle feeding, but at least they have the satisfaction of providing their babies with the best nutrition. If you find yourself in this situation, bear in mind that while it may be worth the effort in the first few months, when most of breast milk's physiological and immunological advantages are achieved, the benefits are less obvious after that.

At Work

If you're going to work soon after Lucy is born, you may want to pump breast milk at the office. This is a good alternative to nursing, especially during the first six months. After that, you should weigh the diminishing benefits of feeding Lucy breast milk against the stress of pumping at work. Most mothers don't tremendously enjoy pumping, but they seem to find it tolerable after they get the hang of it. Unfortunately, very few workplaces are designed to accommodate this activity. Having said that, I've seen many working mothers successfully and happily pump breast milk at work for a full year.

Here are some tips I've gathered from these dairy queens:

- Enjoy your maternity leave without pumping, and start just a few days before going back to the office. Stockpiling pints of surplus milk in anticipation won't make a difference, and it will offset your production.
- Pump only what Lucy's likely to eat the next day while you're at work. You'll probably get an average of twelve ounces in two to three sittings. In the first few months, this will be enough to keep her happy throughout the day.

- In the first week or two, Lucy's caretaker will invariably report at the end of the day that you did not leave enough breast milk. This is partly because Lucy will suck more readily on a rubber nipple and because your caretaker is assuming that when Lucy fusses she's probably hungry.
- If you find you don't have enough milk, keep in mind that formula is not poison. It's the next best thing to breast milk, and if bottle feeding relieves your stress level at work, it's worth it to give Lucy a couple of ounces of formula a day.

After six months, when Lucy starts eating solid foods, breast milk, while still beneficial, is no longer crucial. At this point, pump what's comfortable and supplement with formula. Even if you stop pumping altogether, you can continue breast feeding at night and during weekends.

r

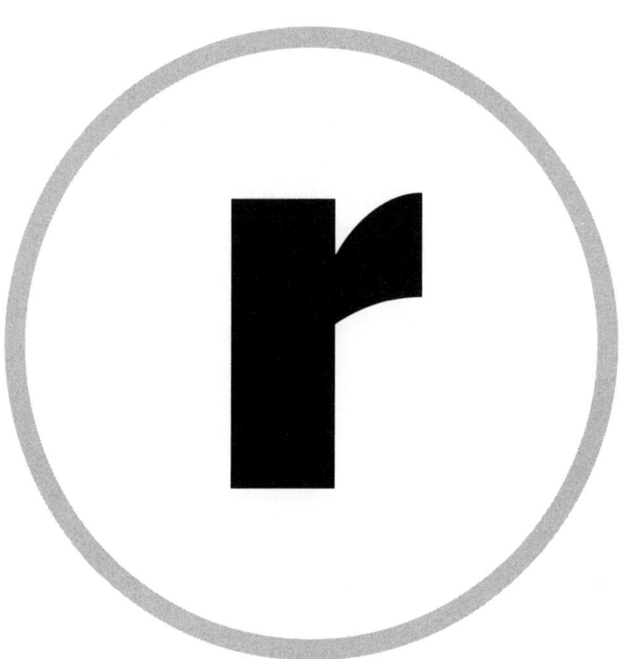

Reading

In the early years of Jimmy's life, read to him as often as possible. It's the second gift of life from parents to children, and you'll be amazed to see how a ten-page story can trigger a whole cornucopia of thoughts and dreams inside his little head. Plus, reading gives him contact with you as well as playful interaction and undivided attention.

On the other hand, you shouldn't worry too much about how long it takes Jimmy to learn to read. Reading is an important cognitive milestone, of course, but the time frame varies tremendously from one kid to the next. Yes, early reading may be a sign of intelligence, but late reading hardly indicates a lack of intelligence. Unfortunately, many school systems are based on standardized reading scales that put undue stress on both parents and children. Although some children learn to read quite early, and some will even teach themselves, as a parent you should focus only on instilling a love of learning and a sense of joy and excitement about books.

Reflux

See also | **Spitting Up; Vomiting**

Have you ever wondered why the food in your stomach doesn't come down when you stand on your head? It's because your stomach sphincter tightens up. If it does not, you have what doctors call *reflux*, and some of your intestinal content will come back up to create heartburn even if you don't stand on your head. For the past few years, reflux has been a fashionable diagnosis for adults. Everybody seems to have it, and it gets blamed for virtually every upper-body symptom. Now, reflux hysteria has spilled over onto babies. Years ago a baby who cried was just your average baby. Nowadays, a crying baby is a baby with reflux. Here are the facts.

In Infants

Gastrointestinal reflux is the return of food upward through the esophagus and mouth. Technically, every baby on Earth has gastrointestinal reflux; that's why they wear bibs. At this point in a baby's life, the muscle that tightens the top of the stomach is still loose, so some of the milk goes back up, resulting in spitting up. For true reflux to occur there must be vomiting.

Reflux and Overfeeding

Before you or your doctor diagnoses Lucy with reflux, be absolutely certain that you're not overfeeding her. Why would you be overfeeding her? Hmmm, let's see. Maybe Lucy has a cranky moment and you think she's hungry. She isn't, but she takes the bottle or the breast as a pacifier. And as she swallows what comes out of the nipple, her belly becomes distended, causing her even more discomfort. And you feed her even more because she's still cranky, until she can't handle it anymore and she vomits.

This scenario, all too typical in young babies, can lead to a misdiagnosis of reflux. If you see yourself in that little story, try not to respond to each crying episode by giving food [**See:** Colic]. On the other hand, if you are confident that she has not been overfed but she's still vomiting frequently, she may indeed have real reflux.

Real Reflux

The true reflux that doctors refer to when they're talking about infants occurs when the stomach sphincter muscle is abnormally weak, and food is delivered back through the mouth in the form of projectile vomit almost every time Lucy is fed. (Vomiting is different from a little spitting up.) If Lucy turns out to have reflux, it's not a problem as long as she's gaining weight steadily; it will improve naturally by the time she is eight months old or so. In the meantime, there are some measures you can take to limit the regurgitation:

- Take pauses and burp her during feeding to allow the milk to settle in the stomach.
- Keep her upright and avoid too much movement or handling for a while after she's done eating.
- Medications such as Zantac, which are supposed to limit acidity, have limited efficacy and should only be used in pronounced cases.

Reflux and Colic

I've seen many babies who were labeled colicky and put on antireflux medication, even though they didn't vomit more than the average (except when overfed, as explained above). The rationale for treating fussy babies with antireflux medication goes something like this: The milk regurgitated from the stomach creates heartburn, and this discomfort makes the baby cry. But this rationale makes no sense: If the milk were regurgitated, there would be no reason for it to stop halfway, so you'd see it come up in the form of vomit. And why would regurgitation hurt these babies more than others? In my opinion, this is yet another of those quick fixes that falsely allows doctors (and parents) to think that they have found a perfect solution to the problem, when there really isn't a failsafe one. Unfortunately, these parents become even more frustrated and disillusioned when the promised improvements don't occur with medications.

In Older Children

Older kids who don't drink coffee, tea, or alcohol; don't smoke; and don't get aggravated at home or at work rarely suffer from reflux.

Respiratory Allergies

See also | **Colds**

Respiratory allergies are triggered when the inner lining of the nose and airway overreacts to an allergen such as pollen or dust. Common symptoms include itchy nose; clear, runny nasal discharge; and teary eyes. When pollen is the problem, the reaction usually starts in summer and continues until pollen levels decrease in the fall. Other common allergens include mold, dander, and feathers. Contrary to common belief, respiratory allergies are relatively rare in children, so they often take the blame for symptoms actually caused by lingering colds. Additionally, it takes several years of exposure for an allergic child to develop the reaction to an allergen, which explains why allergies are even less common in younger kids. In rare cases, an airborne allergen can trigger an intense breathing reaction or a swelling of the airway.

In terms of relief, allergy medicines have side effects that are often worse than the symptoms themselves. Short-term antihistamines work well enough but not long enough, and they can knock children out. Longer-acting antihistamines such as Zyrtec cause less drowsiness but are less effective. And the allergy medicines that claim to last all day, such as Claritin, are about as efficient as sugar water, even if they have no side effects. Nasal steroid sprays also have limited benefits: Their effects wear off fairly quickly, they become less effective with prolonged use, and they carry the risk of various steroid reactions. No big bargain.

The best treatment for allergies remains avoidance of the allergen wherever possible. It's fairly easy if the cause is a carpet, a feather pillow, or a stuffed animal, but harder if it's indigenous vegetation or a beloved pet. Not everyone has the resources (or the desire) to move to Arizona just to avoid local pollens. In the end, your best bet may be the laissez-faire approach: Help Jimmy get used to living with occasional nasal stuffiness without becoming addicted to these allergy medications. For debilitating nasal allergies, you might try allergy shots, but they have their limitations. Jimmy will have to have a lot of these shots before you see a positive effect—*if* you ever see one—since their efficacy is a subject of debate.

Ringworm

Ringworm causes a ring-shaped rash, but it is definitely not a live worm crawling under the skin. Instead, it's a funguslike organism that causes a limited circular scaly lesion with an even scalier edge. The lesion usually grows slowly to no more than a few inches in diameter. The discomfort is minor and external: a slight itching. Ringworm can sometimes be confused with simple dryness of the skin. It is mildly contagious; kids scratch the lesions and then contaminate their friends by touching them with fingers that harbor the fungus under the nails. Ringworm can also be acquired from dogs and cats that go outside. Adults rarely contract it.

Because it's called a worm, this ring-shaped lesion raises more concern than it warrants. It may heal on its own within a few weeks, even without treatment, but upon diagnosis, you can apply an antifungal cream such as Lotrimin, which speeds up the disappearance.

In the northeastern regions of the United States, where Lyme disease is endemic the ringworm rash can be mistaken for Lyme's characteristic "bulls-eye" lesion [**See:** Lyme Disease]. If you have any question about what you're looking at, ask your doctor.

Rolling Over

See also | **Developmental Milestones; SIDS (Sudden Infant Death Syndrome); Tummy Time**

The average baby rolls over at around five or six months of age, but this is hardly a rule. Some babies roll over just after birth; others can't be bothered to try until ten months of age.

A few factors come into play concerning this milestone. First and foremost is size; the more baby mass there is to roll over, the harder it will be. Then there are issues of coordination and muscle strength, which vary from child to child. Finally, there's temperament. Some kids are perfectly happy on their backs and won't attempt a roll until much later on, while wigglier ones try earlier. The whole fuss about rolling over comes from the fact that years ago, pediatricians recommended that kids be laid on their bellies while on the floor or in their cribs. Kids would try to lift their heads to look around for entertainment, of course, but also to improve their view by rolling over as soon as they were able. These days, kids spend the majority of time on their backs because doctors discourage the belly position for fear of SIDS. When Lucy's on her back, she can look at you and play with her mobile, so why would she want to roll?

A friendly word of caution: Don't underestimate Lucy's ability to roll over; she may have more tricks in her bag than you suspect. The first time it happens could be the very moment Lucy is on her changing table and you turn your head for a split second.

Room Temperature

When I first started practicing, I was surprised by how often parents asked me what temperature the baby's room should be. Now, after years, I have finally come up with a concise answer: The perfect temperature for Lucy's room is room temperature. Not too warm, not too cold. In other words, whatever works for you works for her. At night, if you want to make things a bit warmer, I recommend one of those sleeveless sleeping bags, especially for young babies, as there's no risk that it will cover up the head.

As for outside temperatures, you can take Lucy out in frigid winter temperatures. Unlike older kids, babies are easy to keep tightly bundled up. On the other side of the spectrum, heat is also fine; remember, for nine months Lucy lived in a kind of terrarium, with a minimum temperature of 97°F, without any air conditioning.

Roseola

Roseola is a benign viral illness that affects infants and young toddlers and causes a high fever. It tends to appear primarily in spring, and it's rare in children past the age of three. After three or four days, the fever drops drastically, and a faint rash appears on the face and torso for twenty-four hours and then vanishes. No treatment is necessary, except antifever medication for comfort. Happily, once roseola has afflicted your child, it won't usually recur.

Although roseola isn't serious, the high fever it causes can be nerve-wracking, because before the rash appears you don't know what the illness is. But there are some reassuring signs that point to roseola: Children who have it tend to look remarkably healthy considering the intensity of the fever, and they have no other symptoms, save a decreased appetite.

More distressing, the high fever roseola causes may induce febrile convulsions [**See:** Febrile Convulsions]. As dramatic as they look, these seizures are not dangerous for children, and they only happen in kids who are predisposed. Less worrisome but equally disturbing is roseola's notorious tendency to produce a drastic increase in fussiness and neediness. Lucy will want you to hold her all the time. In fact, even when the rash and fever have subsided, Lucy may be tempted to abuse the privilege and try to ride around on your hip all day. In this situation, be prepared to put her down at times and let her work through her own frustration when she has recovered and the rash has faded.

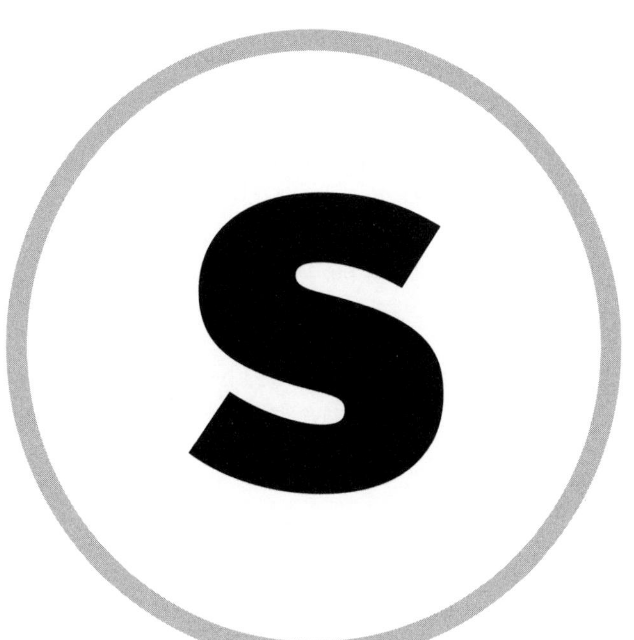
S

Scarlet Fever

See also | **Strep Throat**

Scarlet fever is a scary name for a not-very-scary condition. A variant of strep throat, scarlet fever causes a rash, predominantly on the face and trunk. The rash feels like coarse sandpaper to the touch, and it may be bright red. It may also affect the tongue, causing it to look like a strawberry. You might also see the classic signs of strep throat: a sore throat, swollen tonsils, fever, headaches, and belly pain. Sometimes, however, the rash is so faint and the symptoms so mild that the illness goes undiagnosed.

Scarlet fever is no better or worse than strep throat, and it should be treated in the same way: with a simple course of penicillin prescribed by your pediatrician. In many cases, the entire illness runs its course without any treatment. That said, the standard is to treat even mild episodes in order to prevent any of strep throat's infrequent complications, which include the extremely rare but serious cardiac illness named *rheumatic fever* and kidney problems that can occur when strep is left untreated.

During healing, a mild or pronounced rash may be followed by peeling skin on the hands and feet. The peeling can last for many days, but it's not painful, and it disappears spontaneously.

Schedule

See also | **Bottle Feeding; Breast Feeding; Feeding; Napping; Sleeping**

Some child experts say you should put a baby on a sleeping and feeding schedule beginning at birth. I say that if you follow their dubious advice, you'll waste a lot of time and energy and drive yourself crazy. Lucy has her own schedule. I suggest that you adopt her schedule at first, and then let her slowly adapt to yours.

Sleeping

In terms of sleeping, Lucy initially has no sense of day or night, since she has just emerged from nine months of night. She wakes up whenever her sleep cycle ends, and whenever she wakes up she wants to be comforted, and whenever she wants to be comforted, you feed her. Incidentally, when she wakes up at night, the dark reminds her of her previous environment, where she slept most of the time.

Within a couple of weeks, she is waking up more often during the day than at night, partly because when she wakes you up at night you're less responsive to her, and partly because nature makes us sleep at night.

Eating

As for Lucy's feeding schedule, it starts out all over the map. She can feed for hours on end and then sleep for several hours. Follow her lead. Interfering with her rhythm will just bother her, and in the end she'll only nurse if she wants to anyway.

Babies are wonderfully self-regulating eating machines. The problem is that many books, doctors, nurses, and other experts will advise you to wake up a new baby on a rigid three-hour schedule to offer food. This clinical approach often contributes to breast-feeding failure. If you wake Lucy up to breast-feed and she isn't interested, you may feel a sense of failure and lose confidence in your ability to nurse. Moreover, since she's initially only half-awake, you may be tempted to give her a bottle, which she'll probably take, since it's easier. That will further deepen your sense of failure, and that's when you, like so many mothers I see, will say, "I couldn't breast-feed. I didn't have enough milk."

The best way to synchronize your schedule with Lucy's is to do what other animals do when they have babies. They stay cuddled up together, and when one wakes up, the other one may too, and when everyone wakes up at the same time, they do lunch. If Lucy wants to sleep for four or five hours, let her. If she wakes up ravenously hungry, it just means she needed a long snooze. If she wakes up after just an hour, she may be hungry, or she may not. The best way to know is to offer her food. Over the next week, Lucy will wake up a little more rhythmically (every three hours on average), not because you've imposed that schedule on her but because she is settling into her natural rhythm.

In some instances, this natural method will go awry and lead to a condition I call "overnursing," in which Lucy eats a little, sleeps a little, eats a little, sleeps a little, and so on, all day long. This is very draining for the mother, who loses any opportunity to sleep or recover. That's when I do recommend imposing a schedule [See: Breast-Feeding Problems].

School Anxiety

See also | **Day Care**

I vividly remember bringing our daughter to nursery school for the first time. My wife and I were so apprehensive at the idea of leaving this little thing by herself for a whole two and a half hours. That morning, the family walked to the school with great ceremony, our daughter Abeline in her crisp new floral dress. When we arrived, there were already a dozen kids there, half of them screaming and hanging on to their parents' jackets. After we spent an hour playing with all the toys available, we reached the fateful moment of separation. We kissed her good-bye and snuck out, but we didn't get very far: We looked back to see our little Abeline's blond curly head banging on the window. We ended up going back in and joining a happy group of kids and parents singing "The Wheels on the Bus." We wanted to show Abeline how much fun she could have, so much fun that we ended up staying there all morning and the next morning too.

The first day of school always generates a little bit of fussing; it's a later but lesser form of the same separation anxiety that shows up at eight or nine months. Some kids will have it the first time you leave them in school; others may take a few sessions.

The best way to drop Jimmy off at school is to stay a few minutes and then leave. The message you send when you leave confidently is that you approve of the place, and you approve of leaving Jimmy there, no matter how heartbroken you are. If you try to avoid the unease by prolonging your stay or overexplaining the process, you'll only arouse Jimmy's suspicion and anxiety. When you come back a few hours later, he'll begin to understand that every departure is followed by a return. He'll also start to have a great time.

Interestingly, some nursery schools ask parents to stay with their children for the first few sessions. The intent is to limit the crying at drop-off; teachers don't want their entire classes freaking out at the same time. But this just makes the separation even more difficult. Three weeks later, the parents are still sitting in school for most of the morning and even sneaking out during a moment of inattention, which unnerves Jimmy and increases his fear.

You should treasure those moments of separation anxiety, because they sure won't happen again when you drive your precious student off to college as much as you'd love to stay.

Screening Tests

Newborn Screening

All states now have mandatory newborn screening and testing for a variety of diseases, including HIV and several metabolic conditions. The value of these tests lies in the fact that although these diseases are exceptional, they can all (except HIV) be prevented or at least improved with very simple measures. For example, with congenital hypothyroidism, one of the most common of these rare diseases, a few daily drops of medicine will cure the baby.

The tests are performed by spilling a little blood obtained from Lucy's heel onto a piece of paper. If you never hear back from the hospital, her results are normal. But if something comes up abnormal, the state lab will contact you, your doctor, and the institution where you gave birth. A second blood test will be necessary to confirm the abnormality. Since they analyze some digestive by-products, in order to be accurate these tests must be performed after at least twenty-four hours, the time it takes a newborn to start eating. If you're discharged before the end of the first day, your doctor will redo the test at your first visit.

The number of illnesses included in the test varies from state to state, but the majority of states include the most common of these exceptional diseases. You may run across advertisements for private laboratories that offer additional tests for even rarer diseases; in my opinion there's little benefit in routinely screening newborns for these other almost unheard of diseases, most of which are incurable.

In Children

Years ago, doctors performed a yearly blood test on children to screen for various problems such as anemia or elevated cholesterol. The kids hated it, and it was rarely helpful, since these conditions are so rare. In the end, the medical community decided that the tests were a waste of energy. Nowadays, except for routine lead testing and testing for anemia around the one-year mark, blood tests are performed only in response to specific concerns.

You can minimize the mild pain associated with the drawing of blood from a vein by applying an anesthetic cream twenty minutes prior to the test. The finger prick procedure is more painful, however, and the anesthetic cream won't work as well.

As for other screening tests, we no longer advocate routine tuberculosis tests, unless there's a suspicion of contact. Similarly, we no longer perform annual urine screening tests, unless there's a reason to do so, such as a urinary infection. In our office, this has eliminated the confusion between leftover cups of apple juice and samples!

Sensory Integration

See also | **Autism; Language Acquisition and Late Talking**

This term has recently been used to describe children with a specific set of psychological traits. They are usually highly intelligent or rather hyperperceptive. Their intelligence focuses on specific topics, such as numbers. For example, as early as four years of age they might know every different kind of truck that exists. While their factual retention is excellent, they are a little detached from their environment, and they barely interact with other children. In addition, these kids have a heightened sensitivity to sensory stimuli; for example, they cover their ears when they hear loud noises, and their difficulty handling frustration shows up as loud and frequent tantrums. Finally, physical symptoms may include clumsiness, impaired fine motor coordination, and higher muscle tone, which can result in toe walking [**See:** Toe Walking].

Sensory integration becomes evident in preschool, when such children don't play well with other children or wander around while the others are sitting in a circle. This desire for isolation could be due to hyperperception; a very sensitive child may not be willing to go through the hassle of sharing a toy. At the extreme end of the spectrum of sensory integration lies a rare condition called *Asperger syndrome*, in which a child shows high intelligence in specific areas and develops language but lacks social skills in a way that resembles autism [**See:** Autism].

To date, sensory integration has not been rigorously studied, and as a result it's often a catchall term to describe kids who are a little different. Occupational therapists have provided the primary description of this syndrome through anecdotal observations, since these kids are frequently referred for treatment in an attempt to introduce and reinforce fine and gross motor skills.

If you suspect your child has some of the features of sensory integration, be prudent about labeling and intervening. Most interventions have not been studied thoroughly and can be quite costly. I suggest that you foster social skills in one-on-one interactions rather than in a large group of kids. Enforce boundaries and promote his acquisition of frustration-management skills. Spend the time to answer all his questions patiently, and encourage physical activity, although not necessarily team sports. In my opinion, these children who are slightly unusual follow a different path, but they mature and grow into balanced, intelligent individuals with appropriate social skills.

Separation and Stranger Anxiety

See also | **School Anxiety**

Separation anxiety occurs around six months of age, when Lucy finally realizes that you are not one of her appendages but a separate person who can leave if you so choose. Some kids won't come to this realization until a year or will simply experience very little disturbance when they do. In the textbook cases, Lucy cries each time you put her down, then reaches for you and asks to be picked up again. The more you try to put her down—to help her focus on things other than you—the more upset she gets. Fortunately, this reaction is short-lived. When she requests your attention, you of course play with her or let her hold on to you. But if you've got to go, go—like it or not. Once Lucy realizes the separations aren't permanent, she'll learn not to worry about your departures and to welcome your smiling returns.

Fear of strangers also appears around the six-month mark. Lucy no longer smiles generously at everyone; instead, she bursts into tears at the first sight of someone who isn't an intimate. This is an important developmental phase: Lucy recognizes that not every adult with open arms and a smile is Mommy. The difficulty arises when grandparents or her father fall victim to this new wariness and suffer hurt feelings. If you have to leave her with someone she is uneasy about but whom you trust, do it. Upon your return you may even be disappointed to find that Lucy was perfectly happy with the now-former stranger after just a couple of minutes of crying. If you handle this phase with adult patience and no unnecessary emotion, it will pass within a few months.

Shaking

In Infants

Right after birth, when Lucy hears a loud noise, when you change her diaper, when you pick her up—in short, any time you disturb her—she shakes her arms and legs while extending her limbs in a wide motion that lasts a few seconds. Scientists believe that this is an archaic reflex dating back to our monkey ancestors and that it helped babies hang on as their mommies hopped from tree to tree. The *Moro reflex*, as it is called, is strong at birth, fades rapidly in the first few months, and persists as a fine trembling of the hands even at six months.

Lucy may develop another very cute little motion around eight months called *hand flapping*. When she's upset or scared she'll flap her fingers just as a flamenco dancer would click her castanets. This won't last too long, and you'll miss seeing it when she stops.

In Older Children

A slight shaking of the fingers is normal in kids of all ages. Ordinarily, the cause is hunger or, more precisely, low blood sugar caused by hunger. Beyond that, some children display a slight shaking of the fingers that comes and goes and has no clinical significance.

Sharing

See also | **Biting; Discipline and Boundaries; Hitting**

Why would a young toddler share anything? You never shared anything when you were Jimmy's age either. Young kids want everything, they want it now, and they want it to themselves. Early on, don't expect Jimmy to be gracious and offer to share toys, food, or his place on the coin-operated ride outside the supermarket. Not until the end of the second year does the concept of sharing and taking turns enter a child's mind. Attempting to force the idea too early puts unnecessary pressure on both children and parents, and it may even have the opposite effect.

When a toy should be shared, don't launch into a lengthy explanation about the appropriateness of sharing. Just say it once, and if Jimmy doesn't relinquish the toy, take it away. If that creates havoc, you may want to take the toy away from all of the kids in the group to eliminate any competitiveness. And if Jimmy or any other kids rebel against your ruling by launching into inappropriate behaviors, use the boundary setting described in our comprehensive DISCIPLINE AND BOUNDARIES entry. If you follow this simple approach, I guarantee Jimmy will learn very soon to compromise.

Shoes

See also | **Feet**

Buying the baby's first pair of shoes used to be an important ceremonial event. The whole family went to the store, and an expert salesman in a white coat offered wise counsel about fitting the perfect shoes. A pair with good ankle support came off the shelf, and Jimmy left the store looking even more adorable than when he came in, attempting to move his legs in his stiff new hightops.

Times have changed. These days, we know that when shoes are too rigid they interfere with a child's natural walk. At an early age, footwear need only protect the feet from sharp objects, cold, and heat. But barefoot is best; it increases contact with the ground and therefore improves balance. Consequently, the ideal shoes are soft enough not to interfere with that sensation.

Because Jimmy's tendons are flexible, don't be surprised to see his ankles droop in either direction when he starts walking. This will correct itself when the ankle muscles build up. Stiff shoes with superb ankle supports not only don't help, they also delay the strengthening of his muscles.

Siblings

See also | **Discipline and Boundaries**

After your third month of pregnancy, you decide to break the news to Jimmy. At first, he doesn't seem to care, although it amuses him when you or your husband point to your belly and say "baby." He is quite intrigued with the books you read him that portray big people with big bellies, people his size looking very happy, and even strange hairless new people who are smaller than he is. Several months later, you and your husband suddenly disappear for a few days, and Jimmy stays with grandma, a real treat for him, since he gets plenty of cookies. When you reappear, you have two new things: a noisy little creature who seems permanently affixed to your breast and a new train set for Jimmy. He looks at the train set for a while and then wanders over to the new creature. Within a few days, he notices that the new creature gets lots of attention when it screams, and he wonders if that would work for him too.

Bringing your new baby home is a joyful moment, at least until your older child starts pulling the baby's arm and twisting yours. Kids of any age feel slightly unsettled after the birth of a new sibling. This is due less to jealousy than to a change in routine. Anticipating their reactions will help the whole family deal with the transition more peacefully and smoothly.

At first, Jimmy doesn't mind and even enjoys having the new baby around. But fairly soon, the change in his routine upsets him. At times he's more excited than usual, or he has a harder time controlling his emotions. This also affects how he treats Lucy, and he oscillates between indifference, kindness, and an extreme kindness that is difficult to differentiate from aggression. In other words, while he notices how pleased you are when he pets her, he also notices the reaction he gets from you when he whacks her.

On average, second children arrive about two years after the first. Coincidentally, this is when the older child is in a rambunctious stage and needs his parents to set firm boundaries. Because of your fatigue, guilt, and distraction, Jimmy takes advantage of this new opportunity to push your buttons and drive you crazy. This is the perfect setup for future behavior problems and sibling rivalry if you lose sight of the fact that your main responsibility toward your older child is to deliver a mixture of love and discipline. As hard as it may be, you need to be even more stern and consistent as a parent during this phase.

WHAT TO DO

- **Be very matter-of-fact about the birth of the new baby.** Convey the message that the new arrival benefits everyone, including Jimmy.
- **Try to provide a routine that's like your old one.** Consistency will smooth over many of the problems.
- **Let him touch Lucy, even if he's a little rough.** Sometimes it's not clear if he's petting her or hitting her. But Lucy is tougher than she looks. And when he gets too rough, don't make a big deal, just separate the two of them without showing too much displeasure.
- **Spend extra time with Jimmy** but not in response to misbehavior.
- **Provide some one-on-one activity** without isolating him from the baby.
- **As soon as you can, put the two kids together to share the same room,** even if you have enough space to keep them separate. Cohabitation fosters bonding; the older one gets the sense of protecting the new baby, and the younger one gets a kick out of watching what the older one gets up to. And this way you won't have to divide your time between the two rooms and create jealousy and competitiveness.
- **Implement discipline if necessary.** Don't hesitate to call a time-out; a little bit of crying will help Jimmy lower his frustration.

WHAT NOT TO DO

- **Don't overprepare Jimmy for the birth.** Before age two and a half, he's too young to understand, and even if he does grasp the situation intellectually, that won't help him prepare emotionally.
- **Don't feel sorry for Jimmy;** there is really nothing to be sorry about.
- **Don't force the baby on him** or ask him incessantly if he loves his little sister. Let him develop his own bond.
- **Avoid coming home from the hospital with a bunch of new toys.** It may be sweet, but it could betray your own anxiety, and it puts unnecessary emphasis on his acceptance.
- **Don't give Jimmy attention in response to misbehavior.** Instead, give him attention when he expects it least.

Having a sibling is a blessing for the whole family. For Jimmy it's built-in entertainment and an additional source of affection. It also helps him grow up: As you devote less attention to him, you hover less and encourage his burgeoning independence.

REAL QUESTIONS FROM REAL PARENTS

What is the best time to have a sibling?
There is no good time or bad time. Many child-rearing experts talk about the importance of spacing siblings. This isn't particularly valid. Kids whose siblings follow close behind are just as happy as those with "space."

It's been a few months, and my older child is still hitting the baby once in a while. What should I do?
If Jimmy is still hitting Lucy, it's probably because you gave these episodes too much attention initially. I know it's hard not to overreact to an assault on your new baby, but the more upset you get, the more you'll feed this behavior. Treat this simply as an inappropriate behavior, just like throwing food or knocking over a vase. Give him a simple warning, and if he still disobeys, put him in his room for a few minutes. Then bring him back with no additional comment. By downplaying these events you'll diminish their frequency [**See:** Discipline and Boundaries].

Should I nurse the new baby in front of the older one?
Absolutely. Let Jimmy discover the facts of life, one of which is that a young baby needs to eat.

SIDS (Sudden Infant Death Syndrome)

See also | **Cosleeping; Sleeping Positions**

SIDS, or sudden infant death syndrome, is what we blame for the unexplained death of an otherwise perfectly healthy child at three or four months of age (on average). The causes of SIDS are unknown, and there may be multiple factors. The current leading theory focuses on a defect of the breathing center located in the brain; in some sense, it is thought, these children forget to breathe. Fortunately, this devastating event is rare and has become even rarer in recent years. Based on strong scientific evidence, child-care experts and physicians have cautioned parents against putting children face down to sleep. Back sleeping eliminates the pressure on the nose and mouth that could presumably induce smothering when the baby sleeps on his or her belly.

REAL QUESTIONS FROM REAL PARENTS

But isn't my baby much more comfortable on her belly?
Your baby is more comfortable in the position you get her used to. Put her on her back ten times, and she won't want to be on her belly.

Does it really make a difference?
SIDS is rare, but back sleeping has decreased the risk by half even though doctors don't really understand why. That's a huge decrease, especially when it comes to such a devastating event.

Other than back sleeping, what else can I do to prevent SIDS?
Limit the risk of breathing obstructions in the crib and elsewhere by removing fluffy pillows, stuffed animals, and so on. Also, avoid smoking around the baby; studies have found that secondhand smoke significantly increases the SIDS risk.

How about baby breathing monitors?
They have not been shown to decrease the occurrence of SIDS, but they're certainly responsible for increasing anxiety in parents. I don't recommend them for healthy infants.

When can I stop worrying?
By six months of age the risk becomes extremely low.

What if my baby is able to roll over onto her belly at an early age?
You can't spend the night flipping Lucy onto her back over and over. In any case, she'll probably arrive at this milestone at a stage when SIDS is extremely unlikely.

What are the risks involved in cosleeping?
Some reports claim that it does not affect the risk of SIDS. Some claim that it does, slightly. Personally, I feel it is entirely safe if there are no drugs or alcohol involved and if the parents are not heavy sleepers [**See:** Cosleeping].

What about pets?
The research does not show that pets increase the risk of SIDS [**See:** Pets].

Sign Language

Scientists are always trying to develop special languages to talk with dolphins and gorillas, to make Flipper and Koko understand human conversation through a series of clicks, whistles, and pictograms. Now some people are trying to do the same with babies, designing a sign-language technique specifically for communicating with infants. The rationale behind this? That if babies are grumpy, it's only because they're not adequately understood. This strikes me as comical. There must be some evolutionary reason why babies don't speak; maybe it's so they'll get frustrated with their limited communication skills and learn how to talk. In any case, even when babies do learn this new sign language, they appear to say roughly one thing: "Feed me!" Gee, who'd have guessed?

Sinusitis

See also | **Colds**

Sinusitis, or sinus infection, is an inflammation caused by a bacterial infection of the cavities within the facial bone. Contrary to what you may hear, this illness is quite rare. It is even rarer in younger children, for the simple reason that their sinus cavities are not yet fully formed and therefore cannot be infected. Sinusitis usually includes a significant fever and a thick, persistent nasal discharge in school-age children. Other possible complaints include headaches and a sense of fullness in the face, but these are not reliable symptoms in young kids. Your doctor will treat sinusitis with antibiotics.

Lingering colds with persistent mucus production are often mistaken for sinusitis and treated unnecessarily with antibiotics. This is not appropriate, even if the mucus turns green, which is normal at the end of a cold.

Sitting Up

See also | **Developmental Milestones**

Lucy will generally sit up steadily for the first time around seven months of age. The larger the baby, the more difficult it is; there's simply more mass to heave into a seated position. For this reason, chubby babies achieve this phase of development up to two months later than slimmer babies do.

Size

See also | **Growth Charts; Height; Overweight; Weight Concerns**

As a result of discriminatory cultural norms and prejudices, smaller children can be perceived as fragile, which often creates unnecessary concern. If Jimmy is lean, resist the impulse to fatten him up; this could create future psychological issues with food regulation, and it won't make him eat more anyway. You may want to pull out your baby pictures. I bet one of you was lean as a child, as this trait runs in families. Doctors or parents sometimes introduce high-calorie foods such as peanut butter or shakes as bulking supplements, but these may interfere with the kid's appetite for other, more nutritionally balanced foods.

A chubbier kid is also a healthy kid, as long as you're positive that the weight represents baby fat rather than the early results of a junk-food diet. If Jimmy is on the chunky side, assess the amount of junk food in his diet: foods like cookies, candy, juice, pasta, bread, pizza, potato chips, and sugared cereals. If you're supplying lots of these fattening foods and drinks, cut back. If not, God bless his big fat belly, and keep feeding him normally.

As kids grow up, their constitutions often change, sometimes in just a single year. Your pint-sized beanpole may turn into a very solid citizen, while a chubby kid who doesn't eat junk food can shed that baby fat and grow lean.

Skin Conditions in Infants

See also | **Eczema; Jaundice**

A slew of minor afflictions can ruin Lucy's looks for the first few months of life. Here is an inventory of the various rashes and skin conditions you may see before Lucy starts looking like the baby models in the magazines.

Dry Skin

As a rule, newborns always have dry skin. The epidermis comprises several different layers. In the inner layer, new skin is constantly being formed, while the outer layer is composed of the dead dry skin that is shed permanently. In utero, amniotic fluid keeps this dead skin hydrated so it has no opportunity to dry and peel off. After birth, it's a different story. With no more fluid around, this dead skin now really dries up and sloughs off, and babies can look like reptiles for the first couple of weeks. This dryness won't cause Lucy to suffer. No matter what you do, her skin will appear dry until this outer layer flakes off. A moisturizer will make it look better, but it will also delay the shedding process. Therefore, I recommend that you allow the process to run its course without applying any cream. Wait a few weeks, and it'll be over.

Erythema Toxicum

It's neither toxic nor painful. It's just a few red spots that appear on the face and torso right after birth (as opposed to infant acne, see below). Some spots have a clear liquid pimple in the center. No treatment is required, and these spots vanish spontaneously after a week or two.

Jaundice

You may see a yellow color on Lucy's skin and eyes in the first few days after birth. This is also self-resolving [**See:** Jaundice].

Stork Bites (aka Angel's Kisses)

As the myth goes, the stork's beak leaves a faint and diffuse redness on the back of a newborn's neck when she delivers the baby to you. In reality, these are temporary birthmarks that occur in half of all babies. The condition may also appear on the eyelids or forehead, where it is known as "salmon patches." Either will disappear within a few months.

Strawberry Patches

These birthmarks are much rarer than stork bites. They are intense, well-defined dark red patches that, as the name indicates, look like the surface of a strawberry. Typically the size of a coin, they can occur anywhere on the body, and may be present at birth or appear soon after. The size typically increases with age, stabilizes before the first year, and then decreases, eventually disappearing by age two or three. When they start receding, you'll notice a white area clearing in the center. Even on the face, where they're most noticeable, strawberry patches should be left alone to disappear spontaneously.

Mongolian Spots

This dark blue coloration on the buttocks looks like a large bruise. Sometimes the patch will extend onto the back. More commonly seen on pigmented skin, Mongolian spots disappear after a few years.

Blue Area at the Bridge of the Nose

This is a common concern for parents of fair-skinned babies. A blue coloration appears at the bridge of the nose, between the eyebrows. This is merely due to the veins that are showing under the skin, especially when the baby cries and the pressure makes them more apparent. Within months, the skin gets thicker, and the veins show up less.

Infant Acne

The hormones that are passed in utero to the baby stimulate the newborn's skin and produce the equivalent of hormone-driven teenage acne. Unlike teenagers, babies don't talk back, and their acne won't last long. The process usually shows up after a couple of weeks, peaks at four to six weeks, and decreases, so that by two months it's mostly gone. Acne can be intense; sometimes the face and torso are covered with red areas and pimples. Since a hormonal process is causing the breakout, nothing really helps. Skin cream will only make the whole thing look shinier and more unattractive. And remember, infant acne has positively nothing to do with the maternal diet while breast feeding.

Seborrheic Dermatitis

This characteristic pink and flaky rash sits between and around the eyebrows. A common accompaniment to infant acne, it's also caused by a hormonal process and resolves with no treatment after a few months.

Heat Rash or Prickly Heat

This rash will appear on the face, neck, and diaper area in the form of red and sometimes pimply skin. It results from sweating, and it comes and goes with warm weather. There's no need to do anything about it.

Sleep

See also | **Cosleeping; Family Bed; Napping; Separation Anxiety**

Sleep or the lack of it, is one of the greatest concerns of new parents. After "Is my baby healthy?" the second most commonly asked question is "When is my baby going to sleep through the night?" The answer is (*drum roll, please*) . . . never.

Sleep is not a continuous process. Try to remember how you slept last night. At the end of each of your nocturnal cycles, you woke up (at least five or six times per night), made yourself cozy, rolled onto your other side, and fell back asleep. The same thing happens for Lucy, except that for her, getting cozy means sucking. This starts right after birth. When Lucy is a newborn, every time she rises from slumber, you either feed her or rock her, which puts her to sleep again. After the first ten times, she begins to expect you to soothe her every time she wakes up at the end of her sleep cycle. When do people make the transition from being soothed to sleep by mom to being able to soothe themselves? That's the ten-thousand-dollar question. But when it does happen, that's when Lucy will "sleep through the night."

The First Few Weeks

For the first few days after birth, don't even think about sleeping at night. Lucy is getting used to you, and you're getting used to her. Predictable sleep patterns really aren't a priority at this point. Very young babies seem not to have a sense of day or night, or, even worse, the cycle sometimes seems reversed. Of course, it's not reversed from Lucy's point of view. She just left a pitch-black environment with no cycle to speak of. Until she gets a few weeks older, there is little you can do to keep her up during the day so that she'll sleep more at night. Any attempts to keep her awake will only agitate her. In the meantime, try to sleep when Lucy sleeps, whether she's in your bed or not. If you're breast feeding, your best bet for getting your beauty rest is to learn to nurse on your side while you're half asleep. You won't even need to burp her, since she'll be eating more slowly and therefore swallowing much less air as she nurses. As a rule, never wake her up to feed at night if she's sleeping peacefully.

The First Couple of Months

This period is your best opportunity to make your baby a night sleeper. Here's how.

After a couple of weeks, Lucy is sleeping more at night than during the day. Each waking period ends with a feeding, and nursing is as much about soothing as it is about nutrition. This is more pronounced in breast-fed children, thanks to the physical intimacy of nursing. As time goes on, you've become more accustomed to Lucy's temperament and needs, and she is getting used to the fact that when she has a need you will tend to her.

In the first couple of months, I suggest that you not jump up at her slightest peep and that you ignore her minor whining so she can soothe herself back to sleep. That means letting her wiggle, fuss, or suck on her fist for a while. If she manages to fall back to sleep without your help even once, she's learned the basis of self-soothing, and it will happen more naturally the second time. Of course, if her requests become more persistent, you'll have to feed her.

You can practice this laissez-faire method even if you're cosleeping [**See:** Cosleeping]. While the average parent naturally reaches this point of adjustment around two months after birth, others come to it earlier, and some are still jumping up at every whim, long past the first birthday. Wherever you stand is fine, as long as you understand the implications.

In observing family dynamics, I was puzzled as to why some babies would sleep through the night and others wouldn't. I learned that the parents who were a little less responsive to late-night fussing always had kids who were good sleepers, while the jumpy folks had kids who would wake up repeatedly at night until it became unbearable. For example, when a mother has three kids, it is rarely a question whether or not her third will sleep through the night early on. The family has learned when to react to a fussy baby and when to let her soothe herself back to sleep.

Over the years, I've come to recommend this somewhat laissez-faire attitude regarding nighttime behavior as soon as the shock of birth has passed. This approach is validated by the hundreds of families I see whose babies sleep effortlessly through the night. These parents never have to resort to the ugly "let the baby cry it out" approach described below, and many of them don't even know they've missed out on one of infancy's most nerve-wracking problems. As they say: An ounce of prevention . . .

At Four Months

By now, if Lucy isn't sleeping through the night, I am sorry to report that she's very unlikely to do so on her own. Sooner or later, there's going to be a struggle. You probably already sense that although Lucy eats at night, she's less interested in the food than in the soothing experience it provides.

If you enjoy the cuddling or at least don't mind the fact that Lucy wakes up at night, please skip to the next age group below. If, on the other hand, you feel sleep-deprived and want to handle the situation, I've broken the process down into three simple steps:

1 | Put Lucy in her crib at a reasonable hour (while she's still awake, if possible). The best time is when both of you have had a chance to interact with her for a while after work.

2 | After the bath and the songs, kiss her good night.

3 | Come back the next morning at 7:00 A.M.

I have just heard the collective gasp of thousands of parents: "Are you out of your mind?!" Bear with me. I know this sounds drastic, but it's the only way to get Lucy into the habit of soothing herself rather than relying on you. It's true that the first few days she'll soothe herself to sleep by crying, but eventually she'll sleep just like, well, a baby. The first night she'll cry two to three times, for twenty to thirty minutes (you'll feel like crying too); the second night she'll cry less; and the third even less. By the fourth night, you're home free. Done.

REAL QUESTIONS FROM REAL PARENTS

What if I can't do it?

Again, if you don't mind waking up, then you don't have a problem, and Lucy doesn't either. But as much as I'd like to tell you her sleep patterns will get better, trust me and trust my experience, they won't change on their own.

How long can I let her cry?

Until she falls asleep. It can take an awfully long time. If you last only twenty minutes, you're teaching her to cry for twenty minutes before she gets her soothing.

Can I at least go touch the baby or kiss her, even if I don't feed her?
If you do, she'll see it as a tease, become more upset, and cry even longer because she won't understand why you won't feed her. Babies know nothing of moderation.

How do I know the baby isn't hungry?
She is hungry. But she does not need to eat. After any three- or four-hour fasting period, she'll be hungry. You're hungry in the middle of the night, too; it's just that you learn not to eat because it's good for your belly to take a rest. Well, it's good for hers too.

What about a little water at least?
Only if you want to wake up every couple of hours to give her water.

What about a pacifier?
Same thing.

Would it help if I gave her cereal before bed?
It's a myth that porridge before bedtime helps a baby sleep, since it will be digested in the few hours to come. The same goes for topping off a feeding with a bottle of formula.

Can I feed the baby to sleep?
You can, but it's better not to. Consistency is important, so why would you nurse Lucy to the edge of sleep at 8:00 P.M. but not, say, at 2:00 A.M.? It's a habit you'll have to struggle to overcome, and since you're doing so much struggling as it is, you might as well struggle completely and be done with it. Also, if you're going to struggle, I assure you that things will look much more dramatic to you at 2:00 A.M. than they will at 8:00 P.M. And most of the crying is done early on.

How long will Lucy sleep at this age?
Ten to twelve hours. Straight.

Without eating?
Without eating.

Can I go to her early in the morning?
Again, if you're going to struggle, struggle all the way. Babies are notorious believers in the take-a-mile-if-given-an-inch philosophy. If you give Lucy attention at five-thirty, she'll start looking for you at five. If you slide back to five, she'll test you at four. And so forth. Hold to the schedule, on the other hand, and she'll learn to put herself back to sleep in the morning hours.

Aren't I traumatizing the baby?

At seven in the morning, you'll be surprised to find a happy, smiling baby who loves you and loves to see you. And you'll be rested and happy too. More to the point, your own smiles during the day won't be as forced when you are no longer a zombie.

How about nap time?

Don't worry about nap time. Once Lucy learns to sleep at night, daytime napping will be a breeze.

Is it really this easy?

As I said, after a few days of this, Lucy will sleep through the night. And if you wake up, it will only be because you're surprised that you're sleeping so well. But make no mistake: Be prepared for three or four brutally hard nights. It is never easy to let your baby cry. But once you start, stick to your guns; if you give in halfway through the process, you'll only make it worse.

How do you know all of this?

I learned the hard way. With Abeline, our first daughter, my wife and I took turns on 2:00 A.M. lullaby duty. I spent many nights walking around the loft with Abeline in my arms, singing any French lullaby that my sleep-starved brain could conjure. I wasn't sleeping well at home and even less at work when I was on call. And I was probably just like you, thinking that if she woke up, she was calling us. At ten months, we were so exhausted from soothing her that we finally let her cry it out. Within a couple of days she was sleeping through the night. You'd think we'd have learned our lesson, but we hadn't. With our second daughter, Nora, we made the same mistakes (tending to her every nighttime peep) and later resolved it the same way. It only took us six months to wise up that time. With Fanny, our third one, we let her cry herself to sleep early, just like I told you, and it worked like a charm. She's a perfectly secure little kid who can fall asleep fine on her own. By contrast, Abeline, who got the most soothing before sleeping, still needs her head rubbed every once in a while to get to sleep, just like in the good old days.

I've also learned from the hundreds of sleepless parents to whom I've suggested this method. They initially look at me like I have two heads, but at the next month's visit, they show up with broad smiles and tell me, "That was torture for a few days, but we're so happy we did it!"

At Eight Months

If Lucy doesn't sleep through the night at eight months, she probably spends a good part of the night in your bed, and you most likely breast-feed her a few times a night. You know she feeds at night more for the soothing than for the nourishment, but it's much easier for you and you find it kind of sweet. If you're still happy with this arrangement, skip ahead to the next sleep section. If you're exhausted, though, prepare for action.

Before doing anything to help your eight-month-old sleep, you should take into consideration that at this age, babies are going through what we call separation anxiety [**See:** Separation and Stranger Anxiety]. At four months, when Lucy didn't see you, she had no clue where the heck you were, and she didn't even know you'd left; she had no concept that you're a person separate from her. At eight months, Lucy has figured out not only that you're a separate person but also that you can leave, which troubles her greatly. So if you leave her to cry at night, she knows perfectly well that you're in the other room, and she could feel abandoned. Also, she'll explore what brings you back: not just crying but shrieking, throwing things, even vomiting. (Yes, vomiting; babies that young can upset themselves so much that they vomit.) As a result, you must take a more subtle approach. Here are the instructions for an eight-month-old:

1 | After your normal evening routine, put Lucy to bed at a reasonable hour, after you've both had time to interact with her.

2 | After a few good-night kisses, go out the door without breast feeding her.

3 | When she cries, let her, for ten minutes. Then come back and talk to her for thirty seconds. That's all, just talking. Then leave. No holding, no nursing. The only purpose is to show her that you have not vanished. If she is indeed vomiting, just clean up matter-of-factly and move on.

4 | Repeat the exact same process until she falls asleep. This may take an hour or more.

5 | Each time she wakes up during the course of the night, repeat the same cycle.

6 | In the morning, pick her up and begin the day.

7 | The next night, let her crying jags go a little longer, say, fifteen minutes. Each night, increase that amount of time; eventually, she'll learn to sleep for longer stretches.

Within a few days, Lucy will be sleeping through the night. This process is what people refer to as the *Ferber method*, or *Ferberizing* a baby, and while it's down and dirty, it works.

Warning: If you use this method inconsistently, you not only decrease its chance of success, but you also make things more difficult for you and Lucy later on. She won't know what to believe, and rather than being a source of consistent behavior, you will be an erratic and unpredictable comfort who appears without announcement and without rules.

At One Year of Age

Now the real trouble starts. If Jimmy is not sleeping through the night at a year, you have turned into a mechanical comfort machine and a good one too. You've become very proficient at feeding or soothing him back to sleep at the end of each sleep cycle without too much effort. But unless you still enjoy the ritual, I urge you to do something for yourself. Bypass Ferberizing, since separation anxiety is no longer an issue, and go straight to the cold-turkey method:

1 | After Jimmy's bath and a book, put him to bed.

2 | Kiss him good night. Say "See you tomorrow."

3 | Don't go back in.

Same thing here: After a few nights of that regimen the problem is solved. This is even more brutal than it would have been at four months, because Jimmy can cry much more loudly and even call your name.

Eighteen Months and Beyond

When a toddler is still not sleeping through the night, I rarely find parents who are happy about waking up for soothing duty. Some parents deliberately choose this option as part of a "family bed" philosophy, however, which I totally respect [**See:** Family Bed]. But for those who don't desire such an arrangement, the longer you wait to enforce a sleep regimen, the harder it gets. At this point, Jimmy is probably in your bed for a good part of the night. You should have no doubt that if you're nursing him back to sleep, hunger is no longer the issue; it's all about soothing. And while it may be cute for a two-year-old to end up in your bed night after night, it could be embarrassing when Jimmy turns nine. Also, be aware that nursing a toddler throughout the night often leads to dental decay [**See:** Tooth Rot].

If you want to break the cycle, here's what you need to do:

1 | Put Jimmy into bed after the story, the other story, the kiss, and the last kiss.

2 | Explain that there is a new regimen. Tell him that if he gets out of bed, you're going to bring him right back in. Tell him that the second time he comes out, you're going to close the door or even lock it if he gets out. (By doing this, you're simply staying consistent with your message.)

3 | Follow through on the promise until he falls asleep.

4 | Every time he wakes up, repeat the same cycle. You won't have to close the door any longer, because he won't attempt an escape now that he knows the consequences.
5 | If you live in a multiunit building, you may want to warn those neighbors most likely to overhear the screams. It may seem embarrassing now, but it beats having to explain it all to the cops later.

After two or three days of that routine, the hard part will be done, even if you find him asleep on the floor in his room. But this is no party. Jimmy will scream loudly. To make matters worse, he's old enough to shriek half-sentences and use your name. Again, cry yourself to sleep if you have to, but stay the course. In three days, you will have broken the cycle.

New-Onset Sleep Problems

If a child of any age who's been sleeping well suddenly develops a sleeping problem, fear not. This is common, and it can happen at any age. Suppose Lucy is teething, has a cold, suffers from jet lag, has a bad dream, or goes through any minor upset. Now suppose you pamper her a little more than usual, to alleviate her discomfort. You give her a tour of the house on your hip, you cuddle her more than usual, or you put her in your bed and get cozy with her. This is all natural.

Before you know it, however, she's back to the one-month-old stage again, unable to soothe herself back to sleep. It's unbelievable how quickly this can happen! If you find yourself in this situation, I suggest you reset Lucy's clock as soon as you can to avoid creating a bigger problem. When the triggering event has settled (the pain is gone, the jet lag has waned, the teeth have erupted, etc.), let Lucy whine in her own bed and get back to sleep on her own the way she used to do (see above, under the appropriate age group).

In Summary

Now that you've reached the end of this lesson plan, I hope you can see the wisdom of encouraging Lucy to learn how to soothe herself to sleep early on with the laissez-faire method. Don't be fooled. Kids' sleep issues won't improve on their own. You risk sleep deprivation, guilt, and anger. I've seen parents strain and even destroy their relationship with each other as a result of these issues. If you deal with sleep issues consistently and early, however, you'll profit from your efforts for years.

Sleeping Positions

See also | **Cosleeping; Rolling Over; SIDS; Sleeping; Tummy Time**

Back sleeping is safer. It has decreased the SIDS rate by at least 50 percent. Given these data, the medical profession should be ashamed of having recommended for years that babies sleep on their bellies; the failure to issue a warning sooner cost many infants their lives. Side sleeping has not been studied adequately, but the few studies I have seen suggest that it's not as safe as back sleeping.

REAL QUESTIONS FROM REAL PARENTS

What if my baby is more comfortable on her belly?
This is a common misperception. Lucy becomes most comfortable in the position she experiences the most. Lying on the back is not only safer, it also gives her more visual and manual stimulation.

Can I still put my baby on her stomach once in a while if I supervise?
You can, but there's no reason to do so. She would rather look at you, and contrary to what you sometimes read, "tummy time" is unnecessary for development.

When can I safely put my baby on her stomach?
Lucy will learn to roll over by about five to six months. Once this happens, worrying about turning her back over every time it happens is pointless. It's out of your control.

Snoring and Sleep Apnea

See also | **Adenoids; Tonsils**

Snoring is common in kids, and it's not a problem in itself; it's usually caused by either large adenoids or large tonsils, both of which begin to shrink as early as five years of age, which helps resolve the problem. However, when the snoring includes pauses in breathing that last for more than five seconds and occur several times a night, it could indicate sleep apnea. During these periods of breathlessness, the heart pumps harder to deliver oxygen, which can lead to strain and even enlargement of the heart. The quality of sleep also suffers. If Jimmy experiences episodes of sleep apnea, he'll wake up very tired each morning. If you notice these long pauses in his breathing while he sleeps, mention them to his doctor. The treatment may require surgical removal of the tonsils or adenoids, which will make the apnea subside rapidly.

Note that in kids, sleep apnea has nothing to do with being overweight, as it does in adults.

Soap

See also | **Diaper Rash; Washing a Baby**

Much controversy surrounds the use of soap. Recent studies have shown that soap's antibacterial action contributes to the global growth of especially resistant germs. Still, soap companies have a vested interest in peddling obsessive cleanliness, so they cultivate our obsession with soap. For a baby, soap is just pointless. Babies aren't dirty, and to the extent that they come into contact with dirt, washing with plain water is absolutely fine. Soap removes natural skin oil, which can in turn lead to eczema and diaper rashes.

Sore Throat

See also | **Flu Herpangina; Mononucleosis; Scarlet Fever; Strep Throat**

Sore throats have many causes, including the famous strep bacterium, mononucleosis, and herpangina. Flus and colds can also irritate the throat with repetitive coughing. Whatever the cause of the sore throat, pain medication will relieve it. The only sore throat that warrants antibiotic treatment is strep throat, which can be diagnosed by your doctor with a rapid test.

Soy

See also | **Milk, Cow's**

Fish can contain mercury. Meat can contain hormones. Fruit can contain pesticides. What's a health-conscious parent to do? These days, even soy is controversial. Some studies say the plant estrogens in soy protect against breast cancer, while other studies say those same plant estrogens induce breast cancer. The controversy also stems from the fact that most soy has been genetically modified to increase productivity and resistance to fungi and pests, although toxicity from genetically engineered foods has not been demonstrated conclusively.

Controversies aside, soy is basically a good nutrient. It contains lots of protein, and, although this is not a relevant concern for young kids, it helps decrease cholesterol levels. Soy's high protein content makes it a good meat substitute for vegetarian diets, and babies can eat tofu just as soon as solid foods are introduced. The main drawback to soy is that it doesn't contain much calcium. But that mineral is found in many other foods, such as yogurt, cheese, broccoli, waffles, cereals, calcium-fortified orange juice, and even similarly fortified soy milk. Soy formula has the same nutritional value as dairy-based formula. As for soy milk, you can give it to infants from ten months on, just like cow's milk.

Speech Impediments

See also | **Language Acquisition and Late Talking**

Some young kids speak happily and often, but because of a twist of the tongue they may be unable to pronounce certain words or sounds correctly. For example, Jimmy says "lellow" instead of "yellow." This is a normal part of speech development, and these little variations and idiosyncrasies can last until a child is five or six. They almost always disappear on their own. These twists have less to do with the anatomy of his tongue or palate than with the way he moves his tongue. But don't spend hours analyzing how he moves it, because that's the only way he'll do it for now. If Jimmy has one of these little tongue twists, don't correct the mispronunciation, because he will become more self-conscious. Just speak clearly. Hearing the correct sounds will help him reproduce them when he is more apt. For the same reason, speech therapy won't help, at least not yet.

When Jimmy starts going to school, he'll rapidly learn correct pronunciation from a community of peers. His strongest incentive to enunciate correctly will come when his new best friend turns to him and says, "Huh?" Just being in school with other kids may help him overcome this minor impairment. If Jimmy's pronunciation problems don't clear up, you can consider speech therapy after a year or two of elementary school (or before, if he exhibits mounting frustration).

Spitting Up

See also | **Reflux; Vomiting**

A very normal process for a young baby, spitting up occurs because the muscle that keeps food contained in the stomach is not yet fully developed. Spitting up may be a sign of overfeeding if it happens frequently or in combination with vomiting. Burping a baby doesn't decrease spitting up, and if you're too insistent, it may even make it worse by increasing the pressure on Lucy's belly.

Some babies spit up much more than others, and at the end of the spectrum are those who have what we call *reflux*, a condition in which the stomach muscles are so loose that they can't keep food down. This initially causes spitting up and evolves into vomiting. But remember, the two are quite distinct. As a rule, spit-up lands on your shoulder, and vomit lands on the floor.

Splinters

You should worry less about the actual splinter than about the damage you can cause by acting as an unlicensed surgeon. Generally, it's better to leave splinters in—especially the small ones—than to dig them out. Let the body do its job; in the majority of cases, the splinter will be pushed out or disintegrate within a few days. Attempts at extraction can increase inflammation and the risk of infection. If it's a big splinter and it looks ready to come out, you might be able to remove it with tweezers. Otherwise, your doctor will judge whether it's worth digging for, and he'll do so in a sterile fashion.

Removed or not, splinters bear a small risk of infection, which can be prevented with warm soaks and topical antibiotics. If you see increasing redness at the site, along with pus and swelling, it may require medical attention for possible drainage or an oral antibiotic.

Sterilization

Lucy may be cute, but she's hardly clean, given the various excreta she produces. As a result, there's no need to sterilize anything around your house just because she may come into contact with it. For the same reason, doctors no longer recommend bottle sterilization, at any age. Mothers who are nursing certainly don't sterilize their breasts at each feeding, even if some milk stays on the nipple. The milk sugar and the skin form a perfect growth medium for bacteria. Doesn't seem to bother Lucy!

Stimulation

See also | **Day Care**

"Lucy, look at the birdy in the tree! He says twee, twee, twee, we're so pretty! Say 'My name is Lucy!' Say 'Hi, birdies!' Now say 'Bye-bye, birdies!' We're going to tell daddy we saw some birdies, and we also saw a doggy who said 'Woof, woof!' Big doggy, right Lucy? And then we went to the . . ."

Stimulation is important, but you should offer it organically and normally; periods of playing and laughing should alternate naturally with periods of peace and quiet. At the newborn and infant stages, many parents wonder what kind of stimulation they should provide and may even feel uneasy with moments of silence. Some books recommend a kind of forced stimulation to raise IQ levels, but I doubt they do anything more than introduce a kind of unnatural interaction between parents and kids. You want Lucy to be smart? Just be your usual giggly self. And if you don't feel like giggling, that's okay too. You don't have to talk, sing, or entertain constantly. Add a little kissing and hugging to the mix and hope for the best. You want Lucy to be well coordinated? Just tickle her, roll around with her, give her a ride on your shoulders, and have fun. There's no need to make her raise her back muscles, teach her how to sit just so, and so forth, like some of the books suggest. She'll learn coordination on her own.

As far as toys for new babies go, you can buy plenty of fancy rattles or mobiles at your local museum gift shop. However, you'll notice that Lucy can also remain transfixed by your ceiling fan for a full half hour. Those educational videos targeted at babies are fine as long as you remain clear about their purpose: They give you the time to remember that you actually have an IQ, but they probably won't affect Lucy's.

If you have extra energy to spare, I suggest you store it preciously for the moments when you'll have to read her book to her for the fifth time, to run after her for hours, to sing the same song over and over, and to look up the answers to all her many "whys."

Stomach Bugs

See also | **Diarrhea; Stools; Vomiting**

Besides the drawings, clay works, and other crafts that Jimmy brings home from his nursery school, you should also expect him to bring back a few stomach bugs. Rampant in day-care centers, especially in the spring and fall, stomach bugs are viral infections of the intestine that cause nausea, vomiting, and diarrhea. In children, a bug typically starts with a sudden onset of vomiting, possibly followed by diarrhea. Fever, either high or low, may also be present. Bacteria or parasites can also be responsible for stomach bugs, although less frequently than viruses, and they can produce even more severe symptoms. The main concern with all types of stomach bugs is loss of fluid to vomiting or diarrhea. Younger children especially can become dehydrated very quickly (see below for tips on how to prevent or cure its ill effects).

As far as how your darling might pick up these bugs, let's just say that in medical terms it goes by the poetic name of *feco-oral* or *oro-fecal transmission.*

Vomiting from a Stomach Virus

Vomiting can be quite violent, especially at the onset of the illness. At first, food comes out, but soon there is no more food, only a thin green bile. In general, vomiting won't last for more than twenty-four hours, especially if the fluid is replaced. Even more than diarrhea, vomiting can cause dehydration.

In Infants

Stomach viruses are rare in infants, since tiny tots don't attend nursery school, but when a virus does strike (possibly brought home by an older sibling), vigilance is the key. An infant, especially a young one, can become very dehydrated after just a few hours of vomiting. Keep in mind that other causes of vomiting, such as blockage of the intestine, may be mistaken for a stomach virus.

If Lucy suddenly vomits on more than one occasion (and if it's real vomiting instead of just a little spitting up), you should continue to feed her breast milk or formula in small amounts, and call your doctor for advice.

In Older Infants and Children

With older kids, vomiting can usually be handled at home with simple measures. The goal is to prevent dehydration in the first twenty-four hours by replacing fluids. If you manage to replenish the liquids he's losing, Jimmy's body will do the rest and build its defenses to banish the viral intruder.

WHEN TO WORRY

- **If the vomiting persists for more than twenty-four hours,** especially if it remains intense.
- **If the tiniest amount of fluid makes Jimmy vomit.**
- **If there are signs of dehydration. If Jimmy becomes dehydrated,** he'll appear tired and pale. His eyes will barely stay open, and he'll produce very little urine. These signs indicate that oral rehydration isn't working. You should go to the doctor's office or the hospital so Jimmy can receive intravenous fluids.

WHEN NOT TO WORRY

- **If Jimmy remains active.**
- **If the vomiting recurs once or twice after subsiding for a day or two.** This may indicate that you have been too quick to reintroduce foods that are a little tough on the tummy, such as pizza, despite Jimmy's encouraging cravings.

WHAT TO DO

- **Give Jimmy the tiniest amount of liquid he will tolerate without vomiting,** but give it almost continuously until the vomiting has settled. Use an eyedropper if you have to, and go sloooowly. Too much volume will distend and irritate the intestine, and that will trigger more vomiting.
- **As far as the type of liquid, you can use any soft drink** (cola, ginger ale, sports drink) diluted by half with water and served at room temperature. Commercial rehydration solutions such as Pedialyte are expensive and not really any more effective than sodas at preventing dehydration.
- **For Lucy, you can use small quantities of breast milk or formula** diluted with twice as much water. If she vomits more than a couple of times, switch her to clear fluids, just as you would an older child.
- **Give only fluid until at least six hours after the vomiting ends.** You can then start reintroducing very bland solid foods, such as crackers or dry cereal. Again, go very slowly. If Jimmy tolerates food, you can creep back toward a regular diet. If at any time vomiting begins again, go back to the fluid replacement as explained above.

WHAT NOT TO DO

- **Don't use plain water.** You need to replace minerals, salts, and sugars, along with the water.
- **Don't reintroduce solid foods too quickly.**
- **Don't give cow's milk or full-strength formula** until the vomiting has subsided.
- **Don't use antivomiting suppositories.** They're inefficient and potentially dangerous.

In most cases, vomiting will last for a day or so and then subside. It could be followed by diarrhea, which entails another set of problems [**See:** Below].

Diarrhea from a Stomach Virus

Diarrhea may follow vomiting or appear on its own. It can vary from a few loose stools to very watery stools [See: Stools].

In Infants

Diarrhea is hard to define here, since young infants can normally have up to ten very runny poops per day. A greater frequency than that could represent diarrhea, especially if the constituency is very runny. Since the very young are at greater risk of dehydration, offer small amounts of breast milk or formula, and call your doctor for advice.

In Children

Diarrhea following a stomach virus is messy but usually not serious, though you may be surprised by how long the loose stools persist. Diaper rash is the most common inconvenience. Compared to vomiting, diarrhea rarely causes worrisome dehydration, but there's still a risk.

WHEN **TO WORRY**

- **If there's blood or mucus in the diarrhea**
- **If the diarrhea is extremely frequent** (more than eight times daily)
- **If there are signs of dehydration** [See: Above]
- **If there is a persistent high fever (over 102°F)**

Any of these symptoms could indicate a more virulent bacterial infection or viral strain, which would require medical attention.

WHEN **NOT TO WORRY**

- **When the diarrhea lasts.** This is more the rule than the exception. It can take up to a month after a stomach virus for the stools to return to a normal consistency. This does not mean that the virus is still present; rather, it takes time for the intestine to heal and be able to reabsorb water. Stool analysis or cultures have no benefits, since the infection is gone. Just have patience.

WHAT **TO DO**

- **Feed Jimmy whatever you would normally,** but skip the citrus and acidic vegetables like tomatoes. High-bulk diets have no real value, and since it's going to last for a while, you might as well be feeding him real foods.

▶ **Prevent outbreaks of diaper rash with naked time when practical,** and take the other preventive measures described in the **DIAPER RASH** entry.

For a few days after the vomiting or diarrhea, Jimmy's appetite will usually decrease, and you may even see some of his ribs showing. It could be a while before he goes back to eating with his old enthusiasm and regains the weight he's just lost. If you pressure him to eat, you could end up with a picky eater or a child who overindulges in sweets and starches. If you don't, I promise you that this low-appetite phase will be followed by a period when he'll be voracious, wolfing down everything you put in front of him and calling for more. At that point, you'll see the spaces between his ribs fill in.

Stools

See also | **Constipation; Diarrhea**

Warning: This chapter is not for the faint of heart. It contains foul language and graphic descriptions.

The First Few Days

The first stools are called *meconium*, which is the content of the fetal intestine. Meconium is a thick green substance that the baby passes during birth or shortly after. As Lucy feeds, she'll start producing regular stools. The number of stools at this age can vary and does not give an accurate indication of how well she is feeding. In rare instances, even if a newborn is fed appropriately, you may not see any stools or meconium. If this lack persists over five days, and especially if there is projectile vomiting, the intestinal system could be blocked, which would require medical attention.

The First Few Months

Number

The number of stools varies with age. Initially, the average is one stool after each feeding; over the next few months, the frequency declines. However, variation is so common that these guidelines are largely useless. One infant could have no poops for ten days. Another could produce ten a day. To complicate things, formula-fed babies tend to produce fewer stools than breast-fed babies.

If you see no stools for many days, that does not necessarily indicate a large internal accumulation. Instead, Lucy may just be entirely absorbing the milk, thus producing little waste. As long as there is no belly distension and no vomiting, you don't have to administer laxatives such as prune juice or water; this is not constipation [See: Constipation].

More than ten stools daily could mean diarrhea caused by a stomach virus or, more rarely, intestinal malabsorption. You should run these symptoms by your doctor.

Form and Color

- Watery and even explosive stools are good because they flow smoothly and painlessly. They are often merely the result of undigested excess milk that comes out the other end almost unaffected by its time in the intestine.
- Greenish stools are good, even if they are usually also the result of slight overfeeding (a little too much food is better than not enough). These also represent extra milk that has emerged essentially undigested.
- Poops that are yellow and seedy (featuring small particles that resemble sesame seeds) are good; they fit the textbook description of breast-feeding stools.
- Brown and soft stools are good; they represent a normal variant of breast-milk stools or, more likely, a formula by-product.
- The one case that's not so good and requires attention is when a baby's stool resembles an adult stool: brown and hard. This could be a reaction to extra iron in the formula or, in rare cases, a baby's predisposition to constipation [See: Constipation]. If you're using a formula reinforced with iron, try one without it, since that mineral is not absolutely necessary in formula.

Got all that? Good. Now be prepared to see, at any moment, without any warning, changes in the color, consistency, and frequency of Lucy's poops, as her dietary habits and digestive system evolve.

After Solid Foods Are Introduced

The introduction of solid food firms up the stool's consistency, especially if Lucy starts getting too much starch (such as cereals or potato). The number of poops will also decrease steadily.

In Toddlers

At this age, stools become more regular, averaging one to two each day. Constipation can crop up, especially in the pasta eaters. Alternatively, more frequent bowel movements could mean Jimmy is consuming too much juice or fruit, which have a laxative effect and can give him the runs.

Stool Retention

See also | **Constipation; Toilet Training**

Stool retention is a psychological condition that affects toddlers and young children, particularly boys. Distinct from constipation—again, stool retention is a psychological condition rather than a physiological one—it tends to perpetuate itself, because the parental attention that it generates makes matters worse.

If you haven't been affected by stool retention, it can sound like a joke. What child refuses to go to the bathroom? Trust me, this isn't funny. The problem can take on almost operatic dimensions, as the entire family ends up obsessed with the kid's bowel movements. It's usually associated with constipation or high-pressure toilet training, which further reinforces the retention problem.

How does it start? Well, at the infant stage, defecating is relatively effortless and painless. Then the poops naturally get bulkier, and therefore pooping becomes slightly more painful and involved. This condition is even more pronounced in modern societies, thanks to the excessive starch in the average toddler's diet. The pain of defecation is followed by relief; most kids remember only the relief, but some kids are particularly sensitive to this new pain and become afraid of defecating. They delay pooping to the point of urgency, which only increases their pain. The next time they have to produce a stool, they grow even more apprehensive, holding it in even longer. That's how the cycle starts.

Parental intervention now comes into play. You naturally don't want to see Jimmy in pain, so you try to help out any way you can: encouraging him to push, massaging his belly, giving him juice or another sweet substance as a laxative. This can actually worsen retention by rewarding the problem with retention. Urgency leads to pain, which leads to more urgency, which leads to retention, which leads to more retention. As time goes on, Jimmy will monumentalize the pain and fear of defecation, and these worries can persist for years if you don't break the cycle.

As I have said, children with constipation are more prone to retention, as are children who are subjected to toilet-training pressure. In brief, anything that makes a child hyperaware of his own defecation can contribute. If you deal with the cycle reasonably at this stage, it should go away. Otherwise, you, too, may be in for a long and painful process.

How to Prevent Stool Retention

- When Jimmy first experiences discomfort with bulky stools, let him figure out that he will have to endure some pain, either then or later, since there's nothing you can do to make things better for him.
- Do not pressure him during toilet training [See: Toilet Training].
- Prevent constipation, which usually means avoiding bread, pasta, crackers, and dry cereal. My experience is that high-fiber starches won't help kids, because they're still bulky [See: Constipation].

How to Treat Stool Retention

If you are past the preventive stage and your child is already experiencing mild or moderate stool retention, it's a bit of a challenge to reverse the cycle. To be successful, you need to remove yourself completely from this issue. Your involvement only validates his fears. Since you can't defecate for him, stool retention is his problem, not yours.

WHAT TO DO

- **First, alleviate Jimmy's constipation if he is prone to it.** Keep the starch intake to a minimum. To help soften stools, your doctor will prescribe a temporary laxative, but as soon as the problem subsides, taper off the medication to avoid developing a dependence.
- **The next step is to ignore the problem.** I know this is difficult. You may fear the intestine cannot take the strain of the distension, but rest assured, when Jimmy has to poop there is one outlet available and Jimmy knows perfectly well what to do to relieve the pain; he just has to overcome his fear. If you aren't hovering or asking questions, he'll notice that the drama has disappeared and start wondering why he made such a big deal in the first place.

WHAT NOT TO DO

- **Don't schedule Jimmy to sit on the potty daily.** If he doesn't have to go, he won't be able to, and the feeling of failure will become further entrenched.
- **Don't reward or bribe him when he does go.** This can become a source of reverse pressure; when he doesn't earn the reward, he'll feel like a failure.
- **Don't greet the eventual appearance of stool with excitement or relief.** If he doesn't overcome his fear the next time and you're no longer leaping with happiness, he'll feel like a failure again.
- **Don't get upset.** This will only reinforce his mental block.

There is no quick fix for stool retention once it has set in. Arm yourself with patience, because it takes several weeks to improve this condition, and it can be very stressful for you and your child. This is one situation where the best parenting is no parenting: You have to keep up the appearance of a laissez-faire attitude even if you don't feel it. But don't fret; it will work itself out: by him, of him, and for him.

Strep Throat

See also | **Mononucleosis; Scarlet Fever**

Every winter, there's a strep season. Symptoms include fever (either high or low), a sore throat and difficulty swallowing, red swollen tonsils, headache, a general feeling of fatigue, and belly pain. There may also be a red, sandpapery rash on the face and torso, in which case the condition is called *scarlet fever* (not to be confused with rheumatic fever, a complication of strep). This occurs when the strain of streptococcal bacteria also produces a toxin that causes a rash [**See:** Scarlet Fever].

Strep primarily affects children over five years of age, but younger tots are not immune. In infants, symptoms are mostly limited to fever, and as a result, strep is commonly confused with the flu. Strep infections can be confirmed in minutes with a quick, reliable test. This is particularly useful, because not everything that looks like strep is strep. Several viruses can produce similar symptoms, including the common mononucleosis virus, which does not require antibiotic treatment [**See:** Mononucleosis].

Strep throat frequently goes unnoticed, which means that a lot of people walk around with a scratchy throat and never know they have strep. They may not be symptomatic, but they are contagious, which is one of the reasons strep is so common. In these uncomplicated cases, strep almost always resolves on its own.

Treatment

Your doctor will treat a confirmed case of strep throat with oral antibiotics, not only to alleviate the primary symptoms, but also to prevent potential complications such as rheumatic fever, which occurs when the strep bacteria take up residence in the heart and produce a toxin that damages its valves. Extremely rare in the United States but more common in developing nations, rheumatic fever primarily affects children between the ages of five and ten. Infants never get this rare complication, and toddlers almost never do; for this reason, treatment before five years of age to avoid complications is not so crucial. From five years on, the standard of practice is to treat all confirmed cases. Strep throat can also lead to kidney problems.

The treatment for strep is simple penicillin. There's no need for the newer, more complex antibiotics, since it's one of the only bacteria that has yet to develop antibiotic resistance. There's also no rush to treat strep if the child is not in too much discomfort; early treatment may prevent the body from mounting a natural defense, which could lead to early reinfection.

REAL QUESTIONS FROM REAL PARENTS

When can my child resume school?
The day after the antibiotics begin, if Jimmy feels better. Half the class probably has strep by that point anyway; that's how contagious it is.

Why does my child keep getting strep? It seems like it happens every month during the winter.
Some kids are predisposed to strep, especially those with enlarged tonsils. If it occurs more than five times a year, you and your doctor should consider tonsil removal.

My child just finished an episode of strep, and now he's getting sick again. Why?
This is a common occurrence that has nothing to do with your child's immune system or incorrect antibiotic treatment. Rebound strep happens because children are continually exposed to other infected children during an outbreak, so the second they stop treatment, they're vulnerable again. Sometimes children require one or more courses of antibiotics a few times in a row before the infection clears up.

Why is my child testing positive even though he's not sick?
If your child has had strep a few times and still tests positive without any other symptoms, he could very well be a "strep carrier," which means that he's harboring the strep bacteria in his tonsils, even though he's not manifesting symptoms. The good news is that strep carriers are not contagious, are not at an increased risk for rheumatic fever, and are no more prone to the illness than other children are. Once he's recognized as a strep carrier, he needs no further treatment unless new symptoms appear. Eventually, his body's natural defenses will clear his throat of the bacteria.

Strollers

See also | **Baby Carriers**

You can put a baby in a stroller soon after birth, although you may find baby carriers or slings more convenient and cozy. I have always preferred lighter strollers to the fancy ones that come loaded with canopies, umbrellas, and bottle holders. Using common sense, and taking into account the maturation of her muscle tone, you should be able to figure out how far to recline or prop Lucy up. She won't mind being a little slouched over, even if your neighbors make unwelcome comments. You can use some pieces of hard foam to prop her up and show her off, but as in the crib, be careful to avoid any potential breathing hazards. And even if it's not the law, buckle Lucy in; stroller falls are more common than you might imagine.

Stuttering

See also | **Language Acquisition and Late Talking; Speech Impediments**

Stuttering occurs normally in a large number of children as they acquire more language around age three. This is especially true of kids who are very verbal. Their reach exceeds their grasp, and the words collide in their mouth. If Jimmy is stuttering, let him finish his sentences without correcting him. There is no need for any intervention. After a few months, stuttering disappears in the vast majority of kids. If it does not, or if fluency decreases and verbal tics appear, your doctor will refer Jimmy for a speech evaluation.

Very rarely, some kids become real stutterers; their early speech problems either worsen or go away for a while before recurring. True stuttering, which is more common in boys, can be significantly reduced by various relaxing techniques and speech therapy.

Sucking Blister

This little blister appears in the middle of Lucy's upper lip, probably as a by-product of sucking, and is no cause for concern. This cute little blister will last for about six months, but it always goes away, and when it disappears, it may even be cause for sadness: Your little baby ain't a baby no more.

Sunburn

See also | **Sun Protection**

No matter how careful you are, your child will probably suffer at least a few mild sunburns. A severe burn can be painful and may even be accompanied by fever symptoms. The sun can be tricky: For example, on a long car trip, window glass won't prevent sunburn, and it may even intensify heat and light. If the sunburn is on an extended area of the body, with blistering, it may indicate a second-degree burn. These cases may lead to infection and require a doctor to follow the treatment.

For Minor Burns:

WHAT **TO DO**

- **Give Jimmy pain medication.**
- **Use an over-the-counter** 1% hydrocortisone solution to treat the irritation.

WHAT **NOT TO DO**

- **Don't apply ice.** It will be painful, and it won't help.
- **Don't let Jimmy go back into the sun before the burn heals.** That means until the peeling is done and the new skin isn't bright pink. If he must go out again, make sure he wears a shirt, but be aware that most fabric is only equivalent to about SPF 10, so use a high-SPF sunscreen under the shirt.

Sun Protection

See also | **Sunburn**

The sun isn't always poison. It's even good for the skin in reasonable amounts, and it gives you a free dose of vitamin D. In recent years, as we've become hypersensitive to the risk of skin cancer, people have started blocking the sun to the point of obsession; you can see parents walking down a sunny street with tightly wrapped bundles that, upon closer inspection, turn out to be babies wearing sunglasses.

It's true that in high or prolonged quantities, the sun's ultraviolet rays can have negative long-term effects on skin, ranging from aging to cancer. Although sunscreen is very efficient at preventing burns and is recommended by all skin experts, it has not yet been proven to prevent skin cancer. Similarly, sun exposure is believed to affect the vision later in life, but sunglasses haven't been found to positively decrease the consequences of long-term UV exposure on the eyes.

Applying sunscreen on babies younger than six months is not recommended, because it can be absorbed through their thin skin, and nobody knows if it's harmless or not. At this age, the best sun protection is to keep Lucy in the shade, covered with loose clothing and a hat. As for older children, as soon as they start moving around—since you can't handcuff them to the umbrella—you should keep them covered as well. Apply a sunscreen with SPF 30 generously and evenly to avoid localized sunburns a half hour before sun exposure. Repeat the application every couple of hours. If the kids are playing in water, reapply the sunscreen hourly, because it washes off (even if it's waterproof). The preparations that combine chemical sunscreen (which absorbs UV rays) with a physical sunblock in the form of zinc oxide or titanium dioxide (which block UV rays) have a higher SPF but can leave a temporary white film on the skin.

As for those multicolor shades on Lucy's nose, she may look cool with them, but they'll keep falling off her face. Keeping her hat on her head and all of her in the shade will provide appreciable protection. The experts do recommend sunglasses for older kids who spend prolonged periods in the sun, but if you figure out how to have yours keep them on, please let me know, so I can try your technique on my own kids.

Swaddling

See also | **Colic**

The nurse in the hospital teaches you many things: bathing, diapering, nursing, and swaddling. When she demonstrates the latter, you'll probably be impressed with how neatly she wraps up your little bundle of joy. The technique is simple:

1 | Place the blanket diagonally on a flat surface with the bottom corner pointing toward you and the top corner pointing away from you (like a diamond).

2 | Place Lucy in the middle, and fold down the top corner so her head rests on it. Hold her arms at the middle of her chest.

3 | Take the right corner of the blanket and pull it over her body (to the left), then tuck it in under her.

4 | Now bring the bottom corner up and over the portion of blanket that was the right corner, and tuck it under (the bottom corner should be pointing down now).

5 | Bring the last corner, the leftmost one, up to the right and over Lucy's torso, and tuck it under the other blankets, just under her chin.

As you know, swaddling comforts Lucy by tricking her into believing she is still in the womb. In the first few days of life, it may soothe her and solve some of the problems that feeding and rocking won't. But the trick gets old quickly. After a couple of weeks, as Lucy begins to enjoy her new freedom, she'll much prefer stretching and kicking to being restrained.

Swimmer's Ear

See also | **Ear Infections**

Swimmer's ear is an infection of the outer ear, unlike the middle ear infections. If not for chlorine in pools and cotton swabs poked into wet ears, we'd hardly ever see cases of swimmer's ear. Here's how it develops: Chlorine in the pool water dries the ear, creating an itching sensation; the swab further irritates the skin of the ear canal, which subsequently becomes infected and painful. You can prevent this condition by keeping all things out of little ears before swimming except ear plugs, which can actually help prevent swimmer's ear by keeping the ear canal dry. If Jimmy does come down with swimmer's ear despite all your best efforts, your doctor will prescribe antibiotic ear drops, which should knock it out.

Swimming

Baby-and-me swimming lessons are fun but not tremendously effective for teaching Lucy how to swim. Despite your best intentions, she is unlikely to last more than a few minutes in a swimming pool even if it's warm, and she'll soon let you know that, for her at least, the lesson is over. (In case you were worried, the chlorine is perfectly fine for young babies.)

Children can only handle true swimming at five or six years old, depending on how much they're exposed to water. When children are no longer afraid of immersing themselves and can hold their breath, they're ready to swim. Style comes later.

No matter how talented a swimmer you think your child is, you must watch him or her like a hawk around any pool, both in the water and out, until the early teens. Kids can fall in or worse despite the most sophisticated fences and tarps, and a catastrophe can happen in a split second. This is true of any body of water, from a sink to an ocean.

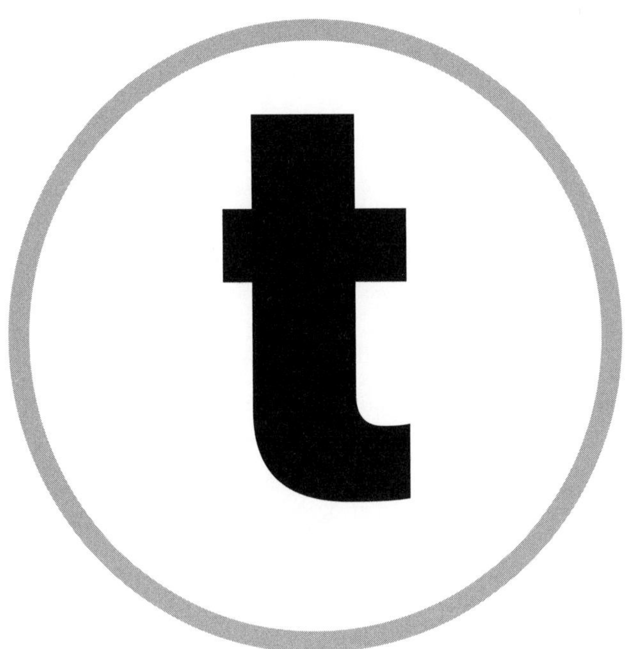
t

Tantrums

See also | **Attention Deficit Disorder (ADD); Discipline**

I just can't believe what I'm seeing. Jimmy, my sweet boy, is at this very moment lying facedown on the floor, screaming his head off. And you know what triggered all that frenzy? I wouldn't let him play with my cell phone, because he's already dropped one in the toilet. What am I supposed to do, change cell phones every month? So now I'm trying to reason with him, but he won't listen and just cries even louder. Okay, okay, Jimmy. Here's the cell phone. Oh my God! He just threw it on the floor. What can I do? I know, I'll give him some ice cream. That'll calm him down."

After the first birthday, children experience frustrations more intensely than previously. This is the period when your little angel turns into a raging monster, complete with the explosive outbursts known as tantrums. These fits can take you by surprise with their violence and shocking ferocity. As bad as they look and sound, however, these meltdowns are in fact a very important developmental milestone. Handled properly, they teach Jimmy how to resolve frustration, which is not a trivial affair.

In the first few tantrums, at least, Jimmy is reacting to a sense of being overwhelmed. The trigger may be having too many choices in a situation, combined with being unable to make a decision. Or it might be that he's getting too much stimulation, especially when he's overtired. With a little experience, you'll learn to sense a tantrum coming on and how to avert it by providing comfort or distraction. At times, however, despite all your efforts, Jimmy will reach a point of no return and go into a full-blown meltdown.

The textbook cases occur around fifteen months of age. Jimmy looks as if the world has collapsed around him; he falls to the floor in a heap and kicks and screams. For a few minutes, he'll vent his frustration and forget completely why he's so mad. Then, magically, he'll stop. During the process, he learns that moments of crisis—even dire crisis—pass. When you were Jimmy's age, you lost control as well, and now you're perfectly capable of sitting in traffic without jumping out of the car and screaming. Frustration management is as essential a skill for a child as walking or talking. And children who master frustration properly now will fare much better later, both cognitively and emotionally.

Though many parental strategies for dealing with tantrums are well intentioned, they can actually reinforce outbursts. Jimmy will most likely interpret any attempts to smooth things over as attention, and he'll come to take malicious pleasure in the trigger: his own meltdown. The tantrums will become more frequent and more intense; children who always get attention for their shows of temper fail to develop the necessary coping mechanisms, and down the line they often become what are informally known as whiners.

Early Tantrums

At Home

- Just ignore them. That means do nothing. Don't distract, don't hug, don't yell. Do nothing. Even if Jimmy is banging his head on the wall, don't interfere. Let him discover on his own that it hurts.
- When you sense a storm coming, try to resist dissuading him with food, candy, or toys.
- When the storm has passed, don't commend Jimmy for calming down. Instead, resume regular business as if nothing has happened.

Away from Home

- Even if you're outside, try your best to ignore the tantrum. This may be a bit challenging and embarrassing, but you won't be the first person in history whose toddler has rolled around on the floor of the supermarket because he wasn't allowed to make a hat from a coffee filter. If it gets out of hand, restrain him in his stroller or the shopping cart with no comment or just leave the store.

If you stick to this laissez-faire routine, Jimmy will experience only a few of these tantrums within the second year of age, and they'll disappear as his coping mechanisms evolve. Then he'll be your little angel again.

Persistent Tantrums

By two years of age, Jimmy should no longer be throwing tantrums. If he is, it's because you have not ignored them and have thus inadvertently reinforced their attention-getting value to him. By this point, a child who hasn't learned to process his own tantrums may lack the coping mechanism necessary for dealing with frustrations. The laissez-faire strategy still applies, but expect trouble. Because you've established a different pattern, Jimmy may not settle for your new Zen approach with equanimity. He'll bang on you instead of the floor when he doesn't get his usual attention. Don't ignore violence toward yourself or someone else; this is inappropriate behavior and should be disciplined. But don't give it undue attention either [See: Discipline and Boundaries].

Long-Lasting Effects of Tantrums

If tantrums aren't handled tactfully at the toddler stage, they can last well into childhood and even beyond. They take the form of explosive outbursts that occur when a child encounters a trivial frustration. Usually, this results from inconsistent parental reactions to the tantrums of a temperamental toddler. Parents who practice a grab-bag methodology—sometimes ignoring, sometimes punishing, sometimes soothing, sometimes rewarding—disrupt their child's need for consistent behavior and predictable reactions. This variable approach not only destabilizes the relationship between parent and child, it also can destabilize the child's own internal mechanism, resulting in emotional fragility. If the child's predisposition to temper reaches extreme proportions, it becomes disruptive both at school and at home.

Child psychologists or teachers frequently raise the question of attention deficit disorder with regard to a kid who lacks frustration-management skills [**See:** Attention Deficit Disorder]. Occasionally, these well-intentioned professionals drive parents to medicate a kid for a problem he doesn't have.

It's not too late to teach your child how to cope with frustration, although the longer you wait, the harder it becomes. As I outlined above, strict indifference to temper remains vital to the process except when it leads to inappropriate behavior such as violence, in which case you must clearly set boundaries.

Tap Water

See also | **Fluoride**

In the United States, at least, tap water is safe enough for watering the garden, bathing, drinking, and putting into your baby's formula. The EPA constantly monitors public drinking water for safety and contamination. Bottled waters, while popular, are rarely necessary; they testify more to the triumph of marketing than to any real problems with public water. (In fact, bottled waters are more frequently contaminated with bacteria and chemicals than their tap cousins are, because the agency in charge of monitoring bottled waters, the FDA, does a less thorough job than the EPA does.)

Tap water sometimes appears cloudy or colored, not because it's dirty but because it may bear trace deposits from pipes or storage containers. These deposits are unappealing, of course, but they aren't toxic. Just let the water run for a little while to flush out sediments. The occasional strange odor in tap water derives not from toxicity but from gas buildup in the pipes. Water filters, which are almost as big an industry as bottled water, supposedly purify the water by removing heavy metals like mercury and lead as well as other bacteria and impurities. In reality, tap water contains none of those things anyway, so you may not want to spend money on an essentially superfluous system. Finally, tap water contains appropriate levels of fluoride, which filters do not remove.

Teeth

See also | **Biting; Cavities; Dentist; Feeding; Gums; Teething**

New Teeth

Baby's first teeth represent a very important milestone and often a source of immense joy for parents, though seldom for the baby. Teeth hurt a little when they pierce through the gums, and at first they don't even help with solid foods [**See:** Below]. Those sharp front incisors, for instance, are designed to bite into hard food, which is still off-limits at the time that teeth generally emerge. So initially, their purpose seems to be purely aesthetic.

Unlike horses, babies can't be "aged" by the number of teeth they have: There is neither a specific timetable nor an absolute order of appearance. On average, the first tooth erupts around six months, but some kids get theirs as early as four months of age, while others have none for a nerve-wracking eighteen months. All are perfectly normal. In the latter case, the teeth come in rapidly thereafter and in clusters, rather than one by one.

Parents tend to worry about late teethers. It doesn't help that in the old days pediatricians "scientifically" monitored the arrival—both order and timing—of their patients' teeth. This was a waste of time; teeth always show up eventually.

Also be aware that not everything that feels or looks like a tooth in Lucy's mouth is one. A white lump that is merely a discoloration of the gum or a bump on the gum can trick you into thinking that Lucy is cutting a tooth.

As much as the fussed-about dental debut may cause pride and excitement in a baby's extended family, breast-feeding mothers have mixed feelings about it: ouch. Not to worry; a prompt but gentle disengagement for a couple of minutes sends a clear message: biting = no food. Even the youngest of brains can rapidly compute that equation, and harmonious nursing generally resumes. On a related note, if you scream when Lucy bites you, she'll bite even more just for the reaction. I know it's difficult not to scream when you're in pain, but it's well worth your effort, since proper conditioning will spare you further sneak attacks [See: Biting].

Crooked Teeth

If Lucy's new fangs initially erupt crookedly, don't be concerned; this is normal. First teeth sometimes come in pointing every which way, often with huge spaces between them. Fortunately, they tend to straighten up with age and do not, in this early state, foretell an eventual need for braces.

Teeth and Feeding

Lucy doesn't need a whole set of teeth to eat solid foods. In fact, she can do it with no teeth at all. A small scientific experiment will reassure you of this. Place your index finger in your baby's mouth between the gums and wait a few seconds. Now try to remove your hand without lifting the whole baby. Gums are strong, and they are pretty efficient at chewing. So go ahead with the solid food when it's time [See: Feeding].

Tooth Color

Erupting teeth are sometimes slightly yellow, and they might stay that way for a while, though healthy teeth will get whiter. You can tell when yellow teeth are a sign of tooth decay, because the enamel is also rugged. A gray tooth usually results from a blow to a baby tooth and subsequent bleeding within the enamel. It will stay this color until it falls out.

Tooth Injuries

If a baby tooth gets knocked out, skip the dentist and proceed directly to the tooth fairy, because it won't be reinserted. Adult teeth, on the other hand, can be reinserted if you act quickly enough. If you're near a dentist when an adult tooth is dislodged, go there with the child and the tooth. If you're not close by, rinse off the tooth and try your best to preserve it by putting it in milk until you reach a medical facility. Partially broken teeth, whether baby teeth or adult teeth, are discarded and repaired with a crown.

Tooth injuries can also cause small wounds in the mouth, but these usually heal well and rarely get infected. A large wound that accompanies a tooth injury would require medical attention [See: Gums].

Teeth Grinding (Bruxing)

One evening you hear an incessant mechanical rumble coming from somewhere in the house. You look around for broken appliances, but slowly realize that the noise is coming from Jimmy's bedroom. As you softly approach your sleeping darling, you realize, to your astonishment, that he's making the noise by ferociously grinding his teeth. You never knew a kid could do that! It's amazing how loud it is. You wake him up gently, but two minutes later he's at it again. You wonder why: Is he overtired? Is preschool too challenging? Did we toss the pacifier too soon? It's decided: you're taking him to the dentist in the morning . . . if he has any teeth left by then.

This is what the dentist will tell you: Teeth grinding, or bruxing, is common in toddlers and young children. It can be loud and may occur almost every night. It can also be slightly abrasive to the front teeth, which may lose enamel. Bruxing does not indicate an emotional imbalance or stress, as it may later in life; in toddlers, it's caused by muscles contracting and twitching during an active phase of sleep. Adults who grind their teeth at night wear mouth guards to prevent abrasion, but these devices are not practical for kids. Luckily, Jimmy still has his baby teeth, and they'll be replaced by beautiful new ones long after the grinding phase has ended.

Teething

***A**t three and a half months, Lucy liked to chew on her hands and drool. Her favorite activity was sucking on her fists for a good part of the day. At least all of Auntie Jane's bibs came in handy! Sometimes Lucy would begin with a very discreet chewing, which gradually escalated into an all-out kicking and crying frenzy. The next-door neighbor, who knew somebody who had a baby once, confidently diagnosed her fits as "teething episodes," but we looked all over her mouth and couldn't find any teeth at all. Daddy went to the drugstore and brought back a local anesthetic gel, homeopathic tablets, teething rings, and even pain medication. Lucy tried them all, but in the end she just went back to chewing on her fists.*

No wonder. Miss Lucy is experiencing what Dr. Freud termed the *oral stage of development*, for which acetaminophen is ineffective. Before this point, until about three months, she was engaged in the *adaptive stage*: learning to take in and cope with new sensations. Now that she has it all figured out, she is ready for the *exploratory stage*. This is the kickoff of one of humankind's eternal goals: the relentless search for pleasure. So far, her mouth has been the source of her most pleasurable sensations—namely, food and comfort—so that is where she begins her quest. And when Lucy asks herself "What should I explore first?" her answer is "My hands!"

Since the hands are readily available, they're the ideal territory for Lucy to explore. With age, the salivary glands become increasingly productive, and the result is a copious stream of saliva, or drool. Sometimes all this new oral stimulation can be overwhelming for Lucy, and that's what makes her so agitated. Parents may misinterpret these signs as symptoms of teething discomfort when in fact they are just a little bit of "oral staging." There is no need for medication.

Okay, so that isn't teething, you say. Then what exactly *is* this "teething" process everyone talks about? True teething starts around six to eight months of age and may last until all the back teeth are in (roughly two to three years of age). Teething episodes, which occur especially around nap time or bed time, are not as painful as you imagine. The combination of being overtired and the mild throbbing she experiences in her gums around the newly erupting teeth makes her extra whiny. For a few days at a time, Lucy will chew harder than usual on her hands and act seriously bent out of shape until she falls asleep.

Treatment Options

In the old days, rubbing Johnny Walker on the gums was the treatment of choice; it made everybody happy, and teething babies slept like angels. Nowadays, babies can skip the cocktail hour because pain medication has substantially improved the outcome of teething episodes. It's very effective but, like all medications, should be used sparingly. Don't pump Lucy up with acetaminophen at the first onset of crankiness. Only use meds when the pain seems truly overwhelming, and then use the highest recommended dosage, which will be safe and more efficient.

- A teething ring, a frozen bagel, carrots, or any other finger food will provide temporary relief as well, but you may become tired of picking them up after Lucy has thrown them on the floor for the umpteenth time.
- Topical anesthetics such as Oragel, a less concentrated form of what your dentist uses, decrease the pain, but they numb the mouth for half an hour or more. For a baby, this translates to a lot of drooling, which is a combined effect of the loss of feeling and a decrease in the swallowing reflex.
- Homeopathic tablets, which contain a small amount of sugar and an infinitesimal dilution of belladonna, an organic anesthetic, have their diehard fans, including my wife, who gave large quantities to all three of our daughters. It's hard to know whether the temporary relief is merely due to the sweet taste of the tablets or the effect of the belladonna. I can't speak against them, but I don't recommend them either.
- The laissez-faire approach may be your best option at times, since most so-called teething moments will resolve after a few minutes of rocking Lucy to sleep. I've seen many parents who say their baby never experienced teething pain. My suspicion is that they simply attributed whining caused by teething to general baseline whining.

Common Myths About Teething

Teething causes fever.

There is no physiological basis for this argument. When the dentist works on your gums, you don't go home with a fever, do you? Conversely, however, a fever will magnify the throbbing pain of teething. Benign febrile illnesses are rather common at this age and may easily coincide with teething.

Teething occurs mostly at night.

Well, nighttime is also when kids are most likely to be overtired and more sensitive to their throbbing gums. There is one caveat you should be aware of when the whole teething business starts: If you carry Lucy on your shoulder for several hours, put her in your bed, or otherwise pamper her when she's teething, Miss Lucy will still want that nightly shoulder ride or a spot in the cozy "mommy-daddy" bed even after the episodes have subsided. Many parents tell me, "My kid was a great sleeper until eight months of age, when he started teething. Now he wakes up four times a night!" As natural as it is to want to reduce your child's discomfort, I advise you to resume the regular routine as soon as things seem settled, even if it involves a little bit of night fussing.

I see the teeth coming through, and it must be so painful!

Actually, once you can see the teeth, chances are that much of the discomfort has passed, since it's the pressure of the teeth against the inside of the gums that causes the pain.

In Summary

Teething pains are a baby's first growing pains. They come and they go, but in the end, they'll make your little one stronger.

Testicles

Undescended Testicles

In the male fetus, testicles form around the thirtieth week of gestation. In a female fetus, those same structures become ovaries. The testicles usually descend during the first year of life, but if one or both remain in the belly after the first birthday, a surgeon needs to rectify this rare disorder by bringing them down.

Water in the Testicles

In some instances, liquid from the intestine leaks into the scrotum, which fills with fluid and makes the testicles appear swollen. This condition is not painful, and it generally resolves after a few months. If it persists through the end of the first year, your doctor may recommend a simple surgery.

Testicular Hernia

If you discover one day that Jimmy's scrotum is very swollen, this most likely represents a testicular hernia, which means that a defect has opened a gap between the scrotum and the abdomen, allowing some of the intestine to slip downward and into the sac. Unlike fluid in the testicle, this swelling appears and disappears over the course of the day, primarily on one side, as the intestinal content moves back and forth through the opening. The swelling will be more prominent when Jimmy cries, because crying increases the pressure in the abdomen and pushes the intestine into the scrotum.

A testicular hernia can occur at any age. It's not painful, but it carries the danger of intestinal twisting or obstruction. Although surgery is required to repair this condition, it's not an emergency unless the intestine gets pinched, which would be accompanied by signs of blockage, sudden vomiting, and belly distention.

Retractile Testicles

In some cases, as in cold weather or cold water, for example, descended testicles retract slightly into the scrotum. Once you know they have descended, don't worry if you sometimes can't feel them. They haven't gone far, and they'll be back.

Testicular Pain

At any age, a sudden onset of intense pain in a child's testicles could be a sign that the vessel that feeds them has twisted, jeopardizing blood flow and risking the entire testicle. This is an emergency, and surgery must be performed within a few hours to save the organ. Fortunately, this torsion is very rare in children under five years, and it's even rarer in infants, in whom you can't precisely localize a sudden onset of pain.

Thermometers

See also | **Fever**

Before I tell you about the best thermometer you can use, let me explain why you need one. If you were to call me because Jimmy has a fever, I would ask if he is slightly warm (101°F range) . . . very warm (103°F range) . . . or boiling hot (104°F and above). And I would be much more interested in any details you could provide that might point to the origin of his illness. Finding the fever's cause ranks much higher in importance than the number on the thermometer, since the difference between 101°F and 101.7°F isn't going to make a huge difference in temperature management.

REAL QUESTIONS FROM REAL PARENTS

What do I take my child's temperature with?

A child's temperature is fairly obvious to the touch. Start with the thermometer at the end of your arm: your hand. If Jimmy feels warm, you can then use a store-bought thermometer to gauge the number.

Which kind?

Precision is not crucial, so a cheap electronic thermometer or an old-fashioned glass one will do the job just fine, as will a disposable strip. The worst thermometers—those that go into the ear like some kind of science-fiction device—also happen to be the most expensive. The consumer versions of these devices give falsely high readings, which can panic parents. If Lucy receives one as a present, don't open the box. Go to the store and exchange it for a simpler and more accurate one. While you're there, you can also pick up a few rattles and toys with the money you're saving.

Where?

Under the arm, in the mouth, on the forehead—these are all good spots, depending on where your thermometer is supposed to go. I don't recommend rectal readings; even if they are more accurate by half a degree, they could be painful and risky on a wiggly child.

How often?

Once you've established that Jimmy has a temperature and you're reasonably comfortable that you've addressed the fever's source, there's no need to monitor the temperature obsessively. A flu, for example, will produce two to three days of high fever, and charting it along the way won't add anything to the treatment. Instead, pay closer attention to signs that could indicate complications, such as vomiting or lethargy [**See:** Flu].

What's the panic number?

The numerical value of the temperature is not the crucial point. No matter what you may have heard, a very high temperature is not dangerous for the brain, nor is it necessarily indicative of a severe illness [**See:** Fever].

Thrush

A mild fungal overgrowth in the mouth, thrush results in whitish deposits that look like cheesy white curds on the sides of the tongue and the inner cheeks. It is often confused with milk staining, which is a thick, homogeneous, white buildup found only on top of the tongue. Thrush generally affects young babies and rarely shows up in kids over a year old.

Thrush does not cause much discomfort or interfere with feeding, and it usually resolves on its own. It is slow to grow and slow to disappear, with or without treatment, and the whole process can take a few weeks. If it lingers, your doctor will prescribe an oral antifungal suspension such as Nystatin. Dip a cotton swab in the suspension and rub it liberally onto the lesions a few times a day until they clear. Some people swear by acidophilus, an alternative treatment that is supposed to restore the normal flora of the mouth, but the condition tends to resolve on its own, so it's difficult to evaluate what helps and what does not.

While thrush isn't a big problem for the baby, it can trouble nursing mothers, because the fungus that causes the condition may irritate the breast [**See:** Breast-Feeding Problems].

Thumb Sucking

See also | **Pacifier**

Whether breast feeding or not, whether using a pacifier or not, some children will suck their thumbs. The reason? Just what you'd imagine: oral comfort, plain and simple. Thumb sucking occurs in perfectly well-balanced babies and usually has no negative consequences. While it's true that it may push the front baby teeth slightly forward, thumb sucking won't affect the permanent ones unless it persists beyond age five, which is extremely rare. The habit usually lasts a few years and disappears on its own if you manage not to interfere. Also, think about it: Thumb sucking has at least one advantage over a pacifier: You don't have to wake up several times a night to plop a thumb back into Lucy's mouth.

WHAT **TO DO**

- **Offer other forms of oral comfort**—bottle, breast, and optional pacifier—on demand so Lucy is not deprived of sucking opportunities.
- **If thumb sucking occurs, ignore it.** Since it's her own thumb, you have very little say in the matter if Lucy decides it's right for her.

WHAT **NOT TO DO**

- **Don't attempt to distract Lucy's hand.**
- **Don't use restrictive devices or sour solutions on the thumb.**
- **Don't remove her thumb each time it goes into her mouth.**

In Older Children

In very rare cases, thumb sucking persists beyond the age of four, usually as a result of negative parental reinforcement, i.e., too much attention, discouragement, and worry over the behavior. This late in development, thumb sucking can misalign the permanent teeth and cause a later need for braces. Unfortunately, breaking the habit is difficult. The only efficient tactic to use with Jimmy is the same one you'd use with Lucy: ignore it. Peer pressure—namely, being called a baby by other kids—will be a far more effective deterrent than anything you might muster.

Tics

Tics are involuntary muscle movements caused by some form of tension. Appearing as early as three years of age, tics tend to be temporary and more prevalent in children who are intelligent and high achievers. Eye blinking, throat clearing, shoulder shrugging, nose rubbing, and nervous coughing all qualify as tics, and all of them generally diminish in intensity when a child concentrates. Though many tics are minor, they can be awkward and socially disabling.

If Jimmy happens to develop a tic, you should deal with it by not dealing with it; ignoring the behavior is the only way to avoid reinforcing it. Don't reveal your own anxiety. Take the laissez-faire approach: Pretend you don't notice the tic. If he has a high-strung personality, encourage noncompetitive activities that will help alleviate his tension.

On average, tics last a few months. If they gain in intensity or last longer, bring the condition to your doctor's attention. In extremely rare cases, these involuntary movements could point to Tourette's syndrome, a condition characterized by intense tics and occasional involuntary verbal outbursts.

Toilet Training

Okay, get ready for this. No matter what you may have heard or read, toilet training is unnecessary. Children learn to move on from diapers, not because they are run through drills but because they become sensitive to the increasing discomfort of marinating in their own dirty diapers. Just like any other milestone, this occurs naturally as a normal part of a child's development, and it does not require training.

Oddly, modern technology delays the process somewhat; today's diapers, which are superabsorbent and designed to fit perfectly, don't cause the same discomfort that diapers did in years past. I bet one of the reasons you're toilet trained is that you grew tired of walking around with a soggy, stinky diaper around your waist. Nowadays, children are less motivated to graduate from this phase as quickly. This delay may make you wonder if Jimmy is ever going to be out of his diapers. Compounding the issue, day-care centers and preschools often impose toilet-training ultimatums for enrolling children, not so much for your child's benefit as for their own convenience.

The truth is that all children will be done with diapers eventually, some earlier than average, some later. But the child-care industry and certain behavioral psychologists have conspired to create a huge amount of pressure for children and parents alike. I recommend that you merely help Jimmy decide when he wants to be clean and offer a little assistance along the way. My laissez-faire toilet-training method, scientifically tested on my own three children, goes something like this:

1 | Once Jimmy becomes aware of his daily waste production, around eighteen months of age, he'll start to let you know when his diaper is full. This is a fine time to start the process.

2 | Buy a potty, and set it on the floor in the bathroom next to the adult toilet. There's no need to discuss the function of this new piece of furniture.

3 | Let him run around naked as often as you can and wherever it's practical. Not only is this the best way to prevent diaper rashes, it will make him much more conscious of what comes out of him. Unless you have expensive carpeting, it makes little difference whether you swab the floor or swab his butt.

4 | Now let him go about his normal business. Occasionally, he'll stop playing to go number one or two. The first few times, he'll be surprised to see what comes out of him and may even enjoy the novelty, but that will wear off quickly when he slips in his own urine. Soon enough, when he feels the urge, he'll look around for a place to satisfy his needs where he won't be bothered by them later. That's when he'll remember the new piece of furniture.

5 | Because Jimmy vaguely remembers seeing you—his role model—sit on the toilet, he'll mimic you.

6 | Before he has fully mastered his potty, he might ask you for a diaper when he feels the urge. Oblige without comment. This is just as good as going to the potty.

7 | If the process becomes too messy or starts to drag on, you may have started too early. Give it a few weeks and try again.

WHAT NOT TO DO

- **Don't pressure Jimmy.** Pressure can be as subtle as a suggestion. It is at best pointless and at worst can delay the process and even lead to stool retention, a dramatic situation wherein kids withhold their stools intentionally [See: Stool Retention]. If your child's day-care center or preschool pressures you, just pay your tuition on time, tell the director that Jimmy's almost there, and stand by him supportively.
- **Don't reward or bribe him because he went to the potty.** Jimmy is definitely smarter than a pet and will figure out that you have a major stake in his bladder and bowel elimination. As part of the toddler exploration stage, he'll try to reverse the circuit and figure out what happens when he does not use the potty. Also, rewards become a form of pressure, because he will start to feel punished without them.
- **Don't make him watch toilet-training videos or read toilet-training books.** They are boring and unproductive.
- **Don't suggest that Jimmy sit on the potty** when he's not feeling the urge. He won't understand what he is doing there if he does not have the need.
- **Don't rush him onto the potty** if he starts urinating or defecating elsewhere in the house. You probably won't get him there in time, and these mad dashes will introduce unnecessary commotion.

▶ **Don't worry if he suffers occasional setbacks** after achieving some control. It's not always a perfect process.

If you stick to this method, most kids will naturally achieve control between the second and the third years, first with urine and then with defecation. When they are comfortable with the potty, the transition to a real toilet happens relatively slowly but spontaneously.

Resisting Toilet Training

If Jimmy is still not on the potty by his third birthday, don't panic; it may just be a matter of time. Just like every other milestone, there are wide variations in when kids reach it. But there is also the possibility that Jimmy has grown so comfortable in diapers that he feels no need to change his habits. Worse, you could also have been mildly pressuring him without realizing it, which can act as a deterrent. By four years of age, if Jimmy has not achieved bowel control, there is no doubt that he is almost certainly responding to one of these outside stimuli. In that case, here is a modified laissez-faire approach that will solve your problem:

1 | Buy some training diapers. They are much less absorbent than normal diapers and therefore more uncomfortable.

2 | Teach him to put the diaper on himself, and place the pile of extras within his reach.

3 | During the day, let him run around in underwear or, when possible, naked.

4 | If he asks for a diaper, remind him where they are.

5 | If he goes in his underwear, don't rush to change him.

6 | If he goes in the potty, don't praise him with all the pent-up relief in your heart. The aim here is to maximize his discomfort and his autonomy.

Again, don't push and don't nag. Just calmly send the message that he should use the potty for his own benefit rather than yours. If Jimmy is in preschool he'll just have to wear a training diaper until he gets "trained." Little by little, Jimmy will discover the primary reason for toilet training: comfort. The older a child is and the more entrenched his habits, the longer the training may take. But it will always work if you are rigorously consistent.

Night Training

Children also learn to control their bladders at night. After a few months of relatively steady control during the day, you can let Jimmy try a night without diapers. If he stays dry, then that's that. If he doesn't, back off and try again a few weeks later. The majority of children will achieve night bladder control in the third year. Some kids remain bed wetters until much later on [**See:** Bed-Wetting].

Wiping

After your child has achieved bladder and bowel control, teach wiping. The main purpose of wiping is to avoid underwear staining. In that sense, it's a cosmetic habit rather than a medical one. Teach it patiently, and don't worry if it's slow going at first.

There is an additional dimension to this process for girls: Many parents believe that if girls wipe from back to front, they increase the risk of urinary tract infections. This is highly unlikely. The proximity of the two orifices ensures that the vagina is regularly contaminated with stool. Therefore, you just have to trust that whoever designed the human plumbing system has accounted for this by protecting the vagina from becoming infected by small amounts of fecal matter. If that were not the case, Lucy would have to be on antibiotics as long as she's wearing diapers.

Tongue

Tongue Tie

In the past, pediatricians routinely recommended cutting the frenulum of the tongue, the thin membrane that links it to the lower palate, if it was shorter than average at birth. They believed that this condition, known as "tongue tie," could impede nursing and even hinder language development later in life. Why take a chance, they figured.

Here's why. Go to the nearest mirror. Pull your tongue out, lift it up, and look underneath. See how thin and stretchy the membrane is? You'll see that even if yours were a little shorter, it would hardly restrict your tongue's range of motion. The so-called tongue tie is a misnomer: Apart from a rare condition in which the tongue is tethered to the palate with a thick membrane that truly restricts motion, a thin, short membrane is merely a normal anatomical variant.

You may occasionally encounter a doctor or lactation specialist who still recommends clipping to solve any existing breast-feeding problems or to prevent speech impairment [See: Breast-Feeding Specialist]. Neither medical research nor my personal experience supports any benefits from this procedure. Simply admire the mobility of your kid's tongue, even if the membrane is relatively small. You'll save money, and you'll spare Lucy an unnecessary and painful procedure.

Geographic Tongue

This is another normal variant of the tongue. In some older kids, areas of the tongue's surface appear slightly whiter than others, thus forming a design that resembles a map. Taste is unaffected, and the tongue usually becomes uniform with time.

Tonsils

See also | **Adenoids; Snoring and Sleep Apnea; Sore Throat; Strep Throat**

Tonsils are glands in the back of the throat that develop around the third year of age. Along with the adenoids, which are located higher up, they are designed to trap and eliminate the germs we inhale. On occasion, especially in school-age kids, the tonsils become infected by the very germs they're meant to destroy, and either strep or a virus will cause fever or sore throat or both. In spite of these rare occurrences, most kids will live in perfect harmony with their glands. However, others may experience ongoing problems.

Recurrent Throat Infection

Some tonsils are especially susceptible to germ trapping, and affected kids will develop multiple strep infections throughout the year. As a result, they'll miss considerable amounts of school and have to endure countless courses of antibiotics.

Enlarged Tonsils

If they become enlarged, the tonsils can obstruct the airway and cause snoring at night. Snoring in itself (even if it is loud) and the size of the tonsils are not so much the problem, since these glands will naturally shrink within a couple of years and the snoring will subside. However, if the enlargement causes sleep apnea (a condition in which your child's breathing stops several times a night for periods of five seconds and then resumes with a couple gasps), bring it to your doctor's attention. This could have repercussions on Jimmy's heart, which must work harder to supply his body with oxygen during episodes of apnea [**See:** Snoring and Sleep Apnea].

If your child experiences at least five to seven episodes of strep throat a year or is diagnosed with sleep apnea, your doctor will probably suggest tonsil removal. This surgery, done under general anesthesia, is safe but more uncomfortable than adenoid removal, with more postoperative pain and a slight risk of bleeding [See: Adenoids]. The operation dramatically reduces recurrent strep infections and sleep apnea. An increasingly popular new laser technique is supposed to offer faster recovery and fewer complications.

Toothbrushing

See also | **Cavities; Dentist**

Many baby books advise you to brush your baby's teeth as early as six months of age. If there are no teeth yet, they tell you to brush the tongue, brush the gums . . . brush anything in sight. What's the point of brushing teeth that aren't even there? Babies eat every couple of hours on average, so even in your wildest dreams you couldn't hope to keep Lucy's mouth clean. Also, as anybody who has actually tried to stick a toothbrush into a baby's mouth can testify, there is no way to do this gracefully. The same goes for gauze pads or those cute toothbrush finger puppets. And if Lucy lets you in there briefly, your chances of doing anything efficient are close to zero. If you're too pushy, you run the risk of creating a permanent aversion to toothbrushing. In young children, limiting sweets is a far more efficient means of cavity prevention.

Don't bother with toothbrushing until about twelve to fifteen months, when Lucy actually has a significant number of teeth and likes imitating anything you do. Now is the time to buy her a cool-looking toothbrush and, during her bedtime routine, let her pretend she's brushing her teeth while you do yours. As she grows older, she'll find this ritual pleasant, and she'll gradually become better at it. Then you can show her the right brushing techniques and how to floss.

As for toothpaste, use kids' formulas. Regular toothpastes have too much fluoride, which can be toxic in high amounts for kids, who would rather eat it than spit it out.

Tooth Rot

A toddler's teeth may rot if he's allowed to drink milk throughout the night, not just before sleeping but all night long. The baby teeth bathe in milk sugars, which rot them away. If you catch the decay early enough, you can save the teeth, but if not, they must be extracted so the rot doesn't spread to the adult teeth waiting below the gums. The extraction generally involves sedation or even anesthesia, since toddlers don't open wide willingly.

I'm sure you can see why you'll want to avoid the need for such measures. To prevent tooth rot, you must not feed your child breast milk or formula during the night. Even if you could brush the kid's teeth all day long, it wouldn't prevent the rot if you were still feeding at night. In my experience, a last bottle, or nursing before sleep, won't cause tooth rot.

The problem is that feeding is usually related to sleeping disturbances, meaning that if you remove the bottle or refuse to nurse, you'll have a very angry toddler. If this describes your situation, please refer to the SLEEP entry to learn how to deal with a difficult sleeper.

Now let's clear up another important issue. In certain books and Web sites that preach breast power, you'll read that only bottle feeding is responsible for tooth rot in toddlers. Because of this fallacy, I have seen dozens of mothers unhappily surprised to discover their breast-fed kids' teeth rotting. Don't be misled. Breast feeding is great, and everyone agrees on that, but all-night feeding sessions can predispose a toddler to tooth decay, whether bottles or breasts are involved [**See:** Breast Feeding].

Travel in Exotic Places

See also | **Bug Bites; Immunizations**

Traveling with kids to exotic locations may present some risks and require some preparation.

t

Bug Bites

In places where mosquitoes and other bugs are fierce, mosquito netting is a must. When it comes to repellents, the most effective ones are also the most toxic (all of them contain the chemical DEET). Still, you may have no choice: use the children's preparation, but use it sparingly.

Bug bites are more likely to become infected in moist climates, especially if scratching irritates them further. Use antihistamines like Benadryl to take the edge off the itching, and prevent infection with topical over-the-counter antibiotic creams. You may also ask your doctor to prescribe an oral antibiotic just in case one of these bites becomes infected despite your preventive measures.

Malaria Prevention

If you read the Centers for Disease Control and Prevention guidelines (at www.cdc.gov), you'll learn that antimalaria drugs are recommended in many countries, some of which may surprise you. Consult your doctor to find out if the drugs are really necessary, since you're unlikely to be roughing it in the jungle with a young baby. If you do need it, the malaria pill is taken weekly, starting one week before the trip and continuing until a month after. In high-risk areas, even young babies can take it (crushed), although it is always easier to keep a baby under a net for prevention.

Food Poisoning

Especially in warm climates, unfamiliar germs may contaminate food, causing severe vomiting and diarrhea and possibly dehydration. If you or anyone in your party becomes ill in this way, practice continuous rehydration with diluted room-temperature sugar sodas, as you would for any stomach bug [**See:** Stomach Bugs]. For vomiting, give as much fluid as often as you can in small quantities to prevent further vomiting. Antivomiting and antidiarrhea medications are not recommended for children, as they are generally inefficient or even harmful. If your child is unable to keep fluid down, find a local doctor, since intravenous fluid replenishment may be required.

Flus and Colds

Your children can get flus and colds in warm climates just as they can at home. Bring along some fever-reducing medications, such as acetaminophen or ibuprofen.

Vaccinations

Most places you visit don't require additional immunizations, but the hepatitis A vaccination is recommended for travel in Central and South America, Africa, and most of Asia. The disease is more debilitating for adults than it is for children, in whom it is often asymptomatic or mild. To be effective, the hepatitis A vaccine must be administered a couple of months before exposure.

The yellow fever vaccine is still mandatory in some remote, undeveloped parts of the world, and a vaccine against Japanese encephalitis is advised for travelers who visit certain rural parts of Asia. Visit the CDC site (www.cdc.gov) for more specifics.

Tummy Time

See also | **Rolling Over; Stimulation; SIDS (Sudden Infant Death Syndrome)**

If you look at old baby pictures, you'll see tots lying happily on their bellies, graceful as skydivers, with their arms spread wide and backs impressively muscled. Their toned physiques resulted from the belly position advised by pediatricians, which required babies to raise themselves up in order to look around.

These days babies are made to lounge on their backs as a precaution against SIDS [**See:** SIDS]. But on the other hand, doctors, baby books, and various childcare experts now strenuously recommend "tummy time" for young babies to strengthen those back muscles they no longer exercise. The trouble is that when you put Lucy on her belly to play, she immediately becomes aggravated and tries to roll over to the position she's used to: facing up. I don't blame her; I can't think of any reason why you should subject infants to this workout.

Since there's no need to strengthen any specific muscle group, I advise you not to act as Lucy's personal trainer. Skip the tummy time, and tickle her tummy so she'll exercise her giggling muscles instead.

Twins

The particular thing about twins is that . . . well, obviously, there are two of them. That means twice as much love but also twice as much feeding and twice as many diaper changes. On the other hand, each twin quickly learns to consider the other a companion, and within a few weeks they won't rely as much on you for entertainment as a single baby would. Of course, with that companionship comes the issues of sharing, hitting, biting, and sibling rivalry that affect all children. Please refer to the specific sections concerning each of these problems.

Nursing Twins

Although most mothers with twins end up relying on a hybrid of bottle feeding and nursing, it is perfectly possible to nurse twins entirely from the breast; after all, there are two of those too. The same basic principles of breast feeding apply [**See:** Breast Feeding]. If you're attached to the idea of breast feeding, use the smallest amount of formula supplementation that you can. Ideally, you'll quickly get the hang of feeding both twins at the same time. This is the only way to get a little rest. Also, while mothers of single babies are advised to feed strictly on demand, I recommend that mothers of twins feed on a more rigid schedule (every two and a half to three hours on average), more for the mom's benefit than for the babies'.

URINARY INFECTIONS

Urinary Infections

In Infants

Urinary infections are rare. In babies, they are caused chiefly by a malformation that allows the reflux of the contaminated urine in the bladder to return to the kidney and infect it. Kidney infections usually cause high fevers, poor appetite, and vomiting. Because these same symptoms apply to many other illnesses (e.g., flu and stomach virus), diagnosing a kidney infection can be challenging. Upon suspicion, your doctor will ask for a urine sample, which must be obtained as cleanly as possible, because germs on the skin can skew the results. The doctor can avoid skin contamination by inserting a tiny tube into the baby's bladder. It may be hard to believe, but this uncomfortable procedure doesn't hurt Lucy or Jimmy much.

Urinary infections generally respond very well to antibiotics. After a documented episode, further tests are necessary to determine whether the urinary system is malformed. If reflux is the issue, depending on the degree, surgery is sometimes recommended to prevent the permanent kidney damage that may follow repeated infections.

In Toddlers and Older Children

Bladder Infections

Older kids are more prone than infants to bladder infections, which show up with or without a fever as painful urination. In case of such an infection, the urine turns cloudy and smelly. A sample makes diagnosis easier, and at this age a "clean" sample is more easily achieved: Jimmy just has to pee into a cup.

In little girls, simple vaginal irritation is often mistaken for a bladder infection, since urination is painful when it drips onto the irritated vagina [See: Vagina]. Two side notes: "Improper wiping" has not been proven to cause urinary infection, and uncircumcised boys don't have a much higher risk of urinary infections.

Kidney Infections

Kidney infections in older children are rarer but not unheard of. The kid will have a high fever (in the 103°F range) and lower-back pain but may not experience pain on urination. In either case, the doctor will treat the condition with an antibiotic and recommend acetaminophen or ibuprofen for the pain and fever. In slightly older children, kidney infections are less likely to be associated with malformations than they are in infants.

V

Vagina

See also | **Urinary Infections; Washing**

In Newborns

The vaginas of little babies always appear puffy at birth, and there may be thick white or even bloody discharge (the equivalent of menses) for the first couple of weeks. This is due to the stimulation of the baby's vagina by maternal hormones. Clean it as you would the diaper area, with water.

In Infants and Toddlers

Vaginal Fusion

In a small percentage of young children, the lips or labia of the vagina will partially fuse together. Unlike women, girls do not have vaginal secretions, so they are likely to experience dryness, irritation, and possibly fusion. Soap, aggressive cleansing, and even diaper rashes also increase the dryness and further contribute to the disorder. Urination is unaffected.

Vaginal fusion causes no symptoms, and it resolves on its own when girls get older and their vaginal secretions prompt the labia to open spontaneously. Prior to this, some doctors prescribe a topical hormonal cream to increase vaginal secretions. I don't; such creams only solve the problem temporarily, and they can have rare side effects such as vaginal bleeding, because the estrogen is absorbed through the skin.

In Older Children

Vaginal Irritation

It is not uncommon, after the toddler stage, for young girls to experience burning in the vaginal area, especially upon urination. When this happens, your girl feels like urinating frequently, but nothing comes out. There could be a slight redness and sometimes a smelly greenish discharge. You may initially fear a urinary tract or vaginal infection, but this is probably not the case.

Blame the burning and discharge on simple vaginal irritation. Soap and bubble baths in particular can dry out the vagina of a little girl, which becomes itchy and then irritated. She pees frequently because she perceives the pain as a need to urinate, but any urine she produces stings a little and makes her think she needs to pee more. The genital exploration that starts as early as three years of age may contribute significantly to the irritation [**See:** Masturbation].

Although vaginal irritation is not the same as a urinary infection, doctors often incorrectly treat the irritation with antibiotics, because germs from the skin contaminate the urine sample and cause inaccurate readings. You can help prevent this condition and the possible misuse of antibiotics by limiting your daughter's soap and bubble baths, applying a soothing ointment like petroleum jelly, and cutting her fingernails short. The symptoms should disappear within days. If, after a week, the pain persists or even increases, or if she develops a fever, take her to the doctor to eliminate the possibility of a urinary or vaginal infection.

For an older girl, a persistent, heavy, malodorous discharge with occasional blood may indicate that Lucy has inserted something into her vagina, which requires medical attention.

Vegetarian Diet

See also | **Feeding**

As a rule, I encourage parents to feed their kids the same diet they feed themselves. A vegetarian diet is perfectly healthy at any age as long as it provides the same amounts of protein found in meat- or fish-based diets. This is relatively easy to achieve, since proteins can be found in lentils, peas, and beans; dairy products; eggs; nut and seed purées such as peanut butter or tahini; and soy products such as tofu or veggie burgers.

Some kids, especially young girls, spontaneously adopt a vegetarian diet on their own, often as part of a trend they pick up at school. Don't tell your little Buddhist, but this usually lasts no more than a year. As long as you ensure that she gets adequate and diverse nutrition from such foods as those listed above, you need not try to force or convince her to eat meat. She will grow up just fine, even if this phase lasts longer than a year.

Vitamins

The American Academy of Pediatrics does not recommend vitamin supplements for children. Why? Because there's no proven benefit. Children who have a reasonably varied diet don't need vitamin supplements, since common foods contain plenty, and the body absorbs them more effectively from food than from pills. This is even true of some otherwise unhealthy foods: Sugared cereals, while not ideal in many respects, are fortified with plenty of vitamins and minerals. Whatever you may have heard, vitamins don't stimulate the appetite, help kids gain weight, or prevent colds and flus. If you're a vitamin aficionado, however, the recommended doses won't do any harm even if they won't do any good.

Vitamin C

Vitamin C proponents think that it prevents heart disease, cancer, anemia, diabetes . . . The list goes on. It's true that vitamin C is a very important nutrient that contributes to vital functions, but deficiency is rare because it's available in so many foods, including such kid favorites as oranges, strawberries, and bell peppers. For that reason, supplements are unnecessary. In fact, very large doses can be toxic, so if you must keep those tasty chewable vitamin C lozenges in the house, keep them well away from your kids.

As for cold prevention, there's no tangible evidence that extra vitamin C has any effect.

Vitamin D

In a recent report, the American Academy of Pediatrics renewed its recommendation that all breast-fed babies receive additional vitamin D to prevent rickets, a bone disorder caused by severe deficiency of this vitamin. Until the late seventies, doctors made the same recommendation. As a result, many mothers opted to feed their babies D-fortified formula. How good could breast milk be if it lacked such an important nutrient?

There are a few reasons to take that recommendation with a grain of salt. While it is true that breast milk provides a low concentration of vitamin D, it provides the nutrient in a more efficient form. Furthermore, the vitamin can be synthesized through the skin using nothing more exotic than a few hours a week of exposure to sunlight.

The American Academy of Pediatrics based this report primarily on a study showing a slight increase of rickets in a small sample of breast-fed African-American infants. But the study is flawed in the sense that it did not take into consideration such important factors as poverty levels or the mothers' nutritional status. Statistically, dark-skinned children are more likely to live in poverty, in housing where light is deficient, and their mothers are more prone to have a deficient diet.

In my opinion, the recommendation that all babies should take supplemental vitamin D based solely on these findings is erroneous and will probably once again serve the formula industry. Also, a few drops of vitamin D for everyone won't address the overall problems for African-American children living in poverty.

If you're nursing, I recommend you eat well and take daytime strolls, not only to ensure vitamin D production but also to prevent you from going stir-crazy no matter what your skin color happens to be.

Vitamin K

Doctors administer vitamin K to every newborn at birth for the prevention of an extremely rare but dramatic bleeding disorder that affects predisposed children during the first days of their life. Since you can't tell in advance who is at risk, every baby receives the vitamin. Many parents are wary of the administration of vitamin K, probably because they perceive a needle in their newborn's thigh as an unpleasant welcome to the world. This is understandable, but the vitamin and the injection are both completely safe, and Lucy is screaming for a thousand reasons other than the needle.

Vomiting

See also | **Spitting Up**

In Infants

Occasional Vomiting

The primary reason for occasional vomiting (once or twice a day) is overfeeding, which frequently occurs if you attempt to soothe Lucy with a nipple (yours or the bottle's). Remember, just because she takes it doesn't mean she's hungry. If you suspect overfeeding is causing her to vomit, offer less food. If the problem does not subside, see below.

Repetitive Vomiting

Repetitive vomiting, especially after a large feeding, could indicate reflux, a condition in which food does not stay in the stomach [**See:** Reflux]. Much rarer but more serious is a blockage of the intestine called *pyloric stenosis*, especially in young infants. In this case, vomiting starts around two to three weeks of age and worsens to the point that the baby vomits even the smallest amounts of food swallowed. Both conditions require medical attention, and the latter requires prompt surgical correction.

In Older Children

In older children, stomach bugs are the most frequent cause of occasional vomiting [**See:** Reflux]. Ongoing vomiting is rare, and it requires medical evaluation.

W

Walkers

See also | **Legs**

You probably took your first steps in a walker. Years ago, baby walkers were everywhere, but these days they are hard to find in stores, due to fears of injury. Not only can a kid fall down the stairs while using a walker, but also prolonged usage has been found to temporarily bow toddlers' legs and actually delay walking. Even if you don't have stairs, walkers are a mixed blessing. They give very young children the power to go places they shouldn't go and touch things they shouldn't touch. But if you're vigilant about all these dangers and like the idea of a walker, you could always smuggle one in for Lucy. The physical repercussions are somewhat overstated; unless you leave her in the device for eight hours a day, her legs won't become bowed, and she'll learn to walk just fine.

Walking

The moment at which Jimmy goes from the monkey stage to upright walking is a major step in his evolution. Though the average kid walks at around thirteen months, there is a wide disparity in when kids reach this milestone. Some pick up and go as early as eight months; others take much longer. If a child is not yet walking by fifteen months, parents often become a little nervous. If, over the next few months, the child still remains on all fours, parents really start to worry. But in reality it can take a good twenty months for a child to walk. Put plainly, Jimmy will walk when Jimmy is ready. It has more to do with coordination and brain maturation than with muscular strength, which varies widely from kid to kid. Eventually, everybody learns how to walk, barring physical impairment.

Doctors and parents often make late walkers the subjects of unnecessary interventions. For example, I recently saw an eighteen-month-old girl who was not yet walking. A developmental specialist had prescribed an MRI of the brain, even though she had no underlying conditions. She just had a slightly lower muscle tone in her legs, as many kids do. Her grandmother and I were confident that she was just taking her own sweet time. We managed to convince the worried parents to hold off on the MRI, and just two months later, they didn't have time to worry any more; they were too busy chasing their daughter, who was running all around the house.

I commonly see doctors and other health-care professionals recommend that parents "train" late walkers to walk. This is a waste of time. There is little you can or should do to speed up the learning process, and if Jimmy feels pressured by your earnest interest in his locomotion, it may interfere with his natural desire to try.

If Jimmy is a late walker, my best advice is to wait patiently and just enjoy the extra time you have on your hands while he's still down on all fours, walking on his.

Warts and Molluscum

Warts are viral growths that look like small scaly patches on the hands and feet. Children often have one or two of these dermatological extrusions, sometimes a few more. Other wartlike lesions known by the ugly name of *molluscum contagiosum* are small, hard bumps with a white head. Molluscum can either be single or in the hundreds, and they can appear anywhere on the body. As viral growths, they are slightly contagious from child to child, but adults rarely get them.

Both warts and molluscum are painless, but as with everything else that sticks out, kids tend to pick at them and make them bleed slightly, spread locally, or even become infected.

By far the best treatment for these intruders is to leave them alone and let the body's natural defenses take over. If you're patient enough, they *always* go away on their own, and they won't spread all over the body. Generally, they vanish within a few months but can take as long as a year or two. The same is true of molluscum, except that these might spread whether you treat them or not. The advantage of the laissez-faire approach is that the lesions disappear painlessly and without irritation or scarring. The next option is to have your doctor freeze them off with one or two applications of liquid nitrogen. The process is slightly painful, and worse, satellite warts can spring up around the site of the initial one, which means that the virus under the skin was not quite dead yet.

Drugstores also sell over-the-counter preparations that promise to make warts disappear within a few weeks if you file the lesions down and apply the compound daily. I don't recommend these approaches, because they are relatively inefficient, they irritate the skin around the wart, and, like freezing, they may induce satellite lesions.

You'll love this last one: The final solution for warts may come from your local hardware store. Some anecdotal reports suggest that applying plain duct tape to warts every day speeds up their disappearance considerably. You can try it, but please don't quote me on this one.

In Summary

Warts are a nuisance but no more than a nuisance. When located in areas where they are bothersome or could easily become irritated, have them frozen and removed by a doctor. Otherwise, let nature take care of them in due time.

Washing

See also | **Diaper Rash; Soap**

Wanna know the best way to wash a baby? With water, lots of it, and nothing else. First of all, unlike older kids, who roll around on the floor all day, newborns simply don't get that dirty. Second, they don't sweat much, and when they do, they don't smell bad. Despite what the makers of infant lotions would have you believe, you don't need soap to wash a baby. In fact, soap—even the "mild" kind from the health food store—dries the skin by washing away not just impurities but also the superficial layer of oil that protects an infant's skin. A tepid bath in plain water is ideal; rub Lucy's skin gently with your bare hand or a soft sponge and dry her just as gently with a soft towel. Don't bother with moisturizing lotions; they're useful primarily for counteracting the drying effects of soap. For hair care—if there *is* any hair—you can use a mild shampoo at the end of the bath if you want. But again, babies don't build up enough oils and sebum to make shampoo necessary; plain water works just as well.

Most parents accept the plain-water approach when it comes to a baby's arms and back but look at me suspiciously when it comes to the diaper area. Let me repeat: Use water, lots of it, and nothing else. The drying effects of soap along with too much rubbing can actually lead to diaper rash. The best way to wash Lucy's little bum is to put it under the sink faucet. The running water washes impurities off the skin without requiring any rubbing and, in the case of girls, reduces soiling of the vagina. With my three girls, I quickly mastered the technique and was able to perform diaper changes in record time. I let the running water do the job instead of me but took full credit for the fact that their butts were spotless.

Now, how often should a baby be bathed? It need not be a daily event. In the first few weeks of life, many infants aren't too crazy about getting wet; for those, a quick sponge bath under running water is just as efficient. As Lucy gets a few weeks older, reintroduce the idea of a formal bath once in a while. She will eventually enjoy it, as all kids do. One good trick to make that first experience pleasant: Dip yourself in the bath while holding her against your body, especially if you're the mother. Breast feeding in a bath is heaven, at least for your baby.

Water, Drinking

In Infants

Breast milk and formula are both about 90 percent water. Still, rumors persist that you should give "100 percent water" between feedings. The problem with 100 percent water is that it lacks the all-important 10 percent: the nutrients in milk. If you're breast feeding, you should drink lots of water yourself to help replenish your fluids, but Lucy gets enough water from milk or formula. This is true in hot weather as well. Extra water is unnecessary until six to eight months of age. Unlike adults, who can forget to drink fluid, a baby's diet is all liquid and therefore poses no risk of dehydration.

There are other myths about water. Some suggest you give Lucy sugar water to stimulate her intestinal movement and induce stool production despite the fact that it's very normal for a baby to go many days without pooping [**See:** Stools]. You don't have to resort to hydration for this purpose, and that method doesn't really work anyway. Others advise giving her a bottle of water as a pacifier. A regular pacifier will do just as well.

If, after all these arguments, you still wish to give your young baby water, go right ahead; in small quantities, it certainly won't do any harm.

In Infants and Toddlers

While continuing to provide formula and/or breast milk, begin giving Lucy water around eight months, the age at which she's eating a significant amount of solid foods. Water is always preferable to juice, partly because it helps prevent the development of a sweet tooth and doesn't reduce appetite. Her daily water requirement is whatever quantity she takes, as long as you offer it at meals and snacks and in between if the weather is warm.

Weight Concerns

See also | **Breast Feeding; Formula**

In the First Days

I'm not sure why we're still in the habit of weighing babies daily in the hospital. In the first few days of life, newborns will normally lose up to 10 percent of their birth weight. (For the sleep-deprived among you, this amounts to about a pound for an average eight-pounder). If you're breast feeding, recording that weight loss may feel discouraging and incite you to plump Lucy up with a little formula, which could interfere with the breast-feeding process [**See:** Breast Feeding].

Rest assured, the weight Lucy is losing represents mostly water, not muscle or fat. In utero, the water content of a baby's body is significantly higher, and she sheds it almost immediately after birth. At this early stage, the percentage of weight loss doesn't reflect the baby's ability to feed, so there is no reason to record it.

In the First Month

By ten to fifteen days of age, weight becomes a better assessment of intake, since most newborns have returned to their birth weight. There are variations: Some newborns will be several ounces above their birth weight, which is reassuring and never indicates overfeeding. Some may still weigh significantly less than their birth weight, and although this is not necessarily cause for alarm, the question is whether the intake is adequate.

For bottle-fed babies, this is no-brainer: you just count the ounces going in. After a couple of sleepy days, a newborn typically ingests about twenty to thirty ounces per day. If Lucy is consuming this much and keeping it down, she's in good shape.

Assessing a breast-fed baby's intake is a little trickier. If Lucy nurses spontaneously about eight times within a twenty-four-hour period, and if you're changing a few wet diapers a day, these are good signs that breast feeding is going well. The appearance of several seedy and liquid stools is also an encouraging sign, but it's not essential; newborns can absorb almost all the milk's nutrients and produce very little waste. Overall, the best sign that Lucy is eating enough is if you feel your breasts fill in before feedings and experience occasional leaking and if she's nursing fairly happily and sleeping between feedings.

Some babies may take up to three weeks to reach their birth weight even when they're feeding enough. If, however, Lucy is fretful between feedings, sucks voraciously on her fists, urinates small amounts, and if you don't feel your breasts filling up, this may indicate that you're not producing enough. If you have any doubt, here's a simple method to determine whether she is hungry or not. Offer her formula once after nursing and see what happens. If she is ravenous and gulps down the whole six-ounce bottle, then at least you know you are probably not producing enough milk. On the other hand, if she eats only a small amount or nothing and falls asleep on the bottle, your breast milk production is probably sufficient.

Many factors lead to insufficient production: You're tired, the task of having to keep a human being alive with your milk is daunting, your hormones are acting up . . . you name it. In any event, the resulting anxiety and stress impede your production. Once you've established that your production may be insufficient, the first thing to do is to supplement with formula. Many mothers are wary of formula supplementation because they associate it with a sense of failure and think it means the end of breast feeding. Happily, this is not true. Temporary supplementation alleviates most of your stressors and lets you regain confidence, so you can relax and begin producing enough milk. I recommend the following method for supplementation and for returning to breast feeding exclusively, once you've determined that you're producing enough milk.

- At first, supplement every feeding with unlimited formula but only after having offered Lucy the breast for a good twenty minutes even if it's a struggle. Any formula variety will do [See: Formula].
- Each day, after a successful nursing session, skip one supplementation.
- Do this daily, until you're no longer supplementing at all. As the days go by,

Lucy will rely more and more on the breast and less on the formula. Within ten days you have a very good chance of returning to breast feeding exclusively.

I'd be lying if I told you that this always works according to plan. At times Lucy will end up relying more on formula than on breast milk. But you have no choice; if she isn't thriving because of insufficient lactation, she must be fed in some other way. Pumping your breasts to stimulate production could be counterproductive. On one hand, it may stimulate lactation, but on the other hand it's so cumbersome that it might increase your stress level instead. See what works for you.

Note: If the signs indicate that you aren't producing enough, Lucy's weight must be monitored biweekly by your doctor until she is gaining adequately.

In the First Six Months

Babies come in all shapes and sizes. It is a misconception that a chubby baby will eat more than a slim one. Like adults, babies have different metabolisms and different growth curves.

In the first six months of life, I weigh babies monthly. On average, Lucy will gain one to two pounds each month. But there is always room for variation (I've seen cases where a baby gains up to four pounds a month), and it's not necessarily an indication that Lucy is being overfed. Babies are wonderfully regulated eating machines; if you feed them too much, you get it right back in the form of spit-up. Formula-fed babies tend to be a little plumper than breast-fed babies, so adjust your expectations accordingly.

If she's gaining less than a pound a month, that could be a warning sign that Lucy is not eating enough. Low weight gain is far less common in formula-fed babies, both because it's easier to overfeed with a bottle—the food is more available—and because formula is more fattening. As a rough guideline, average formula intake is in the three- to four-ounce range for a month-old baby, and it gradually increases to the six- to eight-ounce range for a six-month-old.

If you're nursing, you obviously can't ascertain exactly how much she's eating. The signs that indicate whether Lucy is getting what she needs are the same as those described above. If Lucy feeds every couple of hours, if your breasts are full before feeding and empty after, if she is not wailing all day in hunger, and if she sleeps peacefully between feedings, these are reasonable indications that you are meeting her demand. Her output can also be an indication: If you see plenty of urine and some stools (the latter number can vary greatly), she's getting enough. In these cases, there's no reason for formula supplementation. Some babies simply gain weight slowly, even though they're getting enough nutrients. If you have any doubt as to whether you're producing enough, supplementation with formula (as described above) may be necessary. Your doctor will monitor your baby's weight until it reaches the desired level.

After Six Months

Between six and twelve months, babies will gain around a pound a month. If you look at a growth chart, you'll see that during this phase, the curve flattens out. This is desirable; if Lucy's length and weight continued to double every few months, you would soon end up with a gargantuan creature in your nursery. This flattening of the curve is even more pronounced in babies who are on their way to becoming slim. At this age, these healthy infants reveal themselves to be future lean toddlers by gaining a little less weight than their peers do.

By now, if the weight gain is insufficient, it is extremely unlikely that breast milk production is the cause. If Lucy were hungry she could practically ask for food, at least in her own language. Therefore, in the rare event that abnormal stunting of the weight occurs, your doctor would search for other digestive causes.

The introduction of solid food at around six months has little effect on weight gain at first. Until eight to ten months, a good part of the calories continue to come from the liquid diet. As before, parents of plumper babies should not worry about overfeeding at this age. Just make food available, and Lucy will self-regulate. The same strategy goes for the slim kids.

Wheat

See also | **Food Reactions**

We are raised to believe that "bread is the staff of life." Most Western cultures base their diets on wheat in one or more forms: bread, pasta, couscous, tortillas, etc. Yet wheat is under attack. Alternative-health books, magazines, and sometimes even baby books devote long articles to wheat, preaching caution and raising alarms about possible adverse reactions. Following this trend, some parents may be tempted to design wheat-free diets even if they haven't noticed a problem. Wheat-free diets are hard to maintain, since the grain is found in pasta, bread, and cereals, of course, but also in many foods that contain thickeners and extenders: soup, sauces, and so on.

This fear of wheat is unjustified. Allergies and intolerance to wheat are far rarer than you've probably been led to believe. Wheat allergy (in the sense of a real allergic reaction) is exceptional. Only a few cases have been recorded in medical literature. And if your kid turns out to be one of those rare specimens who is allergic to wheat, the only way you'll find out for sure is by including it in the diet and waiting for a reaction [**See:** Food Reactions].

Wheat intolerance, or *celiac disease*, is a bit more common. Though not an allergy, it is usually confused with one. Rather, it describes the inability to digest gluten, the source of protein in wheat (and potentially other grains like barley, rye, and even oats). The degrees of severity vary when it comes to wheat intolerance, and the condition's onset is unpredictable: A child might handle wheat perfectly well for months before showing signs of intolerance. Typical symptoms include a bloated belly after eating (more than the regular toddler potbelly), irritability (more intense than your average temper tantrum), and persistent diarrhea. In severe cases, height or weight gain may slow down. If you suspect Jimmy has celiac disease, the diagnosis can be clarified through lab tests. The treatment is strict avoidance of wheat—more easily said than done. It's extremely hard to avoid the "staff of life," and you should only impose that abstinence on your child if he tests positive for celiac disease.

Two small notes about wheat-free diets: First, I've seen many breast-feeding mothers eliminate wheat from their diet because they were made to believe that any wheat they ingest is passed along to their babies through breast milk. This is false. Wheat deprivation may make you feel simultaneously saintly and irritable, but it has no effect on the baby. In addition, there's a common conception that wheat exacerbates eczema, so parents will sometimes place children with eczema on wheat-free diets. I have not seen any positive effect in this indication either.

Wipes

See also | **Diaper Rash; Washing**

You can find a bewildering array of baby wipes for sale in your grocery store. What you may not know is that wipes are basically your average table napkins, kept moist in a plastic box with a mild alcoholic agent or fragrance added. For newborns, it's best to avoid packaged wipes altogether; they tend to dry the skin and provoke diaper irritation by dissolving and rubbing away the thin natural layer of protective oil. For butt care at home, I recommend using plain running tap water [**See:** Washing]. A few months later, when Lucy's skin is a bit tougher, wipes are fine to use for the sake of convenience when you're out and about. You can even take the homemade version on the road: Moisten a bunch of napkins with water, throw them in a plastic bag, and guess what? You've just created your own natural wipes and saved a good deal of money.

Witching Hour

See also | **Colic; Sleep**

Every evening at the stroke of seven, Lucy puts on the same show. She dons her black dress, pointy hat, and crooked warty nose and commences shrieking long witchy shrieks. At first you think she's hungry, so you feed her, but instead of calming down, she hisses at you. You wonder if she wants a cuddle, so you rock her gently. She calms down a bit until she scratches your back with her witch's long nails. So you feed her again, and this time she spits out green witch's spit while her face turns red. You go back to rocking . . . until you hear the clock strike twelve eerie chimes.

Lucy's trick ain't no treat. Whoever called this the witching hour wasn't too far from the truth, if not for the fact that it can last way more than an hour. How it happens: At the end of the day, your little witch releases the tension brought on by overstimulation.

This cycle starts on average two weeks after birth, when Lucy seems to be such a good girl but is in fact merely recovering from her delivery trauma by sleeping most of the time. When she awakens to the world, she receives much more stimulation than she ever had in your belly, and that's a bit too much for her. At the end of the day, she lets you know by letting it all out. The problem arises when you automatically think she is hungry and feed her. Although she takes the nipple and what comes with it for comfort, she isn't hungry. Overfeeding causes belly distention and more discomfort. Then you think she wants cuddling, so you rock her, which brings even more stimulation. The cycle continues late into the night, until everyone in the family collapses from exhaustion.

Since the initial problem is overstimulation, the goal is to reduce it. Once you've established that she isn't hungry and doesn't need cuddling, allowing her to cry out her frustration is your only way to break the cycle. In brief, let her cry for five or ten minutes. If she falls asleep, you've won. If she doesn't, try again with a little cuddling. If she settles down, you're good. If not, she hasn't fully vented her frustration yet. Let her cry another five or ten minutes. Eventually, she'll get a chance to cool off and fall asleep and dream about the good old in-utero days [**See:** Colic].

If you handle the witching hour properly, it will actually last less than an hour and will in fact disappear altogether at around two to three months of age, as Lucy acclimates to her new environment. And the little witch will change back into a little princess.

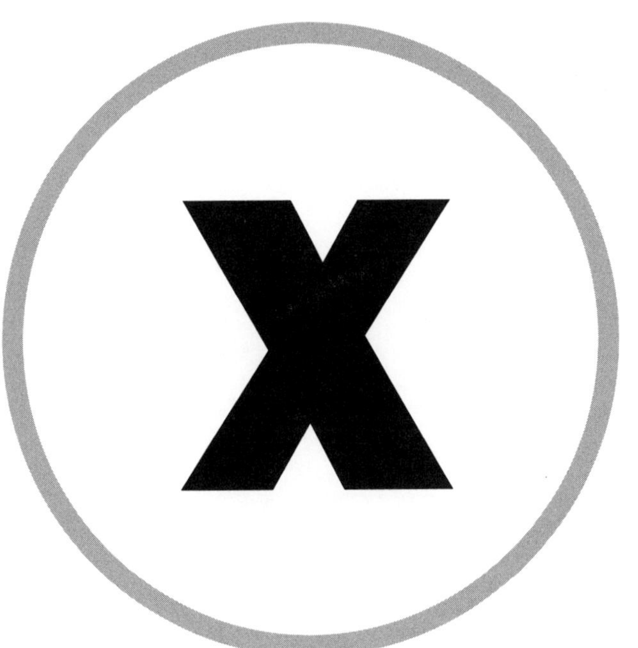

X RAYS

X Rays

X rays are used to diagnose fractures, and they're also helpful for viewing a child's lungs and other soft tissue. You may be hesitant about subjecting your child to the radiation produced during the procedure. Used infrequently, X rays are extremely safe, and the benefits gained from the information they provide far outweigh the possible risk of radiation. If your doctor recommends an X ray, do not hesitate. Of course, repetitive X rays are to be avoided, because the cumulative effect of many irradiations can be harmful, but even CT scans, which consist of a series of X rays, are considered perfectly safe. MRIs, or magnetic resonance imaging scans, do not expose a child to any radiation; they use magnetic fields, which are harmless. Both CT and MRI scans may require sedation, since the procedures require the child to stay still for twenty minutes or so [**See:** Anesthesia].

ZE END

Ze End

Voilà! It's the end of the alphabet and the end of the book.

But I hope it's also a new beginning for you, an opportunity to embrace this softer approach to child care. You've got my song in your head by now:

Kids are tough,
tune them up
fix what needs fixing
stand by them
stand up to them
Your love will take care of the rest.

I also hope that The New Basics *has given you the confidence to relax and trust your intuition, so that when it comes to the health of your child, you'll rely less on this book or any other.*

Thank you for letting me make this house call. I am delighted to have been part of this important time in your life. My warmest wishes to you and your family.

Index